Birds of
Southern India

• Helm Field Guides •

Birds of Southern India

Richard Grimmett
Tim Inskipp

Illustrated by Clive Byers, Daniel Cole, John Cox,
Gerald Driessens, Carl D'Silva, Martin Elliott, Kim Franklin,
Alan Harris, Peter Hayman, Craig Robson,
Jan Wilczur, Tim Worfolk

CHRISTOPHER HELM
A & C BLACK · LONDON

THE COLOUR PLATES
Clive Byers 75–78, 81, 83–87
Daniel Cole 1–3, 18–20, 24, 25 (part), 71
John Cox 21–22, 25 (part)
Gerald Driessens 17, 72 (part), 73
Carl D'Silva 8–16, 23, 52–57, 58 (part), 60–64, 74, 82
Martin Elliott 34–38
Kim Franklin 40 (part), 41 (part)
Alan Harris 39, 41 (part), 42 (part), 43–44, 48–49, 65–70
Peter Hayman 26–33
Craig Robson 72 (part), 79–80
Jan Wilczur 4–7, 50–51, 58 (part), 59
Tim Worfolk 40 (part), 42 (part), 45–47

Front cover and title page illustrations by John Cox

© 2005 text by Richard Grimmett and Tim Inskipp
© 1998, 2005 illustrations by Clive Byers, Daniel Cole, John Cox, Gerald Driessens,
Carl D'Silva, Martin Elliott, Kim Franklin, Alan Harris, Peter Hayman, Craig Robson,
Jan Wilczur, Tim Worfolk
© 2005 photographs by Tim Loseby

Published 2005 by Christopher Helm, an imprint of A & C Black Publishers Ltd.,
37 Soho Square, London W1D 3QZ

0-7136-5164-4

A CIP catalogue record for this book is available from the
British Library

www.acblack.com

Edited and designed by D & N Publishing, Lowesden Business Park,
Hungerford, Berkshire.

Printed in Thailand by Imago.

10 9 8 7 6 5 4 3 2 1

Contents

FOREWORD 6

INTRODUCTION 8

How to Use this Book 8

Descriptive Parts of a Bird 10

Geographical Setting 12

Main Habitats 12

Important Bird Species 14

Migration 17

Birdwatching Areas 17

NATIONAL ORGANISATIONS 20

INTERNATIONAL ORGANISATIONS 24

REFERENCES 26

Acknowledgements 28

GLOSSARY 28

SELECTED BIBLIOGRAPHY 30

FAMILY SUMMARIES 32

COLOUR PLATES AND SPECIES ACCOUNTS 46

APPENDIX 220

TABLES 230

INDEX 234

FOREWORD

M. ZAFAR-UL ISLAM AND ASAD R. RAHMANI
BOMBAY NATURAL HISTORY SOCIETY, MUMBAI, INDIA
www.ibcnetwork.org and www.bnhs.org

India is one of the top ten richest countries in terms of biodiversity. Its immense bio-logical richness includes more than 600 species of amphibians and reptiles, 350 species of mammals and over 1200 species of birds. Southern India contributes much to this diversity and is a fabulous region for the enjoyment and study of birds.

Much of the peninsula of India is constituted by the Deccan plateau, extending from 12° to 21° north with a mean elevation of about 600 m, reaching 900 m in the Vindhyas and Satpuras. Extending down the eastern side of the peninsula, from Orissa south to Tamil Nadu, are the Eastern Ghats. This range of hills and mountains has a mean ele-vation of about 400 m, with the highest peak of 1750 m in the Bilingirangan Hills that form the Ghats' southernmost extension. The deciduous forest, scrub and grasslands of this region support a number of very special Indian endemics, including Grey Junglefowl *Gallus sonneratii*, Painted Francolin *Francolinus pictus*, Rock Bush Quail *Perdicula argoondah*, Painted Bush Quail *Perdicula erythrorhyncha*, Yellow-throated Bulbul *Pycnonotus xantholaemus*, Sykes's Lark *Galerida deva* and Green Avadavat *Amandava formosa*. It also has some grasslands where relict populations of Indian Bustard *Ardeotis nigriceps* and Lesser Florican *Sypheotides indica* are found.

Critical conservation issues in this region are habitat loss and degradation, including the impact of shifting cultivation, and the impact of invasive plants such as *Eupatorium* and *Lantana*. Hunting, and trapping for the bird trade continue to have a negative impact on bird populations. Large areas in this region are protected, either as national parks or wildlife sanctuaries, or through community-driven protection with the help of the forest department. There is an urgent need to protect more grassland areas in the Deccan for the conservation of the rapidly declining Indian Bustard. One of the most important conservation research priorities is to find and protect wintering areas of the Lesser Florican, since most of its wintering sites are likely to fall in this zone. This can-not be done unless satellite tracking is used.

Of great significance for India's considerable biological diversity are the Western Ghats, a range of mountains that extend along the western side of the Indian peninsula for about 1600 km, with the highest peak at Anamudi (2700 m). The Western Ghats support 16 endemic species of bird found nowhere else in the world and, as further tax-onomic work is undertaken, this number is likely to increase. The lowland evergreen and semi-evergreen rainforests probably once extended onto the coastal plain to the west of the Ghats, but almost all forest below 500 m has long been cleared. The remaining forests face severe pressures, with an expanding human population giving rise to increased ille-gal encroachment into forest lands, livestock grazing, and the harvesting of fuelwood and huge quantities of minor forest products such as bamboo and canes. Hydroelectric power and irrigation dams have been built on the steep western slopes of the Ghats, leading to the flooding of primary forest and the establishment of new settlements and new access roads. The high-altitude shola grasslands face numerous onslaughts such as repeated fires and conversion to plantations, but perhaps none is as dangerous as invasive plant species. Scotch broom and wattle have invaded large areas of grassland, especially in the Nilgiris.

The Bombay Natural History Society (BNHS) is meeting the challenges facing birds and their habitats in South India through an integrated programme of species and site conservation and network development. The BNHS has led the way in species surveys and research in India, including pioneering work on threatened species in the south such as the Forest Owlet *Athene blewitti* and Jerdon's Courser *Rhinoptilus bitorquatus* (the latter rediscovered in the 1980s after 86 years by BNHS scientists). For a high proportion of threatened bird species, especially those with restricted ranges and strict habitat requirements, effective site protection and management is the key measure for their survival. To provide a firm foundation for this, the BNHS is implementing the Important Bird Areas (IBA) programme, which has identified about 150 IBAs in the region. More than 50 of these IBAs have no legal protection. Working with the recently established Indian Bird Conservation Network (IBCN), BNHS is promoting IBA monitoring and conservation action. At the national and state level, BNHS will promote IBA conservation through legislation and planning.

BNHS's conservation agenda will be greatly assisted by this Southern India field guide. Field guides play a small but important part in conservation and the wider environmental movement. As a starting point, they encourage more people to take an interest in birds, and through this in the natural world around them. Such interest frequently becomes a commitment to the conservation movement, with interested persons joining conservation organisations and encouraging politicians and administrators to make a greater contribution to nature conservation.

Field guides also help build the technical capacity of individual researchers and research institutions, as well as that of NGOs and governmental conservation agencies. Guides such as this will help, for example, in relation to inventories of protected areas and park monitoring, and will assist with the management of the wildlife trade. The guide will be a tremendous boost to the members of the Indian Bird Conservation Network.

Whilst English is widely spoken in the region, an English-language guide will be inaccessible to the hundreds of millions of Indians who have Marathi, Kannada, Malayalam, Tamil or Telugu as their first language. The planned publication of the guide in these languages, as well as in English, will be of great significance for the region.

INTRODUCTION

Southern India is defined for the purposes of this book as comprising the states of Maharashtra, Andhra Pradesh, Goa, Karnataka, Kerala, Tamil Nadu and Lakshadweep. Little has been published about the avifauna of the Union Territory of Pondicherry and it is here treated with Tamil Nadu. In addition, the Maldives, although not part of India, are included as they are part of a chain of islands extending southwards from Lakshadweep. The region is bounded by northern India to the north, the Arabian Sea to the west, the Bay of Bengal to the east, and Sri Lanka and the Indian Ocean to the south. There are 563 species that regularly occur in the area and a further 91 species have been recorded as vagrants.

HOW TO USE THIS BOOK

Taxonomy and Nomenclature

Taxonomy and nomenclature largely follow *An Annotated Checklist of the Birds of the Oriental Region* (Inskipp *et al.*, 1996). The sequence generally follows the same reference, although some species have been grouped out of this systematic order to enable useful comparisons to be made. In cases where differences in taxonomic opinion exist in the literature, the species limits are fully discussed in that work, to which readers requiring further information should initially refer. The taxonomy differs in several respects based on recent published works that are considered to provide justification for the new treatments. The Long-billed Vulture *Gyps indicus* has been split into two species: Indian Vulture *G. indicus* and Slender-billed Vulture *G. tenuirostris* (Rasmussen, 2001), and only the former occurs in the region. The Indian Spotted Eagle *Aquila hastata* has been split from the Lesser Spotted Eagle *A. pomarina*, with the latter being extralimital (Parry *et al.*, 2002). The Golden-spectacled Warbler *Seicercus burkii* is split into several species, two of which have been recorded in the region: Golden-spectacled Warbler and Whistler's Warbler *S. whistleri* (Alström and Olsson, 1999). The Rufous-winged Bushlark *Mirafra assamica* is split into two species in the subcontinent but only one of these, Jerdon's Bushlark *M. affinis*, occurs in the region (Alström, 1998). The Yellow-legged Gull *Larus cachinnans* has been split into two species: the Yellow-legged Gull *L. michahellis* in Europe and the Caspian Gull *L. cachinnans* further east (Klein and Buchheim, 1997; Liebers *et al.*, 2001).

Colour Plates and Plate Captions

Species that occur regularly in southern India are illustrated in colour and described in the plate captions. Vagrants and very rare species are described in the Appendix, with reference to distinguishing features separating them from other more regularly recorded species where appropriate. The illustrations show distinctive sexual and racial variation whenever possible, as well as immature plumages. Some distinctive races as well as immature plumages are also depicted. Where possible, species depicted on any one plate have been shown to approximately the same scale.

The captions identify the figures illustrated, very briefly summarise the species' distribution, status, altitudinal range and habitats, and provide information on the most important identification characters, including voice where this is an important feature, and approximate body length of the species, including bill and tail, in centimetres. Length is expressed as a range when there is marked variation within the species (e.g. as a result of sexual dimorphism or racial differences).

The identification texts are based on *Birds of the Indian Subcontinent* (Grimmett *et al.*, 1998). The vast majority of the illustrations have been taken from the same work and wherever possible the correct races for southern India have been depicted. A small number of additional illustrations of races occurring in southern India were executed for this book. The text and plates are based on extensive reference to museum specimens, combined with considerable work in the field.

The status of each species is defined as one of the following: a resident, winter visitor, summer visitor, passage migrant or altitudinal migrant. Data on actual breeding records and non-breeding ranges are very few, so it has not been possible to give comprehensive details. Globally threatened species (species at risk of global extinction) are indicated as such, following the BirdLife International Red Data Book (BirdLife International, 2001), with the IUCN threat category given in parentheses.

Key to Distribution and Status Information

AN = Andhra Pradesh GO = Goa
KA = Karnataka KE = Kerala
LS = Lakshadweep MH = Maharashtra
TN = Tamil Nadu MV = Maldives

cp = common passage migrant
cr = common resident
cw = common winter visitor
lcr = locally common resident
lcw = locally common winter visitor
np = not common passage migrant
nr = not common resident
ns = not common summer visitor
nw = not common winter visitor
nwp = not common winter visitor and passage migrant
v = vagrant
xp = extirpated passage migrant
xr = extirpated resident

Plumage Terminology

The figures overleaf illustrate the main plumage tracts and bare-part features, and are based on Grant and Mullarney (1988–89). This terminology for bird topography has been used in the captions. Other terms have been used and are defined in the Glossary. Juvenile plumage is the first plumage on fledging, and in many species it is looser, more fluffy, than subsequent plumages. In some families, juvenile plumage is retained only briefly after leaving the nest (e.g. pigeons), or hardly differs from adult plumage (e.g. many babblers), while in other groups it may be retained for the duration of long migrations or for many months (e.g. many waders). In some species (e.g. *Aquila* eagles), it may be several years before all juvenile feathers are finally moulted. The relevance of the juvenile plumage to field identification therefore varies considerably. Some species reach adult plumage after their first post-juvenile moult (e.g. larks), whereas others go though a series of immature plumages. The term 'immature' has been employed more generally to denote plumages other than adult, and is used either where a more exact terminology has not been possible or where more precision would give rise to unnecessary complexity. Terms such as 'first-winter' (resulting from a

DESCRIPTIVE PARTS OF A BIRD

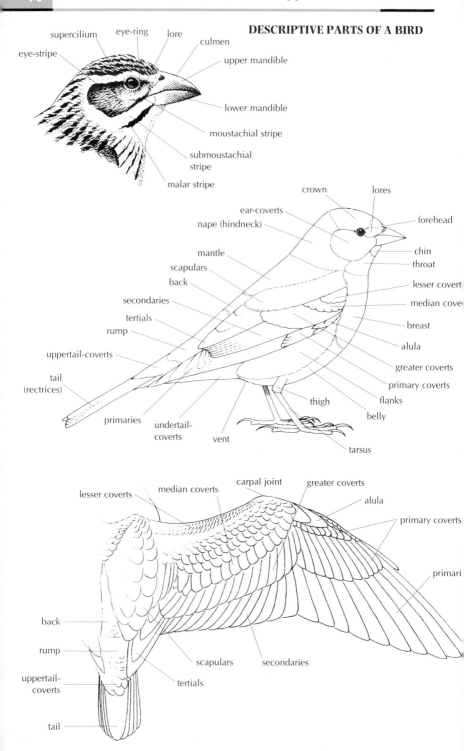

partial moult from juvenile plumage) or 'first-summer' (plumage acquired prior to the breeding season of the year after hatching) have, however, been used where it was felt that this would be useful.

Many species assume a more colourful breeding plumage, which is often more striking in the male compared with the female. This can be realised either through a partial (or in some species complete) body moult (e.g. waders), or results from the wearing-off of pale or dark feather fringes (e.g. redstarts and buntings).

GEOGRAPHICAL SETTING

Climate

On the Kerala coast the annual and daily range of temperatures are small, normally remaining within the range 21°C to 32°C. At the base of the hills the temperature may be slightly higher and lower than these limits. Up on the Western Ghats the climate varies with altitude and aspect but is generally similar to that of a moist temperate region. In winter the temperature may drop to freezing at night, and rise to 20°C during the day.

Despite these variations one feature dominates climate in the region and that is the monsoons. Most of the rain in the region falls between June and September during the southwest monsoon season. During this time cool, moisture-laden winds from the Indian Ocean bring heavy, intermittent rains. Typically, the monsoon begins in Kerala in late May or early June and moves north and west to extend over northern India by the end of June. On reaching the Western Ghats the air rises and cools and the moisture condenses, providing abundant rainfall along this range. The monsoon begins to retreat from the northwest at the beginning of September and usually withdraws completely by mid-October. Rain continues, however, in the southern peninsula, and in the southeast around half the annual rain falls between October and mid-December. This is brought by winds coming from the northeast during the northeast monsoon. The amount of rain varies from year to year, especially over areas of poor rainfall, where it may be as little as 30 to 40 per cent of a normal year. Even when the total monsoon rain in an area is about average, it may fall over a very short period, bringing floods and drought in the same year.

MAIN HABITATS

The bird habitats of southern India can be roughly divided into forests, scrub, wetlands (inland and littoral), marine, grasslands and agricultural land. There is overlap of some habitats, for example mangrove forests can also be considered as wetlands, as can seasonally flooded grasslands. Many bird species require mixed habitat types.

Forests

There is a great variety of forest types in the region. Tropical forests range from coastal mangroves to wet, dense evergreen, dry deciduous and open thorn forests. The forests of the region are vitally important for many of its birds, including both globally threatened and restricted-range species.

Tropical deciduous forests once covered much of the plains and lower hills of the subcontinent, including moist and dry sal and teak forests, riverine and dry thorn forests. Several widespread species endemic to the subcontinent are chiefly confined to these forests, including the Plum-headed Parakeet, which has a preference for moist deciduous forests, and the White-bellied Drongo, which favours open, dry deciduous forests.

Scrub

Scrub has developed where trees are unable to grow in the region, either because soils are poor and thin, or because they are too wet, such as at the edges of wetlands or in seasonally inundated floodplains. Scrub also grows naturally in extreme climatic conditions, such as in semi-desert. In addition, there are now large areas of scrubland in the region where forests have been over-exploited for fodder and fuel collection or grazing.

Wetlands

Wetlands in the region are abundant and support a rich array of waterfowl. As well as providing habitats for breeding resident species, the subcontinent's wetlands include major staging and wintering grounds for waterfowl breeding in central and northern Asia. The region possesses a wide range of wetland types distributed almost throughout, including freshwater and brackish marshes, large water-storage reservoirs, village tanks, saline flats and coastal mangroves and mudflats. The results of the 1987–91 Asian Waterfowl Census, published in 1994 by the Asian Wetland Bureau and the International Waterfowl and Wetlands Research Bureau (now Wetlands International), include detailed distribution maps for 200 Asian wetland species most commonly recorded during the period.

A detailed directory of Indian wetlands compiled by WWF India and the Asian Wetland Bureau describing the values, threats and conservation measures, was published in 1993. Although no data are available, the coastal mudflats and estuaries are thought to be of great importance as staging and wintering areas. Small water-storage reservoirs or tanks are a distinctive feature in India. Aggregations of these tanks provide important feeding and nesting areas for a wide range of waterbirds in some places.

NAGARHOLE.

Grasslands

Some grasslands still exist, especially on the eastern side of the Western Ghats.

Seas

Seabirds in the region comprise mainly gulls and terns, with a few truly pelagic species (e.g. petrels and shearwaters).

Agricultural Habitats

The region is remarkable for the abundance of birds in agricultural habitats in many areas, as a result of non-intensive agricultural systems and low levels of hunting and persecution. Shrikes, Indian Roller, Common Hoopoe, parakeets and birds of prey, for example, can appear abundant on road and rail journeys. This is changing though, as farming becomes more intensive and higher levels of pesticides are applied

IMPORTANT BIRD SPECIES

Restricted-range Species

There is one Endemic Bird Area (EBA) in the region, the Western Ghats EBA, which extends from northern Maharashtra down the western flank of the peninsula to southern Tamil Nadu (Stattersfield *et al.*, 1998). This EBA has 16 restricted-range species, as defined by BirdLife International, all of which are confined to the EBA (and occur nowhere else on the planet). Seven of these species are found in lowland and hill forest to around 1500 m (Malabar Parakeet, Malabar Grey Hornbill, White-bellied Treepie, White-bellied Blue Flycatcher, Grey-headed Bulbul, Wynaad Laughingthrush, and Rufous Babbler), five are associated with montane forest (White-bellied Shortwing,

MUDUMALAI, NILGIRIS.

Black-and-orange Flycatcher, Nilgiri Flycatcher, Rufous-breasted Laughingthrush and Grey-breasted Laughingthrush), whilst Nilgiri Wood Pigeon and Crimson-backed Sunbird are found in both foothill and montane forest. Two restricted range species are associated with the montane grasslands (Nilgiri Pipit and Broad-tailed Grassbird). Two other restricted-range forest birds are non-breeding (winter) migrants to the EBA: Tytler's Leaf Warbler and Kashmir Flycatcher from breeding grounds in the Western Himalayas.

A so-called Secondary Area (see Stattersfield *et al.*, 1998), the Central Indian Forests, an area of dry deciduous forest, is shared between Maharashtra and Madhya Pradesh, supporting one restricted-range species, Forest Owlet.

Globally Threatened Species

Twenty-eight species of southern Indian birds (excluding vagrants to the region) are classified by BirdLife International as globally threatened with extinction (BirdLife International, 2001, 2003). This includes five species that are categorised as Critical (and therefore at extremely high risk of extinction in the immediate future; White-rumped Vulture, Indian Vulture, Jerdon's Courser and Forest Owlet, plus Pink-head-ed Duck which may already have met such a fate. A further four species are categorised as Endangered.

The plight of the two Critical vultures is a very recent phenomenon, with both species suffering an extremely rapid population decline. Recent scientific evidence indicates

PERIYAR FOREST.

that diclofenac (an anti-inflammatory drug) is a major cause of the observed vulture declines (Oaks *et al.*, 2004). Exposure of vultures to diclofenac arises through its veterinary use to treat domestic livestock, with vultures dying after feeding on the carcass of an animal that has very recently been treated with the normal veterinary dose. This decline is causing major problems in rural and urban areas because of the role vultures play in disposing of animal carcasses.

Small populations of the endangered Indian Bustard and Lesser Florican can still be found in southern India. The range of the Indian Bustard is now highly fragmented, and remaining populations continue to be under pressure from agricultural intensification (often facilitated by the extension of irrigation) and overstocking of livestock. Lesser Floricans breed during the monsoon in Maharashtra and areas to the north, and winter in dry, grassy areas throughout the peninsula. Its grassland habitat is under threat due to conversion for agriculture, unsuitable management, overgrazing by livestock, disturbance and the invasive mesquite tree.

Four species, Forest Owlet, Jerdon's Courser, Yellow-throated Bulbul and White-naped Tit, are birds of dry forest and scrub. Such habitat was formerly extensive in southern India, but has been widely cleared for agriculture and forest plantations, and is subject to degradation due to overgrazing and unsustainable exploitation of forest products.

Wetlands in the region support nine threatened species. The region is of particular importance for Spot-billed Pelican, which favour water-storage reservoirs or 'tanks' that are scattered throughout the south. Coastal habitats are important for non-breeding Spot-billed Pelican, but these wetlands are being converted for aquaculture and development.

MUDUMALAI SCRUB.

Three of the resident restricted-range species of the evergreen forests of the Western Ghats EBA, Nilgiri Wood Pigeon, White-bellied Shortwing and Rufous-breasted Laughingthrush, are threatened. These forests are also important for non-breeding populations of the threatened Wood Snipe and Kashmir Flycatcher. Large areas have been cleared for agriculture and plantations (especially tea and coffee), have been impacted by roads and dams, or are being degraded by the collection of timber and fuelwood, and by overgrazing.

MIGRATION

Many species are non-breeding visitors to Southern India. Inland wetlands support large numbers of duck during the winter months, especially Garganey, as well as waders and *Chlidonias* (marsh) terns, whilst coastal habitats provide winter quarters for a wide variety of waders, gulls and terns.

A number of species that breed in the Himalayas winter in Southern India, for example Indian Pitta, Blue-capped Rock Thrush, Large-billed Leaf Warbler and Indian Blue Robin. The region is also host to winter visitors originating in northern and central Asia, including a variety of *Acrocephalus* warblers, pipits and wagtails. Interestingly, Southern India is the main winter destination for Red-headed and Black-headed Buntings.

BIRDWATCHING AREAS

There are numerous areas in southern India that are excellent for birdwatching. For more details, *A Birdwatcher's Guide to India* by Krys Kazmierczak and Raj Singh (1988) is highly recommended.

Borivli (Sanjay Gandhi) National Park, Mumbai, Maharashtra
Location: On the northern edge of Mumbai (Bombay).
Habitat: Forest and scrub, rocky hills, and a reservoir.
Best time to visit: November–March, although worth a visit at any time in the year.
Birds: Grey Junglefowl, Malabar Trogon, Pied Cuckoo, Oriental Dwarf Kingfisher, Indian Grey Hornbill, Brown-headed Barbet, Indian Spotted Eagle, Indian Pitta, Indian Scimitar Babbler, Sulphur-bellied Warbler, Thick-billed Flowerpecker, Loten's Sunbird and Crimson Sunbird.

Goa
Location: 400 km south of Mumbai.
Habitat: A wide variety of habitats in a relatively small area, including forest and scrub, dry grassland, salt pans, agricultural land, and coastal and freshwater wetlands.
Best time to visit: October–March.
Birds: Grey Junglefowl, White-cheeked Barbet, Malabar Trogon, Black-capped Kingfisher, Malabar Grey Hornbill, Greater Painted-snipe, Pallid Harrier, Indian Spotted Eagle, Indian Cormorant, Yellow-browed Bulbul, Malabar Lark, Loten's Sunbird, Purple-rumped Sunbird and Blyth's Pipit. A wide variety of waders, warblers and pipits in winter.

Rollapadu, Andhra Pradesh
Location: 260 km south of Hyderabad.
Habitat: Grassland and agricultural land.
Best time to visit: October–April.

RAJAMALAI.

Birds: Large roost of harriers, mainly Montagu's and Pallid, White-eyed Buzzard, Demoiselle Crane, Indian Bustard, Lesser Florican, larks, including Sykes's Lark and pipits.

Nagarhole (Rajiv Gandhi National Park) and Bandipur, Karnataka
Location: 80 km west of Mysore.
Habitat: Deciduous forest and scrub.
Best time to visit: Throughout the year.
Birds: Red Spurfowl, Grey Junglefowl, White-bellied Woodpecker, Heart-spotted Woodpecker, Malabar Pied Hornbill, Blue-faced Malkoha, Malabar Parakeet, Grey-headed Fish Eagle, Black Ibis and Indian Pitta.

Rajamalai (Eravikulam National Park), Kerala
Location: 12 km from Munnar.
Habitat: Grassland and shola forest.
Best time to visit: Throughout the year.
Birds: Painted Bush Quail, White-bellied Shortwing, Black-and-orange Flycatcher, Nilgiri Flycatcher, White-bellied Flycatcher, Pacific Swallow, Tickell's Leaf Warbler, Large-billed Leaf Warbler, Grey-breasted Laughingthrush and Nilgiri Pipit.

✓ Periyar, Kerala
Location: 110 km south of Bodinayakanur.

Habitat: Evergreen and semi-evergreen forest, grassland and shola forest.
Best time to visit: Throughout the year.
Birds: Grey Junglefowl, Heart-spotted Woodpecker, Great Hornbill, Malabar Trogon, Jerdon's Baza, Black Baza, Rufous-bellied Eagle, Mountain Hawk Eagle, White-bellied Treepie, Rufous-tailed Flycatcher, Yellow-browed Bulbul, Wynaad Laughingthrush and Large-billed Leaf Warbler.

Mudumalai, Tamil Nadu
Location: 90 km south of Mysore.
Habitat: Deciduous forest and scrub, and moist evergreen forest.
Best time to visit: Throughout the year.
Birds: Red Spurfowl, White-naped Woodpecker, Malabar Pied Hornbill, Sirkeer Malkoha, Malabar Parakeet, Jerdon's Nightjar, Indian Pitta, White-bellied Minivet, Malabar Whistling Thrush, Grey-headed Bulbul, Jerdon's Bushlark and Malabar Lark.

Udhagamandalam (Ootacamund), Nilgiris, Tamil Nadu
Location: 90 km northwest of Coimbatore.
Habitat: Shola forest and tea estates.
Best time to visit: November–April.
Birds: Painted Bush Quail, Nilgiri Wood Pigeon, Blue-capped Rock Thrush, Malabar Whistling Thrush, Scaly Thrush, Eurasian Blackbird, White-bellied Shortwing, Kashmir Flycatcher, Black-and-orange Flycatcher, Nilgiri Flycatcher, Large-billed Leaf Warbler, Nilgiri Laughingthrush and Crimson-backed Sunbird.

Top Slip (Indira Gandhi WildLife Sanctuary), Anaimalais, Tamil Nadu
Location: 75 km south of Coimbatore.
Habitat: Evergreen forest, deciduous forest and grassland.
Best time to visit: October–May, best December–February.
Birds: Red Spurfowl, White-bellied Woodpecker, Heart-spotted Woodpecker, Malabar Grey Hornbill, Great Hornbill, Malabar Trogon, Malabar Parakeet, Great Eared Nightjar, Jerdon's Nightjar, Sri Lanka Frogmouth, Rufous-bellied Eagle, White-bellied Treepie, White-bellied Blue Flycatcher, Wynaad Laughingthrush, Dark-fronted Babbler and Black-throated Munia.

Vedanthangal, Tamil Nadu
Location: 85 km southwest of Chennai (Madras).
Habitat: Water tank with mature trees.
Best time to visit: October–March.
Birds: Indian Courser, Oriental Darter, Indian and Little Cormorants, Asian Openbill, Black-headed Ibis, Eurasian Spoonbill and Spot-billed Pelican.

Point Calimere (Kodikkarai), Tamil Nadu
Location: 350 km south of Chennai (Madras).
Habitat: Tidal lagoons, sea coast, salt pans, grassland and scrub.
Best time to visit: October–March.
Birds: Blue-faced Malkoha, Pallas's and Heuglin's Gulls, waders, terns, Lesser and Greater Flamingos and Spot-billed Pelican. Asian Dowitcher and Spoon-billed Sandpiper are occasional winter visitors.

NATIONAL ORGANISATIONS

Bombay Natural History Society (BNHS)
Hornbill House, Dr Salim Ali Chowk, Shaheed Bhagat Singh Road, Bombay 400 023.
Publications: *Journal of the Bombay Natural History Society; Hornbill* magazine (quarterly).
The BNHS was founded in 1883 and is the largest non-governmental organisation in the subcontinent engaged in the conservation of nature and natural resources, education and research in natural history. The society has an invaluable collection of more than 26,000 bird specimens held at its headquarters in Bombay. The society's Nature Education Wing reaches over 10,000 students each year. The Salim Ali Nature Conservation Fund creates awareness, with training programmes for Indian Army officers, journalists and trekkers. Scientists have carried out vital ornithological research, including a national bird-ringing programme and studies on grassland birds.

Salim Ali Centre for Ornithology and Natural History (SACON)
Kalampalayam, Coimbatore, Tamil Nadu 641 010.
Publication: *SACON newsletter.*
SACON came into being in 1990. SACON's objectives are to:

1. study India's biological diversity so as to promote its conservation and sustainable use;
2. study the ecology of the Indian avifauna with special reference to its conservation;
3. foster the development of professional wildlife research in India, by training postgraduates and forest managers; and
4. function as a regional nodal agency for the dissemination of information on biodiversity and its conservation.

Current work includes biodiversity monitoring at Keoladeo Ghana National Park, and monitoring and conservation of the Lesser Florican.

Wildlife Institute of India (WII)
Post Bag No. 18, Chandrabani, Dehradun 248 001.
The WII was set up in 1982. Its objectives are to:

1. train biologists and managers for protected area management and wildlife research;
2. conduct and coordinate applied wildlife research, and evolve techniques relevant to the Indian situation;
3. train education and extension workers to acquire skills in eliciting public support for wildlife conservation;
4. provide consultancy services in conservation matters to government and non-official agencies;
5. create a database leading to a national wildlife information system; and
6. provide conservation orientation courses for those involved in land use management.

Zoological Survey of India (ZSI)
27, Jawaharlal Nehru Road, Calcutta 700 016.
Publications: *Newsletter of the Zoological Survey of India; Records of the Zoological Survey of India, Annual Reports.*
The ZSI was established in 1916 and carries out surveys in the country. Its collections cover the whole of India. The National Zoological Collection of India at Calcutta houses

KERALA BACKWATERS.

more than a million specimens belonging to all the animal groups. Fourteen collecting stations are maintained in different ecological biotopes, such as the Desert Regional Station at Jodhpur and the high-altitude station at Solan.

Indian Bird Conservation Network (IBCN)

The Indian Bird Conservation Network (IBCN) is a network of Indian organisations and individuals who collaborate to promote the conservation of birds in India and, through them, the conservation of biological diversity as a whole. The mission of the IBCN is 'to promote conservation of birds and their habitat through the development of a national network of individuals, organisations and the Government.' The network is made up of partners and a network coordinator who is a staff member of the Bombay Natural History Society.

Some of the IBCN organisational members in the region are as follows:

Andhra Pradesh

Birdwatchers' Society of Andhra Pradesh
PO Box 45, Bangar Hills, Hyderabad 500 034, Andhra Pradesh.
Tel: 6501535, 6612608
Contacts: Siraj Taher and Aasheesh Pittie

Institute of Bird Studies and Natural History
Rishi Valley, Chittoor District 517352, Andhra Pradesh.
Tel: 08571 26037, 08571 68622, 08571 68582
Contact: S. Rangaswami, Director

People's Action In Development
20-1030-2, R.K. Nagar, Co-op. Colony, Cuddapah 516 001, Andhra Pradesh.

Tel: 91 8562 274468
email: paidcdp@hd2.vsnl.net.in
Contact: K. Nageswar Reddy

Karnataka
Atree
#659, 5th Main Road, Hebbal, Bangalore 560 024, Karnataka.
Tel: 080 353 0069
email: kamal.bawa@umb.edu or info@atree.org
Contact: Kamal Bawa

Coorg Wildlife Society
P.B. 111, Madikeri, Kodagu 571 201, Karnataka.
Tel : 08272 23505
Contact: Mr Imran Khan

Hassan Bird Watchers Club
117 Hemalaya, Ravindranagar, Hassan 573 201, Karnataka.
Tel: 08172 68503
Contact: Mr H.P. Mohan, President

Nature Conservation Foundation
3076/5, 4th Cross, Gokulam Park, Mysore 570 002, Karnataka.
Tel : 0821 515601
email: ncf@ncf_india.org
Contact: T.R. Shankar Raman, Executive Director

Wildlife Watch
36 Ramalaya, Subbarama Chetty Road, Basavangudi, Bangalore 560 004, Karnataka.
Tel: 6525466
email: wildlife_watch@vsnl.com
Contact: Ramakrishna Valke

Kerala
Beaks Kerala
Kousthubham Tc5/2097-1, Ugra-ul-10, Ambabmukku, Kowdiar, Trivandrum 695 003, Kerala.
Tel: 341904
Contact: Mr K. Sivakumar, Secretary

Maharashtra
Cobra Adventure and Nature Club
Near Mahadev Temple, Joshi Wada, Yavatmal 445 001, Maharashtra.
Tel: 253571
Contact: Shayam Joshi, Secretary

Ela Foundation
C-9, Bhosle Park, Sahakar Nagar-2, Pune 411 009, Maharashtra.

Tel: 020 4221345
email: satishpandey@hotmail.com
Contact: Dr Satish Pandey

Envirosearch .
B1/102 Nikash Lawns, 140/3 Sus Road, Pashan, Pune 410 021, Maharashtra.
Tel: 020 4007895, 020 5897570
email: envirosearch@vsnl.net
Contacts: Prachi Mehta and Jayant Kulkarni

Green Guards
2541 B, Khasbag, Mangalwar Peth, Kolhapur 416 012, Maharashtra.
Tel: 2645884, 2642013
email: greenguards@hotmail.com
Contact: Prakash M. Bhoje, President

Nashiklub
Sarada Activity Centre, 'Nandinee', Nashik – Pune Road, Nashik 422 011, Maharashtra.
Tel: 0253 2417931, 0253 2417931
email: nasiklub@deshdoot.com

Nature Conservation Society
Sainagar, Shrigonda, Dist. Ahmednagar, Maharashtra.
Tel: 02487 22728
email: nature_shri@yahoo.com
Contact: A.B. Gore

Nature Conservation Society of Nasik
Hemant Vihar, Plot No.13, Savarkar Nagar, off Gangapur Road, Nashik 422 005,
Maharashtra.
Tel: 0253 2341309, 0253 5601832
email: wolfajay@hotmail.com
Contact: Bishwarup Raha, President

Nisarg
C/o Ruturaj S. Joshi, Gurudev Apartments, Ganesh Chowk, Manjavli, Badlapur (West)
421 503, Maharashtra.
Tel: 2673071
Contact: Ruturaj S. Joshi

Nisarg Vidnyaan Mandal Sanstha
138 'Kalpatru' Mahalaxmi Nagar, No. 2 Manewada Road, Nagpur 440 024, Maharashtra.
Tel: 0712 2747606
email: nisargvg@nagpur.dot.net.in
Contact: Vijay L. Ghugey

Sahyadri Nisarga Mitra
Nr. Laxminarayan Temple, At & Po. Tal. Chiplun, Dist. Ratnagiri 415 605, Maharashtra.

Tel: 02355 237115
email: sahyadricpn@rediffmail.com
Contact: Vishwas Katdare, Secretary

Pondicherry
Ecos
50, 1st Cross Street, Rainbow Nagar, Pondicherry 605 011.
Tel: 0413 340806
email: ecos@yahoo.com
Contact: Priya Davidar

Tamil Nadu
Dhan Foundation
18 Pillaiyar Koil Street, Somasundaram Colony, Madurai 625 010, Tamil Nadu.
Tel: 452 2610805
email: dhan@md3.vsnl.net.in
Contact: R. Sreenivasan

Nature Club
Bishop Heber College, Trichirapalli 620 017, Tamil Nadu.
Tel: 0431 2772345
email: reltona@yahoo.com
Contact: Albert Relton

The Nature Trust
22 Madura Kavi Street, East Tambaram, Chennai 600 059, Tamil Nadu.
Tel: 044 22393959
email: thenaturetrust@sify.com
Contact: K.V.R.K. Thirunaranan

Wildlife Association of Ramnad
Chinmaya Vidyalaya, P A C Ramaswamy Raja Matric, Hr. Secondary School, Rajapalayam 626 117, Tamil Nadu.
Tel: 04563 222530
email: cvpacrhs@sancharnet.in
Contact: T.C. Pandian

WWF – India (TSNO)
297 T.T.K. Road, Alwarpet, Chennai 600 018, Tamil Nadu.
Tel: 044 24997107
email: wwftnso@sify.com

INTERNATIONAL ORGANISATIONS

BirdLife International
Wellbrook Court, Girton Road, Cambridge CB3 0NA, UK.
email: birdlife@birdlife.org.uk
Website: www.birdlife.net

Publication: *World Birdwatch* magazine (quarterly).

BirdLife International (formerly the International Council for Bird Preservation) is a network of Partners and Affiliates represented in over 100 countries. BirdLife is the world's leading authority on the status of the world's birds, their habitats and the urgent problems that face them. BirdLife aims to:

- prevent the extinction of any bird species;
- reduce the number of species that are globally threatened;
- enhance the conservation status of all bird species; and
- conserve crucial sites and habitats for birds.

BirdLife has recently completed the *Threatened Birds of Asia: The BirdLife International Red Data Book*, which provides a comprehensive assessment of the status, distribution and conservation needs of threatened birds in Asia. BirdLife is currently working on an inventory of Important Bird Areas in Asia. The Bombay Natural History Society is the BirdLife Partner Designate in India.

Oriental Bird Club (OBC)

P.O. Box 324, Bedford, MK42 0WG, UK.
email: mail@orientalbirdclub.org
Website: www.orientalbirdclub.org
Publications: *BirdingASIA* (half yearly); *Forktail* journal (annual).
The OBC was established in 1985. It aims to:

- encourage an interest in the birds of the Oriental region and their conservation;
- liaise with and promote the work of existing regional societies; and
- collate and publish material on Oriental birds.

The OBC offers grants to nationals in the region to encourage survey work useful for conservation and conservation awareness.

Wetlands International

South Asia Office, A-127, 2nd Floor, Defence Colony, New Delhi 110 024, India.
email: wisaind@del2.vsnl.net.in
Website: www.wetlands.org
Contact: Dr C.L. Trisa
Publication: *Wetlands* (newsletter of Wetlands International).
Wetlands International was created in October 1985 following the merger of the Asian Wetland Bureau with the International Waterfowl and Wetlands Research Bureau. The organisation is committed to promoting the protection and sustainable utilisation of wetlands and wetland resources worldwide. It has been involved in surveys, monitoring and conservation of waterbirds and wetlands since 1954 and has coordinated the Asian Waterbird Census since 1987 (*see* www.wetlands.org/IWC/awc/awcmain.html). It coordinates the Asia-Pacific Migratory Waterbird Conservation Strategy: 2001–2005, which provides an international cooperative conservation framework involving governments, conventions, NGOs, development agencies and local people in the region. This aims to enhance the long-term conservation of migratory waterbirds and their habitats in the region (*see* www.wetlands.org/IWC/awc/waterbirdstrategy/default.htm).

UDHAGAMANDALAM BOTANICAL GARDENS.

World Pheasant Association South Asia Field Office (WPA-SARO)
DLF Phase 3 Gurgaon, Haryana, India.
Publication: *Mor.*
WPA-SARO was established by the World Pheasant Association in April 1992. The main purpose of this office is to further the aims of WPA in the South Asian region. Over the last five years, the office has initiated many short- and long-term field research projects leading to the production of useful data, not only on Galliformes, but also on other birds, mammals and their habitats. The WPA-SARO has also been offering assistance by way of technical, material and financial help.

World Wide Fund for Nature (WWF) India
172-B Lodi Estate, New Delhi 110 023, India.
WWF India was established in 1969 and is the largest of the country's non-governmental conservation organisations. Today, the organisation's mission is 'to promote nature conservation and environmental protection as the basis for sustainable and equitable development'.

REFERENCES

Alström, P. (1998) Taxonomy of the *Mirafra assamica* complex. *Forktail* 13: 97–107.
Alström, P., and Olsson, U. (1999) The Golden-spectacled Warbler – a complex of sibling species, including a previously undescribed species. *Ibis* 141: 545–568.
Anon. (1991) Mangrove conservation. *Hornbill* 1991(4): 20.
Anon. (1996) *Asia-Pacific Migratory Waterbird Conservation Strategy: 1996–2000.*

Wetlands International – Asia Pacific, Kuala Lumpur, Publication No. 117 and International Waterfowl and Wetlands Research Bureau, Japan Committee, Tokyo.

BirdLife International (2001) *Threatened Birds of Asia.* BirdLife International, Cambridge.

BirdLife International (2003) *Saving Asia's Threatened Birds. A Guide for Governments and Civil Society.* BirdLife International, Cambridge.

Collins, N.M., Sayer, J.A., and Whitmore, T.C. (1991) *The Conservation Atlas of Tropical Forests, Asia and the Pacific.* The World Conservation Union. Macmillan, London.

Economic and Social Commission for Asia and the Pacific (1994) *Statistical Yearbook for Asia and the Pacific 1993.* Bangkok.

Gillham, E., and Gillham, B. (1996) *Hybrid Ducks – Contribution Towards an Inventory.* Privately published.

Grimmett, R., Inskipp, C., and Inskipp, T. (1998) *Birds of the Indian Subcontinent.* Christopher Helm, London.

Hussain, S.A. (1996) An overview of recent bird migration studies in India. Abstract. P.1 in Pan-Asian Ornithological Congress and XII BirdLife Asia Conference, Coimbatore, India, 9–16 November 1996.

Inskipp, T., Lindsey, N., and Duckworth, W. (1996) *An Annotated Checklist of the Birds of the Oriental Region.* Oriental Bird Club, Sandy.

Islam, M.Z., and Rahmani, A.R. (2002) Threatened birds of India. *Buceros* 7 (1&2). Compiled from *Threatened Birds of Asia: The BirdLife International Red Data Book* (2001), Cambridge, UK: BirdLife International.

Kazmierczak, K., and Singh, R. (1998) *A Birdwatchers' Guide to India.* Prion Ltd, Sandy.

Klein, R., and Buchheim, A. (1997) Die westliche Schwarzmeerküste als Kontaktgebiet zweier Großmöwenformen der *Larus cachinnans*-Gruppe. *Vogelwelt* 118: 61–70.

Liebers, D., Helbig, A.J., and de Knijff, P. (2001) Genetic differentiation and phylogeography of gulls in the *Larus cachinnans-fuscus* group (Aves: Charadriiformes). *Molecular Ecology* 10: 2447–2462.

Ministry of Environment and Forests (1997) *State of Forest Report 1997.* Forest Survey of India, Dehra Dun.

Oaks, J.L., Gilbert, M., Virani, M.Z., Watson, R.T., Meteyer, C.U., Rideout, B.A., Shivaprasad, H.L., Ahmed, S., Chaudhry, M.J.I., Arshad, M., Mahmood, S., Ali, A., and Khan, A.A. (2004) Diclofenac residues as the cause of vulture population decline in Pakistan. *Nature* 427: 630–633.

Parry, S.J., Clark, W.S., and Prakash, V. (2002) On the taxonomic status of the Indian Spotted Eagle *Aquila hastata. Ibis* 144: 665–675.

Perennou, C., Mundkur, T., Scott, D.A., Folkestad, A., and Kvenild, L. (1994) *The Asian Waterfowl Census 1987–91: Distribution and Status of Asian Waterfowl.* AWB Publication 86. IWRB Publication 24. AWB, Kuala Lumpur, and IWRB, Slimbridge.

Rodgers, W.A., and Panwar, H.S. (1988) *Planning a Wildlife Protected Area Network in India.* Two volumes. Wildlife Institute of India, Dehra Dun.

Sankaran, R. (1995) A fresh initiative to conserve the Lesser Florican. *Oriental Bird Club Bulletin* 22: 42–44.

Shyamsunder, S., and Parameswarappa, S. (1987) Forestry in India – the forester's view. *Ambio* 16: 332–337.

Stattersfield, A.J., Crosby, M.J., Long, A.J., and Wege, D.C. (1998) *Endemic Bird Areas of the World, Priorities for Biodiversity Conservation.* BirdLife International, Cambridge.

WWF India, and AWB (1993) *Directory of Indian wetlands.* WWF India, New Delhi; and AWB, Kuala Lumpur.

ACKNOWLEDGEMENTS

The authors would like to thank once again those who contributed in a major way to the *Birds of the Indian Subcontinent* (Grimmett *et al.*, 1998) and who are acknowledged in that work. Particular thanks go to Carol Inskipp, the second author of this major work and who, owing to pressures of other work, decided not to co-author the North and South India guides – these could not have been produced without her earlier contribution. We are also extremely grateful to M. Zafar-ul Islam and Asad R. Rahmani, of the Bombay Natural History Society, for preparing the foreword and contributing material for the introductory sections. Thanks also go to Clive Byers, Daniel Cole, John Cox, Carl D'Silva, Alan Harris, Craig Robson and Tim Worfolk, who have prepared new illustrations for this edition. RG would like to thank Helen Taylor, and their two children George and Ella, as well as his parents, Frank and Molly Grimmett, for their continued encouragement and support. RG would also like to thank Ani Kartikasari and Meiske D. Tapilatu for their assistance in the preparation of the typescript.

Once again we would also like to thank Robert Kirk, who commissioned the book, and shared our vision to produce accessible guides for the birdwatching public, and to Nigel Redman, Mike Unwin and Julie Bailey of A & C Black, who have managed the project throughout and have skilfully handled the production process.

GLOSSARY

Altitudinal migrant: a species that breeds at high altitudes (in mountains) and moves to lower levels and valleys in non-breeding season.

Arboreal: tree-dwelling.

Arm: the basal part of the wing, from where it joins the body, outwards to the carpal joint.

Axillaries: the feathers in the armpit at the base of the underwing.

Biotope: a particular area that is substantially uniform in its environmental conditions and flora and fauna.

Cap: a well-defined patch of colour or bare skin on the top of the head.

Carpal: the bend of the wing or carpal joint.

Carpal patch: a well-defined patch of colour on the underwing in the vicinity of the carpal joint.

Casque: an enlargement on the upper surface of the bill, in front of the head, as in hornbills.

Cere: a fleshy (often brightly coloured) structure at the base of the bill and containing the nostrils.

Collar: a well-defined band of colour that encircles or partly encircles the neck.

Colonial: nesting or roosting in tight colonies; species that are loosely colonial have nests more widely spaced.

Commensalism: a rare situation where species A benefits from the presence of species B, but where B is indifferent to the presence of A, neither gaining nor losing from that association.

Culmen: the ridge of the upper mandible.

Eclipse plumage: a female-like plumage acquired in some species (e.g. ducks or some sunbirds) during or after breeding.

Edgings or edges: outer feather margins that can frequently result in distinct paler or darker panels of colour in wings or tail.

Endemic: restricted or confined to a specific country or region.

Flight feathers: the primaries, secondaries and tail feathers.

Fringes: complete feather margins that frequently result in a scaly appearance to body feathers or coverts.

Frugivorous: fruit-eating.

Gape: the mouth and fleshy corner of the bill, which can extend back below the eye.

Gonys: a bulge in the lower mandible, usually distinct in gulls and terns.

Graduated tail: where the longest tail feathers are the central pair and the shortest the outermost, with those in between intermediate in length.

Granivorous: feeding on grain or seeds

Gregarious: living in flocks or communities.

Gular pouch: a loose and pronounced area of skin extending from the throat (e.g. in pelicans or hornbills).

Hackles: long and pointed neck feathers that can extend across mantle and wing-coverts (e.g. in junglefowls).

Hand: the outer end of the wing, from the carpal joint to the tip of the wing.

Hepatic: used with reference to the rufous-brown morph of some cuckoos.

Iris (plural irides): the coloured membrane that surrounds the pupil of the eye, which can be brightly coloured.

Jheel: a shallow lake in a low-lying natural depression, usually with floating and submerged vegetation, reedbeds and partially submerged trees.

Lappet: a wattle, particularly one at the gape.

Leading edge: the edge of the forewing.

Local: occurring or common within a small or restricted area.

Mandible: the lower or upper half of the bill.

Mask: a dark area of plumage surrounding the eye and often covering the ear-coverts.

Melanistic: when the plumage is dominated by black pigmentation.

Morph: a distinct plumage type, which occurs alongside one or more other distinct plumage types.

Nomadic: of a wandering or erratically occurring species that has no fixed territory when not breeding.

Nominate: the first-named race of a species, that which has its racial name the same as the specific name.

Nuchal: the hind-neck, used with reference to a patch or collar.

Nullah: a watercourse or ravine, usually dry.

Ocelli: eye-like spots of iridescent colour; a distinctive feature in the plumage of peafowls.

Orbital ring: a narrow circular ring of feathering or bare skin surrounding the eye.

Pelagic: of the open sea.

pH: a measure of acidity: low pH indicates high acidity, high pH low acidity.

Plantation: group of trees (usually exotic or non-native species) planted in close proximity to each other for timber or as a crop.

Primary projection: the extension of the primaries beyond the longest tertial on a closed wing; this can be of critical use (e.g. in the identification of larks or *Acrocephalus* warblers).

Race: subspecies; a geographical population whose members all show constant differences (e.g. in plumage or size) from those of other populations of the same species.

Rectrices: the tail feathers.

Remiges: the primaries and secondaries.

Rictal bristles: bristles, often prominent, at the base of the bill.

Shaft streak: a fine pale or dark line of colour that follows the feather shaft.

Shola: a densely forested ravine on the slopes of the Western Ghats.

Speculum: refers to the often glossy panel across the secondaries of dabbling ducks, which is often bordered by pale tips to these feathers and a greater-covert wing-bar.

Subspecies: *see* race.

Subterminal band: a dark or pale band, usually broad, which lies behind the terminal band of the tail.

Terminal band: a dark or pale band, usually broad, at the end of the tail.

Terrestrial: living or occurring mainly on the ground.

Trailing edge: a darker or paler rear edge of the wing.

Vent: the area around the cloaca (anal opening), just behind the legs (should not be confused with the undertail-coverts).

Vermiculated: finely barred or marked with fine or narrow wavy lines, usually visible only at close range.

Wattle: a lobe of bare, often brightly coloured, skin attached to the head (frequently at the bill base) as in the mynas or wattled lapwings.

Wing linings: underwing-coverts.

Wing panel: a pale or dark band across the wing, broader and generally more diffuse than a wing-bar (often formed by pale edges to the remiges or coverts).

Wing-bar: a narrow and well-defined dark or pale bar across the wing; often refers to a band formed by pale tips to the greater or median coverts (or both, as in 'double wing-bar').

SELECTED BIBLIOGRAPHY

A large number of references were analysed for the information on occurrence and status of birds in the individual states. However, the initial lists were built up from a few key references, which are listed below with the relevant states appended in brackets.

Abdulali, H. (1945) Birds of the Vizagapatam district. *J. Bombay Nat. Hist. Soc.* 45: 333–347. [Andhra Pradesh]

Abdulali, H. (1953) More about Vizagapatam birds. *J. Bombay Nat. Hist. Soc.* 51: 746–747. [Andhra Pradesh]

Abdulali, H. (1981) *Checklist of the Birds of Maharashtra with Notes on their Status around Bombay.* Second edn. [Maharashtra]

Ali, S. (1938) An additional list of birds from Hyderabad State. *J. Bombay Nat. Hist. Soc.* 40: 497–499. [Andhra Pradesh]

Ali, S. (1969) *Birds of Kerala.* Oxford University Press, New Delhi. [Kerala, Tamil Nadu]

Ali, S., and Abdulali, H. (1936–39) The birds of Bombay and Salsette. *J. Bombay Nat. Hist. Soc.* 39: 83–103, 520–530, 679–688; 40: 148–173, 367–381, 628–652. [Maharashtra]

Ali, S., and Whistler, H. (1933–34) The Hyderabad State ornithological survey. *J. Bombay Nat. Hist. Soc.* 36: 356–390, 707–725, 898–919; 37: 124–142, 425–454. [Andhra Pradesh]

Ali, S., and Whistler, H. (1942–43) The birds of Mysore. *J. Bombay Nat. Hist. Soc.* 43: 130–147, 318–341, 573–595; 44: 9–26, 206–220. [Karnataka]

Balachandran, S. (1995) Shore birds of the Marine National Park in the Gulf of Mannar, Tamil Nadu. *J. Bombay Nat. Hist. Soc.* 92: 303–311. [Tamil Nadu]

Barnes, A.M. (1938–39) Birds observed in and near Tambaram, Chingleput district, south India. *J. Bombay Nat. Hist. Soc.* 40: 467–476, 744–747. [Tamil Nadu]

Betts, F.N. (1951) The birds of Coorg. *J. Bombay Nat. Hist. Soc.* 50: 20–63, 224–263. [Karnataka]

Bhamburkar, P.M., and Desai, N. (1993) *Study Report of Mansingh Deo Wild Life Sanctuary (proposed).* World Wide Fund for Nature – India, Nagpur Division, Nagpur. [Maharashtra]

Biddulph, C.H. (1938) The birds of Rameswaram Island. *J. Bombay Nat. Hist. Soc.* 40: 238–256. [Tamil Nadu]

Butler, E.A. (1881) A tentative catalogue of the birds of the Deccan and south Mahratta country. *Stray Feathers* 9: 367–442. [Karnataka, Maharashtra]

Chakravarthy, A.K., and Tejasri, K.P.P.C. (1992) *Birds of Hill Region of Karnataka: an Introduction.* Narbarath Enterprises, Bangalore. [Karnataka]

D'Abreu, E.A. (1935) A list of the birds of the Central Provinces. *J. Bombay Nat. Hist. Soc.* 38: 95–116. [Maharashtra]

Davidson, J. (1898) The birds of north Kanara. *J. Bombay Nat. Hist. Soc.* 11: 652–679, 12: 43–72. [Karnataka]

George, J. (ed.) (1994) *Annotated Checklist of the Birds of Bangalore.* Birdwatchers' Field Club of Bangalore, Bangalore. [Karnataka]

Ghorpade, K.D. (1974) Preliminary notes on the ornithology of Sandur, Karnataka. *J. Bombay Nat. Hist. Soc.* 70: 499–531. [Karnataka]

Grubh, R.B., and Ali, S. (1976) Birds of Goa. *J. Bombay Nat. Hist. Soc.* 73: 42–53. [Goa]

Gururaja, K.V., Aravinda, N.A., and Raghunatha, V. (1993) Checklist of birds of Shimoga and Gudavi. Pp. 77–80 in A. Verghese, S. Sridhar and A.K. Chakravarthy (eds) *Bird Conservation, Strategies for the Nineties and Beyond*. Ornithological Society of India, Bangalore. [Karnataka]

Harris, P. (1996) *Goa, the Independent Birders' Guide*. Eastern Publications, Lowestoft, UK. [Goa]

Hewetson, C.E. (1956) Observations on the bird life of Madhya Pradesh. *J. Bombay Nat. Hist. Soc.* 53: 595–645. [Maharashtra]

Karthikeyan, S., Jayanth, M.S., Hemanth, J., and Sanjay, G.S. (1993) Birds of Dandeli Wildlife Sanctuary. *Newsletter for Birdwatchers* 33: 83–85. [Karnataka]

Koelz, W. (1942) Notes on the birds of the Londa neighbourhood, Bombay Presidency. *J. Bombay Nat. Hist. Soc.* 43: 11–33. [Karnataka]

Koelz, W. (1948) Notes on a collection of birds from Madras Presidency. *J. Bombay Nat. Hist. Soc.* 47: 128–142. [Andhra Pradesh, Karnataka, Kerala, Tamil Nadu]

Lainer, H. (1999) The birds of Goa. *J. Bombay Nat. Hist. Soc.* 96: 203–220, 405–423. [Goa]

Mahabal, A., and Lamba, B.S. (1987) On the birds of Poona and vicinity. *Rec. Zool. Surv. India, Occ. Pap.* 94: 115 pp. [Maharashtra]

Majumdar, N. (1984) On a collection of birds from Adilabad district, Andhra Pradesh. *Rec. Zool. Surv. India Misc. Publ. Occ. Pap.* 65: 63 pp. [Andhra Pradesh]

Neelakantan, K.K., Sashikumar, C., and Venugopalan, R. (1993) *A Book of Kerala Birds*. Part 1. World Wide Fund for Nature – India, Kerala State Committee, Trivandrum. [Kerala]

Nichols, E.G. (1943–45) Occurrence of birds in Madura district. *J. Bombay Nat. Hist. Soc.* 44: 387–407, 574–584; 45: 122–132. [Tamil Nadu]

Prasad, A. (2003) Annotated checklist of the birds of western Maharashtra. *Buceros* 8: 1–174.

Price, T.D. (1980) The seasonality and occurrence of birds in the Eastern Ghats of Andhra Pradesh. *J. Bombay Nat. Hist. Soc.* 76: 379–422. [Andhra Pradesh]

Rahmani, A.R. (1989) *The Great Indian Bustard: Final Report*. Bombay Natural History Society, Bombay. [Andhra Pradesh, Maharashtra]

Rane, U. (1984) Additions 'to the birds of Goa by Robert B. Grubh & Salim Ali JBNHS Vol. 73, No. 1'. *J. Bombay Nat. Hist. Soc.* 80: 638–640. [Goa]

Ripley, S.D., Beehler, B.M., and Krishna Raju, K.S.R. (1988) Birds of the Vishakhapatnam Ghats, Andhra Pradesh. *J. Bombay Nat. Hist. Soc.* 84: 540–559; 85: 90–107. [Andhra Pradesh]

Saha, B.C., and Dasgupta, J.M. (1992) Birds of Goa. *Rec. Zool. Surv. India Misc. Publ. Occ. Paper* 143: 56 pp. [Goa]

Selvakumar, R., Sukumar, R., Narayanaswamy, V., and Baskaran, S.T. (1981) A check list of birds of Guindy Deer Park. *Newsletter for Birdwatchers* 21(8): 3–6. [Tamil Nadu]

Sugathan, R. (1983) Some interesting aspects of the avifauna of the Point Calimere Sanctuary, Thanjavur District, Tamil Nadu. *J. Bombay Nat. Hist. Soc.* 79: 567–575. [Tamil Nadu]

Taher, S.A., and Pittie, A. (1989) *A Checklist of the Birds of Andhra Pradesh*. [Andhra Pradesh]

Taher, S.A., and Pittie, A. (1996) Additions to 'A checklist of birds of Andhra Pradesh'. *Mayura* 11: 1–5. [Andhra Pradesh]

Thomas, J., and Balan, M. (1993) Birds of Annamalai Hills. Pp. 149–150 in A. Verghese, S. Sridhar, and A.K. Chakravarthy (eds) *Bird Conservation, Strategies for the Nineties and Beyond*. Ornithological Society of India, Bangalore. [Tamil Nadu]

Uddin, S.R. (1995) Birds of Cuddapah district, Andhra Pradesh. *Mayura* 10: 28–33. [Andhra Pradesh]

Vyawahare, P.M. (1992) Checklist of birds from Dhule district, Maharashtra, with a note on migratory birds. *Pavo* 29(1–2): 77–106. [Maharashtra]

Vyawahare, P.M., and Kulkarni, A.B. (1987) Checklist of birds from Jaikwadi dam area, Paithan, Aurangabad, Maharashtra. *Pavo* 24: 9–12. [Maharashtra]

Whistler, H., and Kinnear, N.B. (1931–37) The Vernay Scientific Survey of the Eastern Ghats (Ornithological Section). *J. Bombay Nat. Hist. Soc.* 35: 505–524, 737–760; 36: 67–93, 334–352, 561–590, 832–844; 37: 96–105, 281–297, 515–528, 751–763; 38: 26–40, 232–240, 418–437, 672–698; 39: 246–263, 447–463. [Andhra Pradesh, Tamil Nadu]

Zacharias, V.J., and Gaston, A.J. (1993) The birds of Wynaad, southern India. *Forktail* 8: 11–23. [Kerala]

FAMILY SUMMARIES

Some families are divided into subfamilies and some of these are further divided into tribes.

■ ■ ■ Francolins, Spurfowls, Junglefowl and Quails Phasianidae ■ ■ ■

Terrestrial, feeding and nesting on the ground, but many species roost in trees at night. They are good runners, often preferring to escape on foot rather than taking to the air. Their flight is powerful and fast, but, except in the case of the migratory quails, it cannot be sustained for long periods. Typically, they forage by scratching the ground with their strong feet to expose food hidden among dead leaves or in the soil. They mainly eat seeds, fruit, buds, roots and leaves, complemented by invertebrates. **pp.46–51**

■ ■ Whistling-ducks Dendrocygnidae and Swans, Geese and Ducks Anatidae ■ ■

Aquatic and highly gregarious, typically migrating, feeding, roosting and resting together, often in mixed flocks. Most species are chiefly vegetarian when adult, feeding on seeds, algae, plants and roots, often supplemented by aquatic invertebrates. Their main foraging methods are diving, surface-feeding or dabbling, and grazing. They also upend, wade, filter and sieve water and debris for food, and probe with the bill. They have a direct flight with sustained fast wingbeats, and characteristically they fly in V-formation. **pp.52–59**

■ ■ ■ Buttonquails Turnicidae ■ ■ ■

Small, plump terrestrial birds. They are found in a wide variety of habitats with a dry, often sandy, substrate and low ground cover under which they can readily run or walk. Buttonquails are very secretive and fly with great reluctance, with weak whirring beats low over the ground, dropping quickly into cover. They feed on grass and weed seeds, grain, greenery and small insects, picking food from the ground surface, or scratching with the feet. **pp.48–49**

■ ■ ■ Wrynecks, Piculets and Woodpeckers Picidae ■ ■ ■

Chiefly arboreal, and usually seen clinging to, and climbing up, vertical trunks and lateral branches. Typically, they work up trunks and along branches in jerky spurts, directly or in spirals. Some species feed regularly on the ground, searching mainly for termites and ants. The bill of many species is powerful, for boring into wood to extract insects and for excavating nest holes. Woodpeckers feed chiefly on ants, termites, and grubs and pupae of wood-boring beetles. Most woodpeckers also hammer rapidly against tree trunks with their bill, producing a loud rattle, known as 'drumming', which is used to advertise territories and warn off intruders. Their flight is strong and direct, with marked undulations. Many species can be located by their characteristic loud calls. **pp.60–63**

■ ■ ■ Asian Barbets Megalaimidae ■ ■ ■

Arboreal, and usually found in the treetops. Despite their bright coloration, they can be very difficult to see, especially when silent, their plumage blending remarkably well with tree foliage. They often sit motionless for long periods. Barbets call persistently and monotonously in the breeding season, sometimes throughout the day; in the non-breeding season they are usually silent. They are chiefly frugivorous, many species favouring figs *Ficus*. Their flight is strong and direct, with deep woodpecker-like undulations. **pp.62–63**

■ ■ ■ Hornbills Bucerotidae ■ ■ ■

Medium-sized to large birds with massive bills with variable-sized casque. Mainly arboreal, feeding chiefly on wild figs *Ficus*, berries and drupes, supplemented by small animals and insects. Flight is powerful and slow, and for most species consists of a few wingbeats followed by a sailing glide with the wing-tips upturned. In all but the smaller species, the wingbeats make a distinctive loud puffing sound audible for some distance. Hornbills often fly one after another in follow-my-leader fashion. Usually found in pairs or small parties, sometimes in flocks of up to 30 or more where food is abundant. **pp.64–65**

▪ ▪ ▪ Hoopoes Upupidae ▪ ▪ ▪

Hoopoes have a distinctive appearance, with a long decurved bill, short legs and rounded wings. They are insectivorous and forage by pecking and probing the ground. Flight is undulating, slow and butterfly-like.   **pp.66–67**

▪ ▪ ▪ Trogons Trogonidae ▪ ▪ ▪

Brightly coloured, short-necked, medium-sized birds with a long tail, short rounded wings and a rather short, broad bill. They usually occur singly or in widely separated pairs. Characteristically, they perch almost motionless in upright posture for long periods in the middle or lower storey of dense forests. Trogons are mainly insectivorous and also eat leaves and berries. They capture flying insects on the wing when moving from one vantage point to another, twisting with the agility of a flycatcher.   **pp.66–67**

▪ ▪ ▪ Rollers Coraciidae ▪ ▪ ▪

Stoutly built, medium-sized birds with a large head and short neck. Their main diet consists mainly of large insects. Typically, they occur singly or in widely spaced pairs. Flight is buoyant, with rather rapid, deliberate wingbeats.   **pp.66–67**

▪ ▪ ▪ Small Kingfishers Alcedinidae, Large Kingfishers Halcyonidae and Pied Kingfishers Cerylidae ▪ ▪ ▪

Small to medium-sized birds, with large head, a long, strong beak and short legs. Most kingfishers spend long periods perched singly or in well-separated pairs, watching intently before plunging swiftly downwards to seize prey with their bill; they usually return to the same perch. They eat mainly fish, tadpoles and invertebrates; larger species also eat frogs, snakes, crabs, lizards and rodents. Their flight is direct and strong, with rapid wingbeats and often close to the surface.   **pp.68–69**

▪ ▪ ▪ Bee-eaters Meropidae ▪ ▪ ▪

Brightly coloured birds with a long decurved beak, pointed wings and very short legs. They catch large flying insects on the wing, by making short, swift sallies like a flycatcher from an exposed perch such as a treetop, branch, post or telegraph wire; insects are pursued in a lively chase with a swift and agile flight. Some species also hawk insects in flight similar to swallows. Most species are sociable. Their flight is graceful and undulating, and consists of a few rapid wingbeats followed by a glide.   **pp.70–71**

▪ ▪ ▪ Old World Cuckoos Cuculidae ▪ ▪ ▪

Cuculidae have an elongated body with fairly long neck, tail varying from medium length to long and graduated, and quite a long, decurved bill. Almost all Cuculidae are arboreal and eat hairy caterpillars. Male cuckoos of most species are very noisy in the breeding season, calling frequently during the day, especially if cloudy, and often into the night. When not breeding they are silent and unobtrusive, and as a result their status and distribution at this season is very poorly known. Cuckoos are notorious for their nest parasitism.   **pp.72–75**

▪ ▪ ▪ Coucals Centropodidae ▪ ▪ ▪

Large, skulking birds with long, graduated tail and weak flight. Coucals are terrestrial, frequenting dense undergrowth, bamboo, tall grassland or scrub jungle. They eat small animals and invertebrates.   **pp.76–77**

▪ ▪ ▪ Parrots Psittacidae ▪ ▪ ▪

Parrots have a short neck and short, stout, hooked bill with the upper mandible strongly curved and overlapping the lower mandible. Most parrots are noisy and highly gregarious. They associate in family parties and small flocks and gather in large numbers at concentrations of food, such as paddy-fields. Their diet is almost entirely vegetarian: fruit, seeds, buds, nectar and pollen. The flight of *Psittacula* parrots is swift, powerful and direct.   **pp.76–77**

■ ■ ■ Swifts Apodidae and Treeswifts Hemiprocnidae ■ ■ ■

Birds with long pointed wings, compact body, short bill with a wide gape and very short legs. Swifts spend most of the day swooping and wheeling in the sky with great agility and grace. Typical swift flight is a series of rapid shallow wingbeats interspersed with short glides. They feed entirely in the air, drink and bathe while swooping low over water, and regularly pass the night in the air. Swifts eat mainly tiny insects, caught by flying back and forth among aerial concentrations of these with their large mouth open; they also pursue individual insects.   **pp.78–79**

■ ■ ■ Barn Owls and Grass Owls Tytonidae and Typical Owls Strigidae ■ ■ ■

Owls have a large and rounded head, big forward-facing eyes surrounded by a broad facial disc, and a short tail. Most are nocturnal and cryptically coloured and patterned, making them inconspicuous when resting during the day. When hunting, owls either quarter the ground or scan and listen for prey from a perch. Their diet consists of small animals and invertebrates. Owls are usually located by their distinctive and often weird calls, which are diagnostic of the species and advertise their presence and territories.   **pp.80–83**

■ ■ ■ Frogmouths Batrachostomidae ■ ■ ■

Frogmouths have the same cryptic colouring, soft plumage, wide gape and nocturnal habits as nightjars, but differ in some of their habitats. They are more arboreal than nightjars, nesting and roosting in trees and hunting from them at night by pouncing on prey.   **pp.84–85**

■ ■ ■ Nightjars Caprimulgidae ■ ■ ■

Small to medium-sized birds with long, pointed wings, and gaping mouth with long bristles that help to catch insects in flight. Nightjars are crepuscular and nocturnal in habit, with soft, owl-like, cryptically patterned plumage. By day they perch on the ground or lengthwise on a branch, and are difficult to detect. They eat flying insects that are caught on the wing. Typically, they fly erratically to and fro over and among vegetation, occasionally wheeling, gliding and hovering to pick insects from foliage. They are most easily located by their calls.   **pp.84–85**

■ ■ ■ Pigeons and Doves Columbidae ■ ■ ■

Birds with a stout, compact body, rather short neck, and small head and bill. Their flight is swift and direct, with fast wingbeats. Most species are gregarious outside the breeding season. Seeds, fruits, buds and leaves form their main diet, but many species also eat small invertebrates. They have soft plaintive cooing or booming calls that are often monotonously repeated.   **pp.86–89**

■ ■ ■ Bustards Otididae ■ ■ ■

Medium-sized to large terrestrial birds that inhabit grasslands, semi-desert and desert. They have fairly long legs, stout body, long neck, and crests and neck plumes, which are exhibited in display. The wings are broad and long, and in flight the neck is outstretched. Their flight is powerful and can be very fast. When feeding, bustards have a steady, deliberate gait. They are more or less omnivorous, and feed opportunistically on large insects, such as grasshoppers and locusts, young birds, shoots, leaves, seeds and fruits. Males perform elaborate and spectacular displays in the breeding season.   **pp.90–91**

■ ■ ■ Cranes Gruidae ■ ■ ■

Stately long-necked, long-legged birds with a tapering body, and long inner secondaries that hang over the tail. The flight is powerful, with the head and neck extended forwards and legs and feet stretched out behind. Flocks of cranes often fly in V-formation; they sometimes soar at considerable heights. Most cranes are gregarious outside the breeding season, and flocks are often very noisy. Cranes have a characteristic resonant and far-reaching musical trumpet-like call. A wide variety of plant and animal food is taken. The bill is used to probe and dig for plant roots and to graze and glean vegetable material above the ground. Both sexes have a spectacular and beautiful dance that takes place throughout the year.   **pp.90–91**

■ ■ ■ Rails, Gallinules and Coots Rallidae ■ ■ ■

Small to medium-sized birds, with moderate to long legs for wading and short rounded wings. With the exception of the Common Moorhen and Common Coot, which spend much time swimming in the open, rails are mainly terrestrial. Many occur in marshes. They fly reluctantly and feebly, with legs dangling, for a short distance and then drop into cover again. The majority are heard more often than seen, and are most voluble at dusk and at night. Their calls consist of strident or raucous repeated notes. They eat insects, crustaceans, amphibians, fish and vegetable matter. **pp.92–95**

■ ■ ■ Sandgrouse Ptercoclidae ■ ■ ■

Cryptically pattered terrestrial birds resembling pigeons in size and shape. The wings are long and pointed. Most Sandgrouse are wary and, when disturbed, rise with a clatter of wings, flying off rapidly and directly with fast, regular wingbeats. They walk and run well, foraging mainly for small hard seeds picked up from the ground and sometimes also eating green leaves, shoots, berries, small bulbs and insects. They need to drink every day, and will sometimes travel distances to waterholes. Most sandgrouse have regular drinking times which are characteristic of each species, and they often visit traditional watering places, sometimes gathering in large numbers. Most species are gregarious except when breeding. **pp.94–95**

■ ■ ■ Woodcocks, Snipes, Godwits, Sandpipers, Curlews and Phalaropes Scolopacidae ■ ■ ■

Woodcocks and Snipes Subfamily Scolopacinae

Woodcocks and snipes are small to medium-sized waders with a very long bill, fairly long legs and cryptically patterned plumage. They feed mainly by probing in soft ground and also by picking from the surface. Their diet consists mostly of small aquatic invertebrates. If approached, they usually first crouch on the ground and 'freeze', preferring to rely on their protective plumage pattern to escape detection. They inhabit marshy ground. **pp.96–97**

Godwits, Sandpipers, Curlews and Phalaropes Subfamily Tringinae

The Tringinae are wading birds with quite long to very long legs and a long bill. They feed on small aquatic invertebrates. **pp.98–105**

■ ■ ■ Painted-snipes Rostratulidae ■ ■ ■

Painted-snipes frequent marshes and superficially resemble snipes, but have spectacular plumages. **pp.96–97**

■ ■ ■ Jacanas Jacanidae ■ ■ ■

Jacanas characteristically have very long toes, which enable them to walk over floating vegetation. They inhabit freshwater lakes, ponds and marshes. **pp.106–107**

■ ■ ■ Thick-knees Burhinidae ■ ■ ■

Medium-sized to large waders, mainly crepuscular or nocturnal, and with cryptically patterned plumages. They eat invertebrates and small animals. **pp.106–107**

■ ■ ■ Oystercatchers, Avocets, Plovers and Lapwings Charadriidae ■ ■ ■

Oystercatchers, Stilts and Avocets Subfamily Recurvirostrinae

Oystercatchers are waders that usually inhabit the seashore and are only vagrants inland. They have all-black or black-and-white plumage. The bill is long, stout, orange-red and adapted for opening shells of bivalve molluscs. Stilts and avocets have a characteristic long bill, and longer legs in proportion to the body than any other birds except flamingos. They inhabit marshes, lakes and pools, and both feed on aquatic invertebrates. **pp.106–107**

Plovers and Lapwings Subfamily Charadriinae

Plovers and lapwings are small to medium-sized waders with rounded head, short neck and short bill. Typically, they forage by running in short spurts, pausing and standing erect, then stooping to pick up invertebrate prey. Their flight is swift and direct. **pp.108–111**

■ ■ ■ **Crab-plover, Pratincoles and Coursers** Glareolidae ■ ■ ■

Crab-plover Subfamily Dromadinae

The Crab-plover is the only species in this subfamily. Usually found singly, in pairs and in small parties, but with hundreds occurring at traditional roost sites. Mainly crepuscular. Feeds chiefly on crabs, mudskippers and crustaceans which it hunts in plover-like manner.
pp.106–107

Pratincoles and Coursers Subfamily Glareolinae

Coursers and pratincoles have an arched and pointed bill, wide gape and long, pointed wings. Coursers are long-legged and resemble plovers; they feed on the ground. Most pratincoles are short-legged; they catch most of their prey in the air, although they also feed on the ground. All pratincoles live near water, whereas coursers frequent dry grassland and dry stony areas.
pp.110–111

■ ■ ■ **Jaegers, Skimmers, Gulls and Terns** Laridae ■ ■ ■

This family comprises the subfamilies Larinae and Alcinae. Only the subfamily Larinae occurs in Southern India with representatives from three tribes occurring in the region.
pp.112–121

Jaegers Tribe Stercorariini

Aerial seabirds, with a strong, hooked beak, long, pointed wings, short legs, and webbed feet. Jaegers feed by chasing other seabirds, especially terns, until they drop or disgorge their food. They are usually found in marine waters, some distance from land, but are occasionally found inshore and may occur inland after monsoon storms.
pp.112–113

Skimmers Tribe Rynchopini

Skimmers have very long wings, a short forked tail, a long bill and short red legs and toes, and are black above and white below. They frequent rivers and lakes.
pp.114–115

Gulls Tribe Larini

Medium-sized to large birds with relatively long, narrow wings, usually a stout bill, moderately long legs and webbed feet. Immatures are brownish and cryptically patterned. In flight, gulls are graceful and soar easily in updraughts. All species swim buoyantly and well. They are highly adaptable, and most species are opportunistic feeders with a varied diet, including invertebrates. Most species are gregarious.
pp.112–115

Terns Tribe Sternini

Small to medium-sized aerial birds with a gull-like body, but generally more delicately built. The wings are long and pointed, typically narrower than those of gulls, and the flight is buoyant and graceful. Terns are highly vocal and most species are gregarious. There are four groups of terns occuring in Southern India: the Sterna terns, the Chlidonias or marsh terns, and the noddies of the genus *Anous*, plus the unique White Tern of the monotypic genus *Gygis*. The Sterna terns have a deeply forked tail. Sterna terns mainly eat small fish and crabs caught by hovering and then plunge-diving from the air, often submerging completely; also by picking prey from the surface. Marsh terns lack a prominent tail-fork and, compared with Sterna terns, are smaller, more compact and short-tailed, and have a more erratic and rather stiff-winged flight. Typically, marsh terns hawk insects or swoop down to pick small prey from the water surface. Noddies are pelagic terns, with a distinctive wedge-shaped and slightly forked tail. Noddies feed chiefly on small fish, squid, crustaceans and plankton, which they usually catch far out at sea, often feeding on moonlit nights.
pp.116–121

■ ■ ■ Osprey, Hawks, Eagles, Harriers and Vultures etc. Accipitridae ■ ■ ■

A large and varied family of raptors, ranging from the Besra to the huge Eurasian Griffon. In most species, the vultures being an exception, the female is larger than the male and is often duller and brownish. The Accipitridae feed on mammals, birds, reptiles, amphibians, fish, crabs, molluscs and insects – dead or alive. All have a hooked, pointed bill and very acute sight, and all except the vultures have powerful feet with long curved claws. They frequent all habitat types, ranging from dense forest, deserts and mountains to fresh waters.   **pp.122–139**

■ ■ ■ Falcons Falconidae ■ ■ ■

Small to medium-sized birds of prey, which resemble the Accipitridae in having a hooked beak, sharp curved talons, and remarkable powers of sight and flight. Like other raptors they are mainly diurnal, although a few are crepuscular. Some falcons kill flying birds in a surprise attack, often by stooping at great speed (e.g. Peregrine); others hover and then swoop on prey on the ground (e.g. Common Kestrel), and several species hawk insects in flight (e.g. Eurasian Hobby).   **pp.140–143**

■ ■ ■ Grebes Podicipedidae ■ ■ ■

Aquatic birds adapted for diving from the surface and swimming under the water to catch fish and aquatic invertebrates. Their strong legs are placed near the rear of their almost tailless body, and the feet are lobed. In flight, grebes have an elongated appearance, with the neck extended, and feet hanging lower than the humped back. They usually feed singly, but may form loose congregations in the non-breeding season.   **pp.144–145**

■ ■ ■ Tropicbirds Phaethontidae ■ ■ ■

Aerial seabirds which range over tropical and subtropical waters, and nest mainly on oceanic and offshore islands. Graceful pigeon-like flight, with flapping and circling alternating with long glides. Usually solitary, but may congregate with flocks of feeding terns. They feed by first hovering to locate prey (mainly fish and squid), and then plunge-diving on half-closed wings.   **pp.146–147**

■ ■ ■ Boobies Sulidae ■ ■ ■

Boobies are large seabirds. They forage on the wing, scanning the sea, and on sighting fish or squid they plunge-dive at an angle. Flight is direct with alternating periods of flapping and gliding.   **pp.146–147**

■ ■ ■ Anhingas Anhingidae ■ ■ ■

Large aquatic birds adapted for hunting fish underwater. Anhingas have a long, slender neck and head, long wings and a very long tail.   **pp.144–145**

■ ■ ■ Cormorants Phalacrocoracidae ■ ■ ■

Medium-sized to large aquatic birds. They are long-necked, with a hooked bill of moderate length and a long, stiff tail. Cormorants swim with the body low in the water, with the neck straight and the head and bill pointing a little upwards. They eat mainly fish, which are caught by underwater pursuit. In flight, the neck is extended and the head is held slightly above the horizontal. Typically, they often perch for long periods in upright posture, with spread wings and tail, on trees, posts or rocks.   **pp.144–145**

■ ■ ■ Herons and Bitterns Ardeidae ■ ■ ■

Medium-sized to large birds with long legs for wading. The diurnal herons have a slender body and long head and neck; the night herons are more squat, with shorter neck and legs. They fly with leisurely flaps, with the legs outstretched and projecting beyond the tail, and nearly always with head and neck drawn back. They frequent marshes and the shores of lakes and rivers. Typically, herons feed by standing motionless at the water's edge, waiting for prey to swim within reach, or by slow stalking in shallow water or on land. Bitterns usually skulk in reedbeds, although occasionally one may forage in the open, and they can clamber about reed stems with agility. Normally they are solitary and crepuscular, and are most often seen flying low over reedbeds with slow wingbeats, soon dropping into cover again. When in danger bitterns freeze, pointing the bill and neck upwards and compressing their feathers so that the whole body appears elongated. The bitterns are characterised by their booming territorial calls. Herons and bitterns feed on a wide variety of aquatic prey.   **pp.148–153**

▪ ▪ ▪ Flamingos Phoenicopteridae ▪ ▪ ▪

Large wading birds with long neck, very long legs, webbed feet and pink plumage. The bill is highly specialised for filter-feeding. Flamingos often occur in huge numbers and are found mainly on salt lakes and lagoons.   **pp.154–155**

▪ ▪ ▪ Ibises and Spoonbills Threskiornithidae ▪ ▪ ▪

Large birds with long neck and legs, partly webbed feet and long, broad wings. Ibises have a long decurved bill, and forage by probing in shallow water, mud and grass. Spoonbills have a long spatulate bill, and catch floating prey in shallow water.   **pp.154–155**

▪ ▪ ▪ Pelicans Pelecanidae ▪ ▪ ▪

Large, aquatic, gregarious fish-eating birds. The wings are long and broad, and the tail is short and rounded. They have a characteristic long, straight, flattened bill, hooked at the tip, and with a large expandable pouch suspended beneath the lower mandible. Many pelicans often fish cooperatively by swimming forward in a semicircular formation, driving the fish into shallow waters; each bird then scoops up fish from the water into its pouch, before swallowing the food. Pelicans fly either in V-formation or in lines, and often soar for considerable periods in thermals. They are powerful fliers, proceeding by steady flaps and with the head drawn back between the shoulders. When swimming, the closed wings are typically held above the back.   **pp.160–161**

▪ ▪ ▪ Storks Ciconiidae ▪ ▪ ▪

Large or very large birds with long bill, neck and legs, long and broad wings and a short tail. In flight, the legs are extended behind and the neck is outstretched. They have a powerful slow-flapping flight and frequently soar for long periods, often at great heights. They capture fish, frogs, snakes, lizards, large insects, crustaceans and molluscs while walking slowly in marshes, at edges of lakes and rivers and in grassland.   **pp.156–159**

▪ ▪ ▪ Frigatebirds Fregatidae ▪ ▪ ▪

Large aerial seabirds that rarely land on water, and roost and nest in trees and bushes. Agile in the air, and can soar for long periods. Noted for chasing other seabirds, especially boobies, until they drop or disgorge their food, but also capture their own prey by diving to the water surface. They are chiefly storm-driven visitors to the coast, typically during monsoons.   **pp.160–161**

▪ ▪ ▪ Petrels, Shearwaters and Storm-petrels Procellariidae ▪ ▪ ▪

Marine species, coming to shore only to breed. They are typically gregarious, often gathering in flocks at food concentrations. They feed on zooplankton, squid, fish and offal, seized on or below the water surface. Shearwaters and *Bulweria* petrels typically fly by a combination of rapid, rather stiff wing-beats, interspersed with long glides (gliding, or 'shearing', being more pronounced in strong winds). The Storm-petrels have a more fluttering flight.   **pp.162–163**

▪ ▪ ▪ Pittas Pittidae ▪ ▪ ▪

Brilliantly coloured, terrestrial forest passerines. They are of medium size, stocky and long-legged, with short square tail, stout bill and an erect carriage. Most of their time is spent foraging for invertebrates on the forest floor, flicking leaves and other vegetation, and probing with their strong bill into leaf litter and damp earth. Pittas usually progress on the ground by long hopping bounds. Typically, they are skulking and are often most easily located by their high-pitched whistling calls or songs. They sing in trees or bushes.   **pp.164–165**

▪ ▪ ▪ Fairy Bluebirds and Leafbirds Irenidae ▪ ▪ ▪

Small to medium-sized passerines with a fairly long, slender bill with the upper mandible decurved at the tip. All are arboreal, typically frequenting thick foliage in the canopy. They search leaves for insects and also feed on berries and nectar. Their flight is swift, usually over a short distance.   **pp.164–165**

▪ ▪ ▪ **Shrikes** Laniidae ▪ ▪ ▪

Medium-sized, predatory passerines with a strong stout bill, hooked at the tip of the upper mandible, strong legs and feet, a large head, and a long tail with graduated tip. Shrikes search for prey from a vantage point, such as the top of a bush or small tree or post. They swoop down to catch invertebrates or small animals from the ground or in flight. Over long distances their flight is typically undulating. Their calls are harsh, but most have quite musical songs and are good mimics. Shrikes typically inhabit open country with scattered bushes or light scrub. **pp.164–165**

▪ ▪ ▪ **Corvids** Corvidae ▪ ▪ ▪

This is a very large family, represented in Southern India by four subfamilies (in some cases further subdivided into tribes). **pp.166–173**

Subfamily Corvinae

Treepies, Crows Tribe Corvini

These are all robust perching birds that differ considerably from each other in appearance, but have a number of features in common: a fairly long straight bill, very strong feet and legs, and a tuft of nasal bristles extending over the base of the upper mandible. The sexes are alike or almost alike in plumage. They are strong fliers. Most are gregarious, especially when feeding and roosting. Typically, they are noisy birds, uttering loud and discordant squawks, croaks or screeches. The Corvini are highly inquisitive and adaptable. **pp.166–167**

Woodswallows Tribe Artamini

Plump birds with long, pointed wings, short tail and legs, and a wide gape. They feed on insects, usually captured in flight, and spend prolonged periods on the wing. They perch close together on a bare branch or wire, and often waggle the tail from side to side. **pp.168–169**

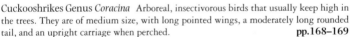

Orioles, Cuckooshrikes, Minivets, Flycatcher-shrikes Tribe Oriolini

Orioles Genus *Oriolus* Medium-sized arboreal passerines that usually keep hidden in the leafy canopy. Orioles have beautiful, fluty, whistling songs and harsh grating calls. Their flight is powerful and undulating, with fast wingbeats. They feed mainly on insects and fruit. **pp.166–167**

Cuckooshrikes Genus *Coracina* Arboreal, insectivorous birds that usually keep high in the trees. They are of medium size, with long pointed wings, a moderately long rounded tail, and an upright carriage when perched. **pp.168–169**

Minivets Genus *Pericrocotus* Small to medium-sized, brightly coloured passerines with a moderately long tail and an upright stance when perched. They are arboreal, and feed on insects by flitting about in the foliage to glean prey from leaves, buds and bark, sometimes hovering in front of a sprig or making short aerial sallies. They usually keep in pairs in the breeding season, and in small parties when not breeding. When feeding and in flight, they continually utter contact calls. **pp.168–169**

Subfamily Dicrurinae

Fantails Tribe Rhipidurini

Small, confiding, arboreal birds, perpetually on the move in search of insects. Characteristically, they erect and spread the tail like a fan, and droop the wings, while pirouetting and turning from side to side with jerky, restless movements. When foraging, they flit from branch to branch, making frequent aerial sallies after winged insects. They call continually. Fantails are usually found singly or in pairs, and often join mixed hunting parties with other insectivorous birds. **pp.172–173**

Drongos Tribe Dicrurini

Medium-sized passerines with characteristic black and often glossy plumage, long, often deeply forked tail, and a very upright stance when perched. They are mainly arboreal and insectivorous, catching larger winged insects by aerial sallies from a perch. Usually found singly or in pairs. Their direct flight is swift, strong and undulating. Drongos are rather noisy, and have a varied repertoire of harsh calls and pleasant whistles; some species are good mimics.   **pp.170–171**

Monarchs Tribe Monarchini

Most species are small to medium-sized, with long, pointed wings and a medium-length to long tail. They feed mainly on insects.   **pp.172–173**

Ioras Subfamily Aegithininae

Small, fairly lively passerines that feed in trees, mainly on insects and especially on caterpillars.   **pp.172–173**

Woodshrikes Subfamily Malaconotinae

Medium-sized, arboreal, insectivorous passerines. The bill is stout and hooked, the wings are rounded, and the tail is short.   **pp.172–173**

■ ■ ■ Thrushes, Shortwings, Old World Flycatchers and Chats Muscicapidae ■ ■ ■

A large and varied family represented by two subfamilies, the second of which is subdivided into two tribes.   **pp.174–185**

Subfamily Turdinae

Thrushes Genera *Monticola, Myophonus, Zoothera* and *Turdus* Medium-sized passerines with rather long, strong legs, a slender bill and fairly long wings. On the ground they progress by hopping. All are insectivorous, and many eat fruit as well. Some species are chiefly terrestrial and others arboreal. Most thrushes have loud and varied songs, which are used to proclaim and defend their territories when breeding.   **pp.174–177**

Shortwings Genus *Brachypteryx* Small, chat-like thrushes with short rounded wings, almost square tail, and strong legs. They are mainly terrestrial, and inhabit low bushes, undergrowth or thickets. Shortwings are chiefly insectivorous and found singly or in pairs.   **pp.182–183**

Subfamily Muscicapinae

Old World Flycatchers Tribe Muscicapini

Small insectivorous birds with a small, flattened bill, and bristles at the gape that help in the capture of flying insects. They normally have a very upright stance when perched. Many species frequently flick the tail and hold the wings slightly drooped. Generally, flycatchers frequent trees and bushes. Some species regularly perch on a vantage point, from which they catch insects in mid-air in short aerial sallies or by dropping to the ground, often returning to the same perch. Other species capture insects while flitting among branches or by picking them from foliage. Flycatchers are usually found singly or in pairs; a few join mixed hunting parties of other insectivorous birds.   **pp.178–181**

Chats Tribe Saxicolini

A diverse group of small to medium-sized passerines. Most are terrestrial or partly terrestrial, some are arboreal, and some are closely associated with water. Their main diet is insects, and they also consume fruits, especially berries. They forage mainly by hopping about on the ground in search of prey, or by perching on a low vantage point and then dropping to the ground onto insects or making short sallies to catch them in the air. Found singly or in pairs.   **pp.182–185**

▪ ▪ ▪ Starlings and Mynas Sturnidae ▪ ▪ ▪

Robust, medium-sized passerines with strong legs and bill, moderately long wings and a square tail. The flight is direct; strong and fast in the more pointed-winged species (*Sturnus*), and rather slower with more deliberate flapping in the more rounded-winged ones. Most species walk with an upright stance in a characteristic, purposeful jaunty fashion, broken by occasional short runs and hops. Their calls are often loud, harsh and grating, and the song of many species is a variety of whistles; mimicry is common. Most are highly gregarious at times. Some starlings are mainly arboreal and feed on fruits and insects; others are chiefly ground-feeders and are omnivorous. Many are closely associated with human cultivation and habitation.   **pp.186–187**

▪ ▪ ▪ Nuthatches Sittidae ▪ ▪ ▪

Nuthatches are small, energetic passerines with a compact body, short tail, large strong feet and a long bill. Nuthatches are also agile tree climbers. They can move with ease upwards, downwards, sideways and upside-down over trunks or branches, progressing by a series of jerky hops. Unlike woodpeckers and treecreepers, they usually begin near the top of a tree and work down the main trunk or larger branches, often head-first, and do not use the tail as a prop. Their flight is direct over short distances, and undulating over longer ones. Nuthatches feed on insects, spiders, seeds and nuts. They are often found singly or in pairs; outside the breeding season, they often join foraging flocks of other insectivorous birds.   **pp.188–189**

▪ ▪ ▪ Treecreepers Certhiidae ▪ ▪ ▪

Small, quiet, arboreal passerines with a slender, decurved bill. There is one representative in the region, the Spotted Creeper. Typically forages by creeping up vertical trunks and along the underside of branches.   **pp.188–189**

▪ ▪ ▪ Tits Paridae ▪ ▪ ▪

Small, active, highly acrobatic passerines with a short bill and strong feet. Their flight over long distances is undulating. They are mainly insectivorous. They probe bark crevices, search branches and leaves, and frequently hang upside-down from twigs. Tits are chiefly arboreal, but also descend to the ground to feed, hopping about and flicking aside leaves and other debris. They are very gregarious; in the non-breeding season most species join roving flocks of other insectivorous birds.   **pp.188–189**

▪ ▪ ▪ Swallows and Martins Hirundinidae ▪ ▪ ▪

Gregarious, rather small passerines with a distinctive slender, streamlined body, long, pointed wings and a small bill. The long-tailed species are often called swallows, and the shorter-tailed species termed martins. All hawk day-flying insects in swift, agile, sustained flight, sometimes high in the air. Many species have a deeply forked tail, which affords better manoeuvrability. Hirundines catch most of their food while flying in the open. They perch readily on exposed branches and wires.   **pp.188–191**

▪ ▪ ▪ Bulbuls Pycnonotidae ▪ ▪ ▪

Medium-sized passerines with soft, fluffy plumage, rather short and rounded wings, a medium-long to long tail, slender bill and short, weak legs. Bulbuls feed on berries and other fruits, often supplemented by insects, and sometimes also nectar and the buds of trees and shrubs. Many species are noisy, especially when feeding. Typically, bulbuls have a variety of cheerful, loud, chattering, babbling and whistling calls. Most species are gregarious in the non-breeding season.   **pp.192–193**

▪ ▪ ▪ Grey Hypocolius Hypocoliidae ▪ ▪ ▪

Grey Hypocolius is the only member of this family. Often forms flocks in winter. Forages chiefly by hopping and clambering about within trees and bushes, feeding mainly on berries. Flight is strong and direct, with rapid wingbeats and occasional swooping glides or high circling. Settles on the tops of bushes and remains still for long periods. Raises nape feathers when excited or alarmed.   **p.228**

■ ■ ■ **Cisticolas and Prinias** Cisticolidae ■ ■ ■

Cisticolas Genus *Cisticola* Tiny, short-tailed, insectivorous passerines. The tail is longer in winter than in summer. They are often found in grassy habitats, and many have aerial displays.   **pp.194–195**

Prinias Genus *Prinia* Prinias have a long, graduated tail that is longer in winter than in summer. Most inhabit grassland, marsh vegetation or scrub. They forage by gleaning insects and spiders from vegetation, and some species also feed on the ground. When perched, the tail is often held cocked and slightly fanned. Flight is weak and jerky.
                                                              pp.194–195

■ ■ ■ **White-eyes** Zosteropidae ■ ■ ■

Small or very small insectivorous passerines with a slightly decurved and pointed bill, a brush-tipped tongue, and a white ring around each eye. White-eyes frequent forest, forest edges, and bushes in gardens.   **pp.194–195**

■ ■ ■ **Warblers, Laughingthrushes and Babblers** Sylviidae ■ ■ ■

A huge and varied family of mostly small species.   **pp.196–205**

Warblers Subfamily Acrocephalinae

A large group of small, active perching birds with a fine pointed bill. Insects and spiders form their main diet; some species also consume berries, seeds and nectar. They usually capture their prey by gleaning from foliage, but sometimes also from the ground. Warblers inhabit all types of vegetation, often in dense habitats.   **pp.196–201**

Bush Warblers Genus *Cettia* Medium-sized warblers with rounded wings and tail that inhabit marshes, grassland and forest undergrowth. They are usually found singly. Bush warblers call frequently, and are usually heard more often than seen. *Cettia* species have surprisingly loud voices, and some can be identified by their distinctive melodious songs. Bush warblers seek insects and spiders by actively flitting and hopping about in vegetation close to the ground. They are reluctant to fly, and usually cover only short distances at low level before dropping into dense cover again. When excited, they flick their wings and tail.
                                                              pp.196–197

Warblers Genus *Locustella* Very skulking, medium-sized warblers with a rounded tail, usually found singly. Characteristically, they keep low down or on the ground among dense vegetation, walking furtively and scurrying off when startled. They fly at low level, flitting between plants, or rather jerkily over longer distances, ending in a sudden dive into cover.   **pp.196–197**

Warblers Genus *Acrocephalus* Medium-sized to large warblers with prominent bill and rounded tail. They usually occur singly. Many species are skulking, typically keeping low down in dense vegetation. Most frequent marshy habitats, and are able to clamber about readily in reeds and other vertical stems of marsh plants. Their songs are harsh and often monotonous.   **pp.196–197**

Warblers Genus *Hippolais* Medium-sized warblers with a large bill, square-ended tail, and rather sloping forehead and peaked crown giving a distinctive domed head shape. Their songs are harsh and varied. They clamber about vegetation with a rather clumsy action.   **pp.196–197**

Tailorbirds Genus *Orthotomus* Have a long, decurved bill, short wings and a graduated tail, the latter held characteristically cocked.   **pp.196–197**

Warblers Genus *Phylloscopus* Rather small, slim and short-billed warblers. Useful identification features are voice, strength of supercilium, colour of underparts, rump, bill and legs, and presence or absence of wing-bars, of coronal bands or of white on the tail. The coloration of upperparts and underparts and the presence or prominence of wing-bars are affected by wear. Leaf warblers are fast-moving and restless, hopping and creeping about actively and often flicking the wings. They mostly glean small insects and spiders from foliage, twigs and branches, often first disturbing prey by hovering and fluttering; they also make short fly-catching sallies. **pp.198–201**

Warblers Genus *Seicercus* These are small and active warblers. They feed in a similar manner to *Phylloscopus* warblers, by gleaning from foliage and twigs and making frequent aerial sallies, but have a broader bill and brighter plumage than those species. **pp.200–201**

Grassbirds Subfamily Megalurinae
Brownish warblers with a longish tail which inhabit damp tall grassland. The males perform song flights in the breeding season. **pp.200–201**

Laughingthrushes Subfamily Garrulacinae
Medium-sized, long-tailed passerines that are gregarious even in the breeding season. At the first sign of danger, they characteristically break into a concert of loud hissing, chattering and squealing. They often feed on the ground, moving with long springy hops, rummaging among leaf litter, flicking leaves aside and into the air, and digging for food with their strong bill. Their flight is short and clumsy, the birds flying from tree to tree in follow-my-leader fashion. **pp.202–203**

Babblers Subfamily Sylviinae, Tribe Timaliini
A large and diverse group of small to medium-sized passerines. They have soft, loose plumage, short or fairly short wings, and strong feet and legs. The sexes are alike in most species. Typically, members of this tribe associate in flocks outside the breeding season, and some species do so throughout the year. Babbler flocks are frequently a component of mixed-species feeding parties. Most babblers have a wide range of chatters, rattles and whistles; some have a melodious song. Many are terrestrial or inhabit bushes or grass close to the ground, while other species are arboreal. Babblers are chiefly insectivorous, and augment their diet with fruits, seeds and nectar. Arboreal species collect food from leaves, moss, lichen and bark; terrestrial species forage by probing, digging, and tossing aside dead foliage. **pp.202–205**

Sylvia Warblers Subfamily Sylviinae, Tribe Sylviini
Small to medium-sized passerines with a fine bill, closely resembling the true warblers. Typically, they inhabit bushes and scrub, and feed chiefly by gleaning insects from foliage and twigs; they sometimes also consume berries in autumn and winter. **pp.200–201**

▪ ▪ ▪ Larks Alaudidae ▪ ▪ ▪
Terrestrial cryptically coloured passerines, generally small-sized, which usually walk and run on the ground and often have a very elongated hindclaw. Their flight is strong and undulating. Larks take a wide variety of food, including insects, molluscs, arthropods, seeds, flowers, buds and leaves. Many species have a melodious song, which is often delivered in a distinctive, steeply climbing or circling aerial display, but also from a conspicuous low perch. They live in a wide range of open habitats, including grassland and cultivation. **pp.206–207**

▪ ▪ ▪ Flowerpeckers and Sunbirds Nectariniidae ▪ ▪ ▪

These birds are represented by two discrete tribes.   **pp.208–209**

Flowerpeckers Tribe Dicaeini

Very small passerines with short beak and tail, and with a tongue adapted for nectar-feeding. They usually frequent the tree canopy and feed mainly on soft fruits, berries and nectar; also on small insects and spiders. Many species are especially fond of mistletoe *Loranthus* berries. Flowerpeckers are very active, continually flying about restlessly, and twisting and turning in different attitudes when perched, while calling frequently with high-pitched notes. Normally they live singly or in pairs; some species form small parties in the non-breeding season.   **pp.208–209**

Sunbirds Tribe Nectariniini

Sunbirds have a bill and tongue adapted to feed on nectar. They flit and dart actively from flower to flower, clambering over the blossoms, often hovering momentarily in front of them, and clinging acrobatically to twigs. Sunbirds usually keep singly or in pairs, although several may congregate in flowering trees, and some species join mixed foraging flocks. They have sharp, metallic calls and high-pitched trilling and twittering songs.
pp.208–209

▪ ▪ ▪ Passeridae ▪ ▪ ▪

Represented in Southern India by four subfamilies: sparrows, wagtails and pipits, weavers and estrildine finches.   **pp.210–217**

Sparrows Subfamily Passerinae

Small passerines with a thick conical bill. There are two genera occuring in the region: *Passer*, the true sparrows, some of which are closely associated with human habitation; and *Petronia*, the rock sparrows, which inhabit dry rocky country or light scrub. Most species feed on seeds, taken on or near the ground.   **pp.214–215**

Wagtails and Pipits Subfamily Motacillinae

Small, slender, terrestrial birds with long legs, relatively long toes and a thin, pointed bill. Some wagtails exhibit wide geographical plumage variation. All walk with a deliberate gait and run rapidly. The flight is undulating and strong. Most wagtails wag the tail up and down, and so do some pipits. They feed mainly by picking insects from the ground as they walk along, or by making short rapid runs to capture insects they have flushed; they also catch prey in mid-air. Song flights are characteristic of many pipits. Both wagtails and pipits call in flight, and this is often a useful identification feature. They are usually found singly or in pairs in the breeding season, and in scattered flocks in autumn and winter.
pp.210–213

Weavers Subfamily Ploceinae

Small, rather plump, finch-like passerines with a large, conical bill. Adults feed chiefly on seeds and grain, supplemented by invertebrates; the young are often fed on invertebrates. Weavers inhabit grassland, marshes, cultivation and very open woodland. They are highly gregarious, roosting and nesting communally, and are noted for their elaborate roofed nests.
pp.214–215

Estrildine Finches Subfamily Estrildinae

Small, slim passerines with a short, stout, conical beak. They feed chiefly on small seeds, which they pick up from the ground or gather by clinging to stems and pulling the seeds directly from seedheads. Their gait is a hop or occasionally a walk. Outside the breeding season all species are gregarious. Their flight is fast and undulating.   **pp.216–217**

■ ■ ■ Finches and Buntings Fringillidae ■ ■ ■

Finches Subfamily Fringillinae

Small to medium-sized passerines with a strong conical bill used for eating seeds. They forage on the ground; some species also feed on seedheads of tall herbs, and blossoms or berries of bushes and trees. Finches are highly gregarious outside the breeding season. Their flight is fast and undulating. **pp.218–219**

Buntings Subfamily Emberizinae

Small to medium-sized, terrestrial passerines with a strong, conical bill designed for shelling seeds, usually of grasses; adults also eat insects in summer. They forage by hopping or creeping on the ground. Their flight is undulating. Buntings are usually gregarious outside the breeding season, feeding and roosting in flocks. Buntings occur in a wide variety of open habitats. **pp.218–219**

Grey Francolin *Francolinus pondicerianus* 33 cm
ADULT Rufous throat with fine dark necklace. Finely barred upperparts with shaft streaking, and finely barred underparts. Sexes similar, but female lacks spurs. Male usually calls from vantage point: a rapidly repeated *khateeja-khateeja-khateeja*. Dry grass and thorn scrub. AN: cr, KA: cr, KE: nr, MH: cr, TN: nr

Painted Francolin *Francolinus pictus* 31 cm
a MALE and **b** FEMALE Rufous-orange face (and often throat), and bold white spotting on upperparts and underparts. Sexes rather similar. Call is a *click...cheek-cheek-keray*. Tall grassland and cultivation with scattered trees; open thin forest. AN: cr, KA: cr, MH: cr, TN: nr

Red Spurfowl *Galloperdix spadicea* 36 cm
a MALE and **b** FEMALE *G. s. spadicea*; **c** MALE *G. s. stewarti* Red facial skin and legs/feet. Male has brownish-grey head and neck, and rufous body. Female has black mottling on upperparts, and barred underparts. Male *stewarti* of Kerala is deeper chestnut-red. Scrub, bamboo thickets and secondary growth. AN: nr, GO: cr, KA: lcr, KE: cr, MH: nr, TN: nr

Painted Spurfowl *Galloperdix lunulata* 32 cm
a MALE and **b** FEMALE Dark bill and legs/feet. Male has greenish-black head and neck barred with white, chestnut-red upperparts, and yellowish-buff underparts with spotting and barring. Female is dark brown, with chestnut supercilium and forehead, and buff throat and malar stripe; lacks red orbital skin. Thorn scrub and bamboo thickets. AN: nr, KA: nr, KE: xr, MH: nr, TN: cr

Common Quail *Coturnix coturnix* 20 cm
a MALE and **b** FEMALE Male has black 'anchor' mark on throat (which may be lacking), and buff or rufous breast with pale streaking. Female lacks 'anchor' mark and has blackish spotting on buffish breast. Song is a far-carrying *whit, whit-tit*, repeated in quick succession. Crops and grassland. AN: v, GO: nw, KA: nw, KE: nw, MH: nr, TN: nw

Rain Quail *Coturnix coromandelica* 18 cm
a MALE and **b** FEMALE Male has strongly patterned head and neck, black on breast, and streaking on flanks. Female smaller than female Common, with unbarred primaries. Song is a loud, metallic and high-pitched *whit-whit*, repeated in runs of three to five calls. Crops, grassland, grass and scrub jungle. AN: nr, GO: v, KA: nr, KE: x?r, MH: nr, TN: nr

1 Blue-breasted Quail *Coturnix chinensis* 14 cm

a MALE and **b** FEMALE Small size. Male has black-and-white head pattern, slaty-blue flanks, and chestnut belly. Female has rufous forehead and supercilium, and barred breast and flanks. Song is a high-pitched, descending *ti-yu* or *quee-kee-kew*. Wet grassland, field edges and scrub. AN: nr, KA: nr, KE: x?r, MH: nr, TN: nr

2 Jungle Bush Quail *Perdicula asiatica* 17 cm

a MALE and **b** FEMALE Male has barred underparts, rufous-orange throat, rufous supercilium edged with white, white moustachial stripe, brown ear-coverts and orange-buff vent. Female has vinaceous-buff underparts, with head pattern similar to male. Rufous throat of female distinct from underparts. Dry grass and scrub, deciduous forest. AN: nr, GO: nr, KA: nr, KE: nr, MH: cr, TN: nr

3 Rock Bush Quail *Perdicula argoondah* 17 cm

a MALE and **b** FEMALE Male has barred underparts, and vinaceous-buff ear-coverts and throat; lacks white moustachial stripe. Female has vinaceous-buff underparts, including throat and ear-coverts, and short whitish supercilium. Head pattern of female is much plainer than in female Jungle. Dry rocky and sandy areas with thorn scrub in plains and foothills. AN: nr, GO: nr, KA: nr, KE: ?, MH: nr, TN: nr

4 Painted Bush Quail *Perdicula erythrorhyncha* 18 cm

a MALE and **b** FEMALE Black spotting on upperparts and flanks, and red bill and legs. Male has white supercilium and throat, and black chin and mask. Female has rufous supercilium, ear-coverts and throat. Scrub in plains and foothills. AN: nr, KA: nr, KE: cr, MH: nr, TN: nr

5 Small Buttonquail *Turnix sylvatica* 13 cm

MALE Very small size and pointed tail. Buff edges to scapulars form prominent lines, and rufous mantle and coverts are boldly fringed buff, creating scaly appearance. Underparts are similar to many Yellow-legged, but very different to those of Barred. Bill grey and legs are pinkish. Has repetitive booming call. Tall grassland. AN: nr, GO: nr, KA: nr, KE: ?, MH: nr, TN: nr

6 Yellow-legged Buttonquail *Turnix tanki* 15–16 cm

a MALE and **b** FEMALE Yellow legs and bill. Comparatively uniform upperparts (lacking scaly or striped appearance), and buff coverts with bold black spotting. Pattern and coloration of underparts very different from Barred. Utters a low-pitched hoot, repeated with increasing strength to become human-like moan. Scrub and grassland, and crops. AN: nr, KA: nr, KE: nr, MH: nr, TN: nr

7 Barred Buttonquail *Turnix suscitator* 15 cm

a MALE and **b** FEMALE Grey bill and legs, and bold black barring on sides of neck, breast and wing-coverts. Orange-rufous flanks and belly clearly demarcated from barred breast. Female has black throat and centre of breast. Utters a motorcycle-like *drr-r-r-r-r-r*, and a far-carrying *hoon-hoon-hoon-hoon*. Scrub, grassland, and field edges. AN: nr, GO: nr, KA: nr, KE: nr, MH: cr, TN: nr

Red Junglefowl *Gallus gallus* M 65–75 cm, F 42–46 cm
a MALE and **b** FEMALE Male has red comb and wattles, orange and golden-yellow neck hackles, blackish-brown underparts, and long greenish-black sickle-shaped tail. In eclipse plumage, male lacks neck hackles and elongated central tail feathers. Female has naked, reddish face, black-streaked golden 'shawl', and rufous-brown underparts streaked with buff. Male's call, at dawn and dusk, is a loud *cock-a-doodle-doo*, very similar to the crowing of a domestic cockerel. Forest undergrowth and scrub. AN: nr, KA: nr, MH: nr

Grey Junglefowl *Gallus sonneratii* M 70–80 cm, F 38 cm
a MALE and **b** FEMALE Male has 'shawl' of white and pale yellow spotting, and golden-yellow spotting on scapulars. Eclipse male lacks neck hackles and elongated tail feathers. Female has white streaking on underparts. Male's call is a loud *kuk-ka-kurruk-ka*, repeated at regular intervals. Forest undergrowth, secondary growth and bamboo thickets. AN: nr, GO: cr, KA: lcr, KE: cr, MH: nr, TN: lcr

Indian Peafowl *Pavo cristatus* M 180–230 cm, F 90–100 cm
a MALE and **b** FEMALE Male has blue neck and breast, and spectacular glossy green train of elongated uppertail-covert feathers with numerous ocelli. Female has whitish face and throat and white belly, and lacks elongated uppertail-coverts. Call is a trumpeting, far-carrying and mournful *kee-ow, kee-ow, kee-ow*. Dense riverine vegetation and open sal forest. AN: nr, GO: nr, KA: lcr, KE: nr, MH: nr, TN: nr

1 **Fulvous Whistling-duck** *Dendrocygna bicolor* 51 cm
a **b** ADULT and **c** JUVENILE Larger than Lesser, with bigger, squarer head and larger bill. Adult distinguished from adult Lesser by warmer rufous-orange head and neck, dark blackish line down hind-neck, dark striations on neck, more prominent streaking on flanks, indistinct chestnut-brown patch on forewing, and white band across uppertail-coverts. Freshwater wetlands. AN: v, GO: v, KA: v, KE: ?, MH: nr

2 **Lesser Whistling-duck** *Dendrocygna javanica* 42 cm
a **b** ADULT and **c** JUVENILE Smaller than Fulvous, and separated from that species by greyish-buff head and neck, dark brown crown, lack of well-defined dark line down hind-neck, bright chestnut patch on forewing, and chestnut uppertail-coverts. Both species of whistling-duck have rather weak, deep-flapping flight, when they show dark upperwing and underwing, and are very noisy with much whistling. Wetlands. AN: nr, GO: cr, KA: cr, KE: cr, MH: cr, TN: nr

3 **Bar-headed Goose** *Anser indicus* 71–76 cm
a **b** ADULT and **c** JUVENILE Adult has white head with black banding, and white line down grey neck, with a black-tipped yellowish bill and yellowish legs. Juvenile has white face and dark-grey crown and hind-neck. Plumage paler steel-grey, with paler grey forewing, compared with Greylag. *See* Appendix for descriptions of Lesser White-fronted Goose and Greylag Goose. Large rivers and lakes. AN: nw, GO: v, KA: nw, KE: v?, MH: nw, TN: nw

4 **Ruddy Shelduck** *Tadorna ferruginea* 61–67 cm
a **b** MALE and **c** FEMALE Rusty-orange, with buffish head; white upperwing- and underwing-coverts contrast with black remiges in flight. Breeding male has black neck-band. Wetlands. AN: lcw, GO: nw, KA: nw, KE: v, LS: v, MH: nw, TN: nw

5 **Common Shelduck** *Tadorna tadorna* 58–67 cm
a **b** MALE, **c** FEMALE and **d** **e** JUVENILE Adult has greenish-black head and neck, and largely white body with chestnut breast-band and black scapular stripe. Female is very similar to male, but slightly duller, and lacks knob on bill. Juvenile lacks breast-band and has sooty-brown upperparts. White upperwing- and underwing-coverts contrast with black remiges in flight in all plumages. Wetlands. AN: nw, KA: nw, MH: nw

6 **Comb Duck** *Sarkidiornis melanotos* 56–76 cm
a **b** MALE, **c** FEMALE and **d** JUVENILE Whitish head, speckled with black, and whitish underparts with incomplete narrow black breast-band. Upperwing and underwing blackish. Male has fleshy comb. Comb lacking in female and she is much smaller with duller upperparts. Pools in well-wooded country. AN: nr, GO: nw, KA: nr, KE: v, MH: nr, TN: nr

Gadwall *Anas strepera* 39–43 cm

a **b** MALE and **c** **d** FEMALE White patch on inner secondaries in all plumages. Male is mainly grey with white belly and dark patch at rear; bill is dark grey. Female similar to female Mallard, but has orange sides to dark bill and clear-cut white belly. Wetlands. AN: nw, GO: nw, KA: nw, KE: v, MH: nw, TN: v

Eurasian Wigeon *Anas penelope* 45–51 cm

a **b** MALE and **c** **d** FEMALE Male has yellow forehead and forecrown, chestnut head and pinkish breast; shows white forewing in flight. Female has rather uniform head, breast and flanks. In all plumages, shows white belly and rather pointed tail in flight. Male has distinctive whistled *wheeooo* call. *See* Appendix for description of Falcated Duck. Wetlands. AN: nw, GO: nw, KA: nw, MH: cw, TN: nw

Mallard *Anas platyrhynchos* 50–65 cm

a **b** MALE and **c** **d** FEMALE In all plumages, has white-bordered purplish speculum. Male has yellow bill, dark green head and purplish-chestnut breast. Female is pale brown and boldly patterned with dark brown; bill variable, patterned mainly in dull orange and dark brown. Wetlands. AN: nw, GO: nw, MH: nw, TN: nw

Spot-billed Duck *Anas poecilorhyncha* 58–63 cm

a **b** MALE and **c** FEMALE Yellow tip to bill, dark crown and eye-stripe, spotted breast and boldly scalloped flanks, and white tertials. Sexes similar, but male has red loral spot and is more strongly marked than female. Wetlands. AN: cr, GO: nw, KA: nr, KE: nw, MH: nr, TN: nr

Northern Shoveler *Anas clypeata* 44–52 cm

a **b** MALE and **c** **d** FEMALE Long, spatulate bill. Male has dark green head, white breast, chestnut flanks and blue forewing. Female recalls female Mallard in plumage but has blue-grey forewing. Wetlands. AN: nw, GO: nw, KA: cw, KE: nw, MH: cw, MV: nw, TN: nw

1

Cotton Pygmy-goose *Nettapus coromandelianus* 30–37 cm

a b MALE, **c** ECLIPSE MALE and **d e** FEMALE Small size. Male has broad white band across wing, and female has white trailing edge to wing. Male has white head and neck, black cap and black breast-band. Eclipse male and female have dark stripe through eye. Vegetation-covered wetlands. AN: cr, GO: nr, KA: nr, KE: nw, MH: cr, MV: v, TN: nr

2

Common Teal *Anas crecca* 34–38 cm

a b MALE and **c d** FEMALE Male has chestnut head with green band behind eye, white stripe along scapulars and yellowish patch on undertail-coverts. Female has rather uniform head, lacking pale loral spot of female Garganey. In flight, both sexes have broad white band along greater coverts, and green speculum with narrow white trailing edge; forewing of female is brown. *See* Appendix for description of Baikal Teal. Wetlands. AN: cw, GO: cw, KA: nw, KE: nw, LS: np, MH: cw, MV: nw, TN: nw

3

Garganey *Anas querquedula* 37–41 cm

a b MALE and **c d** FEMALE Male has white stripe behind eye, and brown breast contrasting with grey flanks; shows blue-grey forewing in flight. Female has more patterned head than female Common Teal, with more prominent supercilium, whitish loral spot, pale line below dark eye-stripe, and dark cheek-bar; shows pale grey forewing and broad white trailing edge to wing in flight. Wetlands. AN: cw, GO: cw, KA: cw, KE: cw, LS: v, MH: cw, MV: nw, TN: cw

4

Northern Pintail *Anas acuta* 51–56 cm

a b MALE and **c d** FEMALE Long neck and pointed tail. Male has chocolate-brown head, with white stripe down sides of neck. Female has comparatively uniform buffish head and slender grey bill; in flight she shows combination of indistinct brownish speculum, prominent white trailing edge to secondaries, and greyish underwing. Wetlands. AN: cw, GO: cw, KA: cw, KE: nw, MH: cw, MV: v, TN: nw

5

Pink-headed Duck *Rhodonessa caryophyllacea* 60 cm

a MALE and **b** FEMALE Male has pink head and bill and dark brown body. Female has greyish-pink head and duller brown body. In flight, pale fawn secondaries contrast with dark forewing, and pinkish underwing contrasts with dark body. Pools and marshes in elephant-grass jungle. AN: ex, MH: ex

1

Red-crested Pochard *Rhodonessa rufina* 53–57 cm

a **b** MALE and **c** **d** FEMALE Large, with square-shaped head. Shape at rest and in flight more like dabbling duck. Male has rusty-orange head, black neck and breast, and white flanks. Female has pale cheeks contrasting with brown cap. Both sexes have largely white flight feathers on upperwing, and whitish underwing. Lakes and large rivers. AN: nw, GO: v, KA: nw, MH: nw, TN: nw

2

Common Pochard *Aythya ferina* 42–49 cm

a **b** MALE, **c** **d** FEMALE and **e** IMMATURE MALE Large with domed head. Pale grey flight feathers and grey forewing result in different upperwing pattern from other *Aythya*. Male has chestnut head, black breast, and grey upperparts and flanks. Female has brownish head and breast contrasting with paler brownish-grey upperparts and flanks; lacks white undertail-coverts; eye is dark and bill has grey central band. Lakes and large rivers. AN: nw, GO: nw, KA: nw, MH: nw, TN: nw

3

Ferruginous Pochard *Aythya nyroca* 38–42 cm

a **b** MALE and **c** FEMALE Smallest *Aythya* duck with dome-shaped head. Chestnut head, breast and flanks, and white undertail-coverts. Female is duller than male, with dark iris. In flight, shows extensive white wing-bar and white belly. *See* Appendix for comparison with Baer's Pochard. Lakes and large rivers. AN: nw, GO: nw, KA: nw, KE: nw, LS: v, MH: cw, MV: v, TN: v

4

Tufted Duck *Aythya fuligula* 40–47 cm

a **b** MALE, **c** IMMATURE MALE, **d** **e** FEMALE and **f** FEMALE WITH SCAUP-LIKE HEAD Breeding male is glossy black, with prominent crest and white flanks. Eclipse/immature males are duller, with greyish flanks. Female is dusky brown, with paler flanks; some females may show white face-patch, recalling Greater Scaup (*see* Appendix) but they usually also show tufted nape and squarer head shape. Female has yellow iris. Lakes and large rivers. AN: nw, GO: nw, KA: nw, MH: nw, MV: nw, TN: nw

1 Eurasian Wryneck *Jynx torquilla* 16–17 cm
ADULT Cryptically patterned with grey, buff and brown. Has dark stripe down nape and mantle, and long, barred tail. Scrub, secondary growth and cultivation edges. AN: nw, GO: nw, KA: nw, KE: v, MH: nw, TN: v

2 Speckled Piculet *Picumnus innominatus* 10 cm
a MALE and **b** FEMALE Tiny size. Whitish underparts with black spotting, black ear-covert patch and malar stripe, and white in black tail. Male has orange on forehead, which is lacking in female. Bushes and bamboo in broadleaved forest and secondary growth. AN: nr, GO: nr, KA: nr, KE: nr, MH: nr, TN: nr

3 Brown-capped Pygmy Woodpecker *Dendrocopos nanus* 13 cm
a MALE and **b** FEMALE Very small. Has fawn-brown crown and eye-stripe, brown coloration to upperparts, greyish- to brownish-white underparts (streaked with brown) and white spotting on central tail feathers. Light forest and trees in cultivation. AN: nr, GO: nr, KA: nr, KE: nr, MH: nr, TN: nr

4 Fulvous-breasted Woodpecker *Dendrocopos macei* 18–19 cm
a MALE and **b** FEMALE White barring on mantle and wing-coverts, and diffusely streaked buffish underparts. Male has red crown, which is black in female. Forest edges and open forest. AN: nr

5 Yellow-crowned Woodpecker *Dendrocopos mahrattensis* 17–18 cm
a MALE and **b** FEMALE Yellowish forehead and forecrown, white-spotted upperparts, poorly defined moustachial stripe, dirty underparts with heavy but diffuse streaking, red patch on lower belly, and bold white barring on central tail feathers. Open woodland and open country with scattered trees. AN: nr, GO: nr, KA: nr, KE: nr, MH: nr, TN: nr

6 Rufous Woodpecker *Celeus brachyurus* 25 cm
a MALE and **b** FEMALE Short black bill and shaggy crest. Rufous-brown, with prominent black barring. Male has scarlet patch on ear-coverts. Broadleaved forest and secondary growth. AN: nr, GO: nr, KA: nr, KE: nr, MH: cr, TN: nr

7 Heart-spotted Woodpecker *Hemicircus canente* 16 cm
a MALE and **b** FEMALE Prominent crest; very short tail. Black-and-white plumage with heart-shaped black spots on tertials. Male has black crown, female has white crown and juvenile has black spotting on white crown. Broadleaved forest and coffee plantations. AN: nr, GO: nr, KA: nr, KE: nr, MH: nr, TN: nr

8 White-bellied Woodpecker *Dryocopus javensis* 48 cm
a MALE and **b** FEMALE Large black woodpecker with white belly. Male has red crown and moustachial stripe; red restricted to hind-crown on female. In flight, shows white rump, white underwing-coverts and small white patch at base of primaries. Forest and secondary growth with tall trees. AN: nr, GO: nr, KA: nr, KE: nr, MH: nr, TN: nr

9 Lesser Yellownape *Picus chlorolophus* 27 cm
MALE Tufted yellow nape, and white spotting on underparts. Male has mainly crimson crown and crimson moustachial stripe. Female has less crimson on crown than male and lacks crimson moustachial stripe. Broadleaved forest and secondary growth. AN: nr, GO: nr, KA: nr, KE: nr, MH: nr, TN: nr

10 Greater Yellownape *Picus flavinucha* 33 cm
a MALE and **b** FEMALE Tufted yellow nape, yellow (male) or rufous-brown (female) throat, dark-spotted white foreneck, uniform underparts and rufous barring on secondaries. Broadleaved forest and forest edges. AN: nr.

Streak-throated Woodpecker *Picus xanthopygaeus* 30 cm
a MALE and **b** FEMALE Scaling on underparts, and white supercilium and moustachial stripe. Male has red crown (black, streaked with grey, in female). Broadleaved forest and secondary growth. AN: nr, KA: nr, KE: nr, MH: nr, TN: nr

Himalayan Flameback *Dinopium shorii* 30–32 cm
a MALE and **b** FEMALE Smaller bill than Greater Flameback, with unspotted black hind-neck, and brownish-buff centre of throat (and breast on some) with black spotting forming irregular border. Centre of divided moustachial stripe is brownish buff (with touch of red on some males). Breast less heavily marked with black than on Greater. Has reddish or brownish eyes, and three toes. Female has white streaking to black crest. Mature broadleaved forest. AN: nr, TN: nr

Common Flameback *Dinopium javanense* 28–30 cm
a MALE and **b** FEMALE Smaller size and smaller bill than Greater Flameback, with unspotted black hind-neck and irregular line of black spotting down centre of throat. Smaller size and bill compared with Himalayan; moustachial stripe lacks clear dividing line (usually solid black, although can appear divided on some and similar to Himalayan). Crown of female is finely spotted with white. Forest. GO: nr, KA: nr, KE: nr, MH: nr, TN: nr

Black-rumped Flameback *Dinopium benghalense* 26–29 cm
a MALE and **b** FEMALE Black eye-stripe and throat (lacking dark moustachial stripe), spotting on wing-coverts, and black rump. Light forest, and groves and trees in open country. AN: cr, GO: cr, KA: lcr, KE: cr, MH: cr, TN: lcr

Greater Flameback *Chrysocolaptes lucidus* 33 cm
a MALE and **b** FEMALE Large size and long bill. White or black-and-white-spotted hind-neck and upper mantle, clean black line down centre of throat and neck, and white spotting on black breast. Moustachial stripe is clearly divided (with obvious white oval centre). Has pale eyes and four toes. Female has white spotting to black crest. Forest and groves. AN: nr, GO: nr, KA: nr, KE: nr, MH: nr, TN: lcr

White-naped Woodpecker *Chrysocolaptes festivus* 29 cm
a MALE and **b** FEMALE White hind-neck and mantle, and black scapulars and back forming V-shape. Moustachial stripe is clearly divided. Rump is black. Female has yellow crown. Light broadleaved forest and scattered trees. AN: nr, GO: nr, KA: nr, KE: nr, MH: nr, TN: nr

Brown-headed Barbet *Megalaima zeylanica* 27 cm
ADULT Fine streaking on brown head and breast, brown throat, orange circumorbital skin and bill, and white-spotted wing-coverts. Streaking almost absent on belly and flanks. Call is a monotonous *kotroo, kotroo, kotroo* or *kutruk, kutruk, kutruk*. Forest, wooded areas and trees near habitation. AN: nr, GO: nr, KA: lcr, KE: nr, MH: cr, TN: nr

White-cheeked Barbet *Megalaima viridis* 23 cm
ADULT Brownish bill. White supercilium and cheeks contrasting with brown crown and nape. Whitish throat and bold white streaking on breast. Call is a *pucock, pucock, pucock*. Wooded areas, gardens and groves. GO: cr, KA: cr, KE: cr, MH: nr, TN: cr

Crimson-fronted Barbet *Megalaima rubricapilla* 17 cm
ADULT Small size. Adult has crimson face, throat and breast, blue band down side of head and breast, and unstreaked green belly and flanks. Juvenile is duller, but shows traces of adult head pattern. Call is very similar to Coppersmith, although possibly softer and quicker, a fast-delivered *poop, poop, poop*... Open wooded country. GO: nr, KA: lcr, KE: lcr, MH: nr, TN: nr

Coppersmith Barbet *Megalaima haemacephala* 17 cm
a MALE and **b** JUVENILE Small barbet with crimson forehead and breast-patch, yellow patches above and below eye, yellow throat and streaked underparts. Juvenile lacks red on head and breast. Voice is a loud, metallic, repetitive and monotonous *tuk, tuk, tuk*. Open wooded country, groves and trees in cultivation and gardens. AN: cr, GO: cr, KA: cr, KE: nr, MH: cr, TN: cr

Malabar Grey Hornbill *Ocyceros griseus* 45 cm
a **b** MALE, **c** FEMALE and **d** IMMATURE Orange or yellowish bill, lacking casque, and broad greyish-white supercilium. Darker grey upperparts than Indian Grey, with pale streaking to crown and sides of head, shorter, darker grey tail and rufous undertail-coverts. Female has black patch at base of lower mandible. Immature has rufous fringes to upperparts. Call is a raucous *waa waa*, and a maniacal laughing *waa...waa...wa-wa-wa-wa-wa*. Open forest. GO: nr, KA: nr, KE: cr, MH: nr, TN: nr

Indian Grey Hornbill *Ocyceros birostris* 50 cm
a **b** MALE and **c** FEMALE Small hornbill with sandy brownish-grey upperparts, long tail that has dark subterminal band and elongated central feathers, and white trailing edge to wing. Prominent black casque and extensive black at base of bill. Female similar to male, but with smaller bill and casque. Territorial call is a loud cackling and squealing *k-k-k-ka-e* or rapid piping *pi-pi-pi-pi-pipipieu...*; normal contact call is a kite-like *chee-ooww*. Open broadleaved forest, and groves and gardens with fruiting trees. AN: nr, KA: nr, KE: lcr, MH: nr, TN: nr

Malabar Pied Hornbill *Anthracoceros coronatus* 65 cm
a **b** MALE and **c** FEMALE Compared with Oriental has axe-shaped casque with large black patch along upper ridge, white outer tail feathers (immatures have black at base, but not so extensive as in Oriental), broader white trailing edge to wing and pink throat-patches. Orbital skin is blue-black on male, pinkish on female. Female's casque similar in shape and patterning to male's, although lacks black at posterior end; bill of female lacks black at tip. Open forest and large fruit trees near villages. AN: nr, GO: nr, KA: nr, KE: nr, MH: nr, TN: nr

Oriental Pied Hornbill *Anthracoceros albirostris* 55–60 cm
a **b** MALE and **c** FEMALE Much smaller than Great Hornbill. Head and neck black. Tail mainly black with white tips to outer feathers. Both sexes have cylindrical casque, and blue orbital skin and throat-patch. Female has smaller casque than male, and has black at tip of bill. Calls include a variety of loud, shrill, nasal squeals and raucous chucks. Mature broadleaved forest with fruiting trees. AN: nr

Great Hornbill *Buceros bicornis* 95–105 cm
a **b** MALE Huge size, with massive yellow casque and bill, and white tail with black subterminal band. Has white neck, wing-bars and trailing edge to wing, which are variably stained with yellow (by preen-gland oils). Sexes alike, although female has white iris (red in male) and lacks black at ends of casque. Calls are loud and raucous, frequently given as a duet, *grongk-gonk, grongk-gongk*, and often becoming louder and more agitated prior to flight; flight call is a loud *ger-onk*. Mature broadleaved forest with fruiting trees. GO: nr?, KA: nr, KE: lcr, MH: nr, TN: nr

Common Hoopoe *Upupa epops* 31 cm

a **b** ADULT Orange-buff, with black-and-white wings and tail, and black-tipped fan-like crest. Voice is a repetitive and mellow *poop, poop, poop*. Open country, cultivation and villages. AN: cr, GO: nw, KA: nr, KE: nr, LS: v, MH: nr, MV: v, TN: cr

Malabar Trogon *Harpactes fasciatus* 31 cm

a MALE, **b** FEMALE and **c** IMMATURE MALE Male has blackish head and breast, pink underparts, and black and grey vermiculated wing-coverts. Female has dark cinnamon head and breast, pale cinnamon underparts and brown-and-buff vermiculated coverts. Immature male has blackish head and breast, and cinnamon underparts; coverts are vermiculated with grey on older birds. Call is a throaty, musical *cue-cue-cue*, and a low rolling *krr-r-r-r* when alarmed. Dense broadleaved forest. AN: nr, GO: nr, KA: nr, KE: nr, MH: nr, TN: nr

European Roller *Coracias garrulus* 31 cm

a **b** ADULT and **c** JUVENILE Turquoise head and underparts, and rufous-cinnamon mantle. Has black flight feathers and tail corners. Juvenile is much duller, and has whitish streaking on throat and breast; patterning of wings and tail helps separate it from Indian Roller. Open woodland and cultivation. AN: v, GO: np, KA: v, MH: np

Indian Roller *Coracias benghalensis* 33 cm

a **b** ADULT and **c** JUVENILE Has rufous-brown on nape and underparts, streaking on ear-coverts and throat, and greenish mantle. In flight, shows turquoise band across primaries and dark blue terminal band to tail. Cultivation, open woodland, groves and gardens. AN: cr, GO: nr?, KA: cr, KE: nr, LS: v, MH: nr, MV: v, TN: cr

Dollarbird *Eurystomus orientalis* 28 cm

a **b** ADULT Dark greenish, appearing black at distance, with red bill and eye-ring. In flight, shows turquoise patch on primaries. Tropical forest and forest clearings. KA: nr, KE: nr?, TN: nr

Common Kingfisher *Alcedo atthis* 16 cm

ADULT Orange ear-coverts. Greenish blue on head, scapulars and wings, and turquoise line down back. Note race resident in the peninsula (illustrated) is a darker blue, less green, on the upperparts compared with the races that are winter visitors to the region, although still not as blue as Blue-eared. Fresh waters in open country. AN: cr, GO: cr, KA: cr, KE: cr, LS: np, MH: cr, MV: v, TN: lcr

Blue-eared Kingfisher *Alcedo meninting* 16 cm

a ADULT and **b** JUVENILE Blue ear-coverts. Upperparts are deeper blue than in Common Kingfisher (lacking green tones to blue of head, scapulars and wings compared with Common); underparts are a deeper orange coloration. Confusingly, juvenile has orange ear-coverts, but otherwise overall coloration is as adult. Streams in dense forest. AN: nr, GO: nr, KA: nr, KE: nr, MH: nr, TN: nr

Oriental Dwarf Kingfisher *Ceyx erithacus* 14 cm

a ADULT and **b** JUVENILE Tiny size. Orange head with violet iridescence, and black upperparts with variable blue streaking. Juvenile duller, with whitish underparts (with orange breastband) and orange-yellow bill. Shady streams in moist broadleaved forest. GO: nr?, KA: v, KE: nr?, MH: ns, TN: nr

Stork-billed Kingfisher *Halcyon capensis* 38 cm

ADULT Huge size and massive red bill. Has orange, orange-buff collar and underparts, and blue upperparts. Has an explosive laugh *ke-ke-ke-ke-ke*; song is a long series of paired melancholic whistles. Shaded slow-moving rivers and streams. AN: nr, GO: nr, KA: nr, KE: nr, MH: nr, TN: nr

White-throated Kingfisher *Halcyon smyrnensis* 28 cm

ADULT White throat and centre of breast, brown head and most of underparts, and turquoise upperparts. Shows prominent white wing-patch in flight. Call is a loud rattling laugh; song is a drawn-out musical whistle, *kililili*. Cultivation, forest edges, gardens and wetlands. AN: cr, GO: cr, KA: cr, KE: cr, LS: v, MH: cr, TN: cr

Black-capped Kingfisher *Halcyon pileata* 30 cm

a ADULT and **b** JUVENILE Black cap, white collar, purplish-blue upperparts and pale orange underparts. Shows white wing-patch in flight. Call is a ringing cackle, *kikikikikiki*. Wetlands and mangroves, mainly coastal. AN: nr, GO: nr, KA: nr, KE: nr, LS: nw, MH: nr, TN: nr

Collared Kingfisher *Todiramphus chloris* 23–25 cm

a ADULT and **b** JUVENILE Dark bill, blue-green upperparts, and whitish collar and underparts. Mainly coastal wetlands. GO: nr, KA: nr, KE: ?, MH: nr

Pied Kingfisher *Ceryle rudis* 31 cm

a ADULT and **b** JUVENILE *C. r. leucomelanura*; **c** MALE *C. r. travancoreensis* A black-and-white kingfisher, with prominent crest. Female has single breast-band (double in male). *C. r. travancoreensis*, of the SW peninsula, has darker upperparts than the widespread *C. r. leucomelanura*. Frequently hovers over water in search of fish. Slow-moving rivers and streams, and lakes and pools in open country. AN: cr, GO: lcr, KA: cr, KE: cr, MH: nr, TN: cr

ecol 02 2017

Blue-bearded Bee-eater *Nyctyornis athertoni* 31–34 cm

ADULT Large bee-eater with square-ended tail, and blue 'beard'. Has yellowish-buff belly and flanks with greenish streaking. Edges of broadleaved forest and open forest. AN: nr, GO: nr, KA: nr, KE: nr, MH: nr, TN: nr

Green Bee-eater *Merops orientalis* 16–18 cm

ADULT Small bee-eater, with blue cheeks, black gorget and golden coloration to crown. Green tail with elongated central feathers. Juvenile has green crown and nape, lacks black gorget and has square-ended tail. Open country with scattered trees. AN: cr, GO: cr, KA: cr, KE: cr, MH: cr, TN: cr

Blue-cheeked Bee-eater *Merops persicus* 24–26 cm

a **b** ADULT Chestnut throat, whitish forehead, turquoise-and-white supercilium and turquoise-and-green ear-coverts. Green upperparts, underparts and tail, although may show touch of turquoise on rump, belly and tail-coverts. Near water in arid areas. AN: v, GO: v, KA: v, MH: cp

Blue-tailed Bee-eater *Merops philippinus* 23–26 cm

a **b** ADULT and **c** JUVENILE Larger than Green Bee-eater, with chestnut throat, green crown and nape, and blue tail. Green upperparts and underparts are washed with brown and blue. Juvenile is like washed-out version of adult; lacks elongated central tail feathers. Near water in open wooded country. AN: nw, GO: nr?, KA: nw, KE: nw, MH: np, MV: v, TN: lcw

European Bee-eater *Merops apiaster* 23–25 cm

a **b** **c** ADULT and **d** JUVENILE Yellow throat, black gorget, blue underparts, chestnut crown and mantle, and golden-yellow scapulars. Juvenile is duller than adult, but still shows chestnut on crown and well-defined yellowish throat. Open country. KA: np, MV: v, TN: v

Eco
Scape

Chestnut-headed Bee-eater *Merops leschenaulti* 18–20 cm

a **b** ADULT and **c** JUVENILE Chestnut crown, nape and mantle, and yellow throat with diffuse black gorget. Tail has slight fork; lacks elongated central tail feathers. Juvenile is like washed-out version of adult, but crown and nape are dark green on some. Open broadleaved forest, often near water. AN: nr, GO: nr?, KA: lcr, KE: nw, MH: nr?, TN: nr

1

Pied Cuckoo *Clamator jacobinus* 33 cm
a ADULT and **b** JUVENILE Adult is black and white with prominent crest. Juvenile has smaller crest, browner upperparts and more buffish underparts. Call is a metallic, pleasant *piu…piu…pee-pee piu, pee-pee piu*. Broadleaved forest and well-wooded areas. AN: ns, GO: ns, KA: nr, KE: nr, LS: v, MH: ns, TN: ns

2

Chestnut-winged Cuckoo *Clamator coromandus* 47 cm
a ADULT and **b** IMMATURE Prominent crest, whitish collar and chestnut wings. Immature has rufous fringes to upperparts. Makes a series of double metallic whistles, *breep breep*. Broadleaved forest. AN: np, KA: np, KE: np, MH: np, TN: nw

3

Large Hawk Cuckoo *Hierococcyx sparverioides* 38 cm
a ADULT and **b** JUVENILE Larger than Common Hawk Cuckoo, with browner upperparts, strongly barred underparts and broader tail banding. Juvenile has barred flanks and broad tail banding; head dark grey on older birds. Call is a shrill *pee-pee-ah….pee-pee-ah*, which is repeated, rising in pitch and momentum, climaxing in hysterical crescendo. Broadleaved forest. AN: np, GO: nwp, KA: v, KE: v, TN: nw

✓*4*

Common Hawk Cuckoo *Hierococcyx varius* 34 cm
a ADULT and **b** JUVENILE Smaller than Large Hawk Cuckoo, with grey upperparts, more rufous on underparts, indistinct barring on belly and flanks, and narrow tail banding. Juvenile has spotted flanks and narrow tail banding. Call is like that of Large Hawk Cuckoo. Well-wooded country. AN: nr, GO: nr, KA: nr, KE: cr, MH: nr, TN: cr

5

Indian Cuckoo *Cuculus micropterus* 33 cm
a ADULT and **b** JUVENILE Brown coloration to grey upperparts and tail, broad barring on underparts, and pronounced white barring and spotting on tail. Juvenile has broad and irregular white tips to feathers of crown and nape, and white tips to scapulars and wing-coverts. Call is a descending, four-noted whistle, *kwer-kwah…kwah-kurh*. Forest and well-wooded country. AN: nr, GO: np, KA: nw, KE: nr?, MH: nr, MV: v, TN: v

6

Eurasian Cuckoo *Cuculus canorus* 32–34 cm
a ADULT and **b** HEPATIC FEMALE Finer barring on whiter underparts than Indian. *See* Appendix for comparison with Oriental Cuckoo. Male's call is a loud repetitive *cuck-oo…cuck-oo*; both sexes have a bubbling call. Forest, well-wooded country and scrub. AN: np, GO: np, KA: np, KE: v, LS: v, MH: nw, MV: nw, TN: nw

7

Lesser Cuckoo *Cuculus poliocephalus* 25 cm
a ADULT and **b** HEPATIC FEMALE Smaller than Eurasian; hepatic female can be bright rufous and indistinctly barred on crown and nape. Call is a strong, cheerful *pretty-peel-lay-ka-beet*. Forest and well-wooded country. AN: np, GO: v, KA: np, KE: v, MH: ns?, TN: np

8

Banded Bay Cuckoo *Cacomantis sonneratii* 24 cm
ADULT White supercilium, finely barred white underparts, and fine and regular dark barring on upperparts. Song is a shrill, whistled *pi-pi-pew-pew*, the first two notes at the same pitch, the last two descending. Dense broadleaved forest. AN: nr, GO: nr, KA: nr, KE: nr?, MH: ns, TN: nr

Grey-bellied Cuckoo *Cacomantis passerinus* 23 cm

a ADULT, **b** HEPATIC FEMALE and **c** JUVENILE Adult is grey with white vent and undertail-coverts. Hepatic female has white underparts with dark barring; lacks white supercilium of Banded Bay Cuckoo, upperparts are brighter rufous with crown and nape only sparsely barred, and tail is unbarred. Juvenile is either grey, with pale barring on underparts, or similar to hepatic female, or intermediate. *See* Appendix for comparison with Plaintive Cuckoo. Song is a clear, interrogative *pee-pipee-pee...pipee-pee,* ascending in scale and pitch; also a single plaintive repeated whistle. Groves and open forest. AN: nr, GO: nr?, KA: nr, KE: nr?, LS: v, MH: ns, MV: v, TN: nr

Drongo Cuckoo *Surniculus lugubris* 25 cm

a ADULT and **b** JUVENILE Black, with white-barred undertail-coverts. Bill fine and down-curved, and tail has indentation. Juvenile is spotted with white. Song is an ascending series of repeated whistles, *pee-pee-pee-pee-pee-pee*. Edges and clearings of forest and groves. AN: nr, GO: ns?, KA: nr, KE: nr, MH: ns?, TN: nr

Asian Koel *Eudynamys scolopacea* 43 cm

a MALE and **b** FEMALE Male is greenish black, with green bill. Female is spotted and barred with white. Song is a loud rising, repeated *ko-el...ko-el...ko-el...ko-el*. Open woodland, gardens and cultivation. AN: cr, GO: cr, KA: cr, KE: nr, LS: nr, MH: cr, MV: cr, TN: lcr

Green-billed Malkoha *Phaenicophaeus tristis* 38 cm

ADULT Greyish-green coloration, green and red bill, red eye-patch, white-streaked supercilium and white-tipped tail. Dense forest and thickets. AN: nr

Blue-faced Malkoha *Phaenicophaeus viridirostris* 39 cm

ADULT Greenish coloration, green bill, blue eye-patch and bold white tips to tail. Scrub and secondary growth. AN: nr, GO: nr, KA: nr, KE: nr, MH: nr, TN: cr

Sirkeer Malkoha *Phaenicophaeus leschenaultii* 42 cm

ADULT Sandy coloration, yellow-tipped red bill, dark mask with white border and bold white tips to tail. Thorn scrub and acacia trees in dry areas. AN: nr, KA: nr, KE: nr, MH: nr, TN: nr

Greater Coucal *Centropus sinensis* 48 cm
ADULT Larger than Lesser, with brighter and more uniform chestnut wings and black under-wing-coverts. Juvenile is similar to adult. Call is a deep *hoop-hoop-hoop-hoop-hoop-hoop-hoop*, descending and then rising towards the end of the series. Tall grassland and thickets near cultivation. AN: cr, GO: cr, KA: cr, KE: cr, MH: cr, TN: cr

Lesser Coucal *Centropus bengalensis* 33 cm
a ADULT BREEDING and **b** IMMATURE Smaller than Greater, with duller chestnut wings, and chestnut underwing-coverts; often with buff streaking on scapulars and wing-coverts. Non-breeding has pronounced buff shaft-streaking on head and body, chestnut wings and black tail; immature similar but with barred wings and tail. Song is a series of deep, resonant *pwoop-pwoop-pwoop* notes; similar to that of Greater, but usually slightly faster and more interrogative. Tall grassland, reedbeds and scrub. GO: v, KA: nr, KE: nr, TN: v

Vernal Hanging Parrot *Loriculus vernalis* 14 cm
a MALE and **b** IMMATURE Small green parrot. Adult has red bill and red rump. Call is a distinctive rasping *de-zeez-zeet*. Moist broadleaved forest. AN: nr, GO: nr, KA: nr, KE: nr, MH: nr, TN: lcr

Alexandrine Parakeet *Psittacula eupatria* 53 cm
a MALE and **b** FEMALE Very large, with maroon shoulder-patch. Male has black chin-stripe and pink collar. Call is a loud, guttural *keeak* or *kee-ah*, much deeper than that of Rose-ringed. Sal and riverine forest. AN: nr, GO: nr, KA: nr, MH: nr, TN: nr

Rose-ringed Parakeet *Psittacula krameri* 42 cm
a MALE and **b** FEMALE Green head and blue-green tip to tail. Male has black chin-stripe and pink collar. Call is a loud, shrill *kee-ah*. Broadleaved forest, wooded areas and cultivation. AN: cr, GO: cr, KA: cr, KE: nr, LS: nr, MH: cr, MV: ir, TN: cr

Plum-headed Parakeet *Psittacula cyanocephala* 36 cm
a MALE, **b** FEMALE and **c** IMMATURE Head is plum-red on male, pale grey on female. Yellow upper mandible, and white-tipped blue-green tail. Call is a high-pitched, ringing *tooi-tooi*. Broadleaved forest and well-wooded areas. AN: nr, GO: cr, KA: nr, KE: nr, MH: nr, TN: cr

Malabar Parakeet *Psittacula columboides* 38 cm
a MALE, **b** FEMALE and **c** IMMATURE Blue-grey head, breast and mantle. Blue primaries, yellow tip to tail. Female lacks blue-green collar of male. Calls contain loud, discordant and jarring or scolding notes, coarser than those of other parakeets. Evergreen and moist deciduous forest. GO: nr, KA: nr, KE: cr, MH: nr, TN: nr

Indian Swiftlet *Collocalia unicolor* 12 cm

 a **b** ADULT Uniform upperparts, with indistinct indentation to tail. *See* Appendix for comparison with Himalayan Swiftlet. Hills. GO: np, KA: nr, KE: cr, MH: nr, TN: lcr

White-rumped Needletail *Zoonavena sylvatica* 11 cm

 a **b** ADULT Small and stocky, with white rump and oval-shaped wings. Whitish belly and undertail-coverts help distinguish it from House Swift. Flight is fast with rapid wing beats, much banking from side to side, interspersed with short glides on slightly bowed wings. Broadleaved forest. AN: nr, GO: nr?, KA: nr, KE: nr, MH: nr, TN: v

Brown-backed Needletail *Hirundapus giganteus* 23 cm

 a **b** ADULT Large size, and fast powerful flight. Mainly brown (including throat) with white lores and white undertail-coverts. *See* Appendix for comparison with White-throated Needletail. Centre of mantle is paler, forming indistinct 'saddle'. Broadleaved forest. GO: nr?, KA: nr, KE: nr, MH: nr, TN: nr

Asian Palm Swift *Cypsiurus balasiensis* 13 cm

 a **b** ADULT Small and very slim, with scythe-shaped wings and long, forked tail (which is usually held closed). Fluttering flight, interspersed with short glides. Mainly brown with paler throat. Open country and cultivation with palms. AN: cr, GO: nr, KA: nr, KE: nr, LS: v, MH: cr, TN: lcr

Alpine Swift *Tachymarptis melba* 22 cm

 a **b** ADULT Large, powerful swift with white throat, brown breast-band and white patch on belly. Mainly hills and mountains. AN: nr, GO: np, KA: nr, KE: nr, MH: nr, TN: nr

Common Swift *Apus apus* 17 cm

 a **b** ADULT Uniform dark brown swift, with whitish throat; lacks white rump. Has prominently forked tail. *See* Appendix for comparison with Pallid Swift. GO: v, MH: v, MV: nw

Fork-tailed Swift *Apus pacificus* 15–18 cm

 a **b** ADULT Blackish swift with white rump and white scaling on underparts. Slimmer bodied and longer winged than House Swift, with deeply forked tail. Open ridges and hilltops. AN: v, GO: nw, KA: np, KE: nw, MH: v, TN: v

House Swift *Apus affinis* 15 cm

 a **b** ADULT Small blackish swift with broad white rump-band. Compared with Fork-tailed is rather stocky, with comparatively short wings, and tail has only a slight fork. Towns and villages. AN: cr, GO: cr, KA: cr, KE: nr, LS: v, MH: cr, MV: v, TN: nr

Crested Treeswift *Hemiprocne coronata* 23 cm

 a **b** MALE and **c** FEMALE Large size, long scythe-shaped wings and long, forked tail. Blue-grey upperparts and paler underparts, becoming whitish on belly and vent. Male has dull orange ear-coverts (dark grey in female). Forest. AN: nr, GO: nr, KA: nr, KE: nr, MH: nr, TN: nr

Barn Owl *Tyto alba* 36 cm

ADULT Unmarked white face, whitish underparts, and golden-buff and grey upperparts. Eyes are dark. Utters a variety of eerie screeching and hissing noises. Generally nocturnal. Usually hunts in flight, quartering the ground and often banking or hovering to locate prey. Roosts in old buildings and hunts in cultivation. AN: nr, GO: nr, KA: nr, KE: nr, MH: nr, TN: nr

Grass Owl *Tyto capensis* 36 cm

a **b** ADULT Similar to Barn Owl, with whitish face and underparts, but upperparts are darker and heavily marked with dark brown. Also shows dark barring on flight feathers, golden-buff patch at base of primaries contrasting with dark primaries, and dark-barred tail. Mottled rather than streaked upperparts, lack of prominent streaking on breast, and black eyes, are useful features to separate it from Short-eared Owl, which may be found in similar habitat. Generally nocturnal, and usually seen when flushed. Tall grassland. AN: nr, KA: nr, KE: nr, TN: nr

Oriental Bay Owl *Phodilus badius* 29 cm

ADULT Oblong-shaped, vinaceous-pinkish facial discs. Underparts vinaceous-pink, spotted with black; upperparts chestnut and buff, spotted and barred with black. Call is a series of eerie, upward-inflected whistles. Dense broadleaved forest. KA: nr, KE: nr, TN: nr

Pallid Scops Owl *Otus brucei* 22 cm

ADULT Compared with grey morph Oriental Scops, is paler, greyer and more uniform. Has less distinct scapular spots, and narrower dark streaking on underparts, which lack pale horizontal panels. Call is a resonant *whoop-whoop-whoop....* *See* Appendix for comparison with Eurasian Scops Owl. MH: nw

Oriental Scops Owl *Otus sunia* 19 cm

a ADULT RUFOUS MORPH and **b** ADULT BROWN MORPH Prominent ear-tufts. Prominent white scapular spots, streaked underparts and upperparts; lacks prominent nuchal collar. Occurs as rufous, grey and brown morphs. Iris yellow. Nocturnal. Call is frog-like *wut-chu-chraaii.* Forest, secondary growth and groves. *See* Appendix for comparison with Eurasian Scops Owl. AN: nr, GO: nr, KA: nr, KE: nr, MH: nr, TN: nr

Collared Scops Owl *Otus bakkamoena* 23–25 cm

ADULT Larger than other scops owls, with buff nuchal collar, finely streaked underparts and indistinct buffish scapular spots. Iris dark orange or brown. Nocturnal. Call is a subdued, frog-like *whuk,* repeated at irregular intervals. Forest, well-wooded areas and groves. AN: nr, GO: nr, KA: nr, KE: lcr, MH: nr, TN: lcr

Jungle Owlet *Glaucidium radiatum* 20 cm

a ADULT *G. r. radiatum*; **b** ADULT *G. r. malabaricum* Distinguished from Spotted Owlet by finely barred upperparts and underparts, rufous barring on wings, and rather plain-looking face. *G. r. malabaricum*, which occurs in the Malabar coastal strip, is more rufous in coloration. Mainly crepuscular. Open forest and secondary growth. AN: nr, GO: nr, KA: nr, KE: cr, MH: cr, TN: nr

Spotted Owlet *Athene brama* 21 cm

ADULT White spotting on upperparts, including crown, and diffuse brown spotting on underparts. Mainly crepuscular and nocturnal. Call is a harsh, screechy *chirurr-chirurr-chirurr...* followed by/alternated with *cheevak, cheevak, cheevak.* Habitation and cultivation. AN: cr, GO: cr, KA: cr, KE: cr, MH: cr, TN: cr

Forest Owlet *Athene blewitti* 23 cm

ADULT Compared with Spotted Owlet has rather dark grey-brown crown and nape, only faintly spotted with white, and lacks prominent white collar of Spotted. Wings (apart from inner coverts) and tail are broadly banded blackish brown and white, with white-tipped remiges and a broad white tail-tip. Breast dark brown, and barring on upper flanks is broader and more prominent; rest of underparts white, much cleaner than on Spotted. Deciduous forest. MH: nr

1 Eurasian Eagle Owl *Bubo bubo* 56–66 cm

ADULT Very large owl, with upright ear-tufts. Upperparts mottled dark brown and tawny-buff; underparts heavily streaked. Mainly nocturnal, but usually perches before sunset and after sunrise in a prominent position on cliff or rock. Call is a resonant *tu-whooh*. Cliffs, rocky hills, ravines and wooded areas. AN: nr, GO: nr, KA: nr, KE: nr, MH: nr, TN: lcr

2 Spot-bellied Eagle Owl *Bubo nipalensis* 63 cm

ADULT Very large owl, with prominent ear-tufts and bold chevron-shaped spots on underparts. Upperparts dark brown, barred with buff. Eyes dark brown. Nocturnal. Call is a deep hoot and a mournful scream. Dense broadleaved forest. GO: nr, KA: nr, KE: nr, MH: nr, TN: nr

3 Dusky Eagle Owl *Bubo coromandus* 58 cm

ADULT Large grey owl with prominent ear-tufts. Upperparts greyish brown with fine whitish vermiculations and diffuse darker brown streaking. Underparts greyish white with brown streaking. Call is a deep, resonant *wo, wo, wo, wo-o-o-o-o*. Generally nocturnal, but emerges from roost about an hour before sunset; sometimes hunts during the day in cloudy weather. Often calls during the day. Well-watered areas with extensive tree cover. GO: nr, KA: nr, MH: nr, TN: nr

4 Brown Fish Owl *Ketupa zeylonensis* 56 cm

ADULT Browner than Dusky Eagle Owl, with dark streaking on dull buff underparts, which are crossed with fine dark barring. Upperparts are brown with dark streaking. Partly diurnal, emerging from roost long before sunset; sometimes hunts during the day. Calls include a soft, deep *hup-hup-hu* and a wild *hu-hu-hu-hu...hu ha*. Forest and well-wooded areas near water. AN: nr, GO: nr, KA: nr, KE: nr, MH: nr, TN: nr

5 Mottled Wood Owl *Strix ocellata* 48 cm

ADULT Concentric barring on facial discs, and white, rufous and dark brown mottling on upperparts; dark brown barring mixed with rufous on whitish underparts. Call is a spooky, quavering *whaa-aa-aa-aa-ah*. Open wooded areas, and groves around villages and cultivation. AN: nr, GO: nr, KA: nr, KE: nr, MH: nr, TN: nr

6 Brown Wood Owl *Strix leptogrammica* 47–53 cm

ADULT Uniform rufous-buff facial discs, with prominent white eyebrows. Has uniform brown upperparts with fine barring on scapulars, and buff underparts with fine brown barring. Nocturnal. Calls include a *hoo-hoohoohoo(hoo)* and a loud eerie scream. Dense broadleaved forest. AN: nr, GO: nr, KA: nr, KE: nr, LS: nr?, MH: nr, TN: nr

✓7 Brown Hawk Owl *Ninox scutulata* 32 cm

ADULT Hawk-like profile. Dark face and rufous-brown streaking on underparts. Nocturnal, often hunting from prominent perch. Call is a repeated, soft, pleasant *oo...ok, oo...ok,....* Forest and well-wooded areas. AN: nr, GO: nr, KA: nr, KE: nr, MH: nr, TN: nr

8 Short-eared Owl *Asio flammeus* 37–39 cm

a **b** ADULT Streaked underparts and short ear-tufts, with buffish facial discs and yellow eyes. In flight, rather long and narrow wings show buffish patch at base of primaries and dark carpal patches. Often seen hunting during the day, quartering low over the ground in a leisurely manner, and hovering or gliding with wings in a V. Grassland and open scrub country. *See* Appendix for comparison with Long-eared Owl. AN: nw, GO: v, KA: nw, KE: nw, MH: nw, MV: nw, TN: nw

Sri Lanka Frogmouth *Batrachostomus moniliger* 23 cm

a MALE and **b** FEMALE Male brownish grey; female more rufous and less heavily marked. Song is a series of loud liquid chuckles. Dense tropical and subtropical evergreen forest. GO: nr, KA: nr, KE: nr, TN: nr

Great Eared Nightjar *Eurostopodus macrotis* 40–41 cm

a **b** ADULT Very large and richly coloured, with prominent ear-tufts. Fine rufous barring on black ear-coverts and throat, dark brown barring on buff underparts, and tail broadly banded with golden-buff and dark brown. Lacks pale spots on wings or tail. Song is a clear, wailing *pee-wheeeu*. Broadleaved moist forest and secondary growth. AN: nr, GO: nr, KE: lcr, TN: nr

Grey Nightjar *Caprimulgus indicus* 27–32 cm

a **b** MALE and **c** FEMALE Grey-brown, heavily marked with black. Compared with Large-tailed, lacks pale rufous-brown nuchal collar, and usually lacks buff or rufous edges to scapulars. (*See also* Table 1 on p.230.) Song is a loud, resonant *chunk-chunk-chunk-chunk....* Forest clearings and scrub-covered slopes. AN: nr, GO: nr?, KA: lcr, KE: cr, MH: nr, TN: lcr

Large-tailed Nightjar *Caprimulgus macrurus* 33 cm

a **b** MALE and **c** FEMALE More warmly coloured and strongly patterned than Grey, with longer and broader tail. Has diffuse, pale rufous-brown nuchal collar, well-defined buff edges to scapulars and prominent buff tips to wing-coverts. (*See also* Table 1 on p.230.) Song is a series of loud, resonant calls: *chaunk-chaunk-chaunk* notes, repeated at the rate of about 100 per minute. Edges and clearings of tropical and subtropical forest. AN: nr

Jerdon's Nightjar *Caprimulgus atripennis* 28 cm

a **b** MALE More warmly coloured and strongly patterned than Grey. Has rufous band across nape/upper mantle, well-defined buff edges to scapulars, and broad, buff tips to black-centred coverts forming wing-bars. Plumage rather similar to Large-tailed, but is generally darker and with more extensive rufous-brown coloration to nape and upper mantle. Appears shorter-winged and shorter-tailed than Large-tailed. (*See also* Table 1 on p.230.) Song is a series of liquid, tremulous calls: *ch-wo-wo*, repeated at the rate of 13–20 per minute. Edges of moist forest and secondary growth. AN: nr, GO: nr, KA: nr, KE: nr, MH: nr, TN: nr

Indian Nightjar *Caprimulgus asiaticus* 24 cm

a **b** ADULT Like a small version of Large-tailed. Has boldly streaked crown, rufous-buff nuchal collar, bold black centres and broad buff edges to scapulars, and relatively unmarked central tail feathers. (*See also* Table 1 on p.230.) Song is a far-carrying *chuk-chuk-chuk-chuk-tukaroo*; short sharp *qwit-qwit* in flight. Open scrub and cultivation. AN: nr, GO: nw, KA: nr, KE: nr, MH: nr, TN: nr

Savanna Nightjar *Caprimulgus affinis* 23 cm

a **b** MALE and **c** FEMALE Crown and mantle finely vermiculated, and often appears rather plain except for scapulars, which are edged with rufous-buff. Male has largely white outer tail feathers, although this can be difficult to see. (*See also* Table 1 on p.230.) Song is a strident *dheet*. Rare, possibly resident; below 250 m. Open forest and scrubby hillsides. AN: nr, GO: nr?, KA: nr, KE: nw, MH: nr

Rock Pigeon *Columba livia* 33 cm
a **b** ADULT Grey tail with blackish terminal band, and broad black bars across greater coverts and tertials/secondaries. Feral birds vary considerably in coloration and patterning. Often in large flocks. Feral birds live in villages and towns; wild birds around cliffs and ruins. AN: cr, GO: cr, KA: cr, KE: nr, LS: ir, MH: cr, MV: ir, TN: nr

Nilgiri Wood Pigeon *Columba elphinstonii* 42 cm
a **b** ADULT Chequerboard pattern on neck, maroon-brown upperparts, uniform slate-grey tail. Moist evergreen forest. GO: nr, KA: nr, KE: nr, MH: nr, TN: lcr

Pale-capped Pigeon *Columba punicea* 36 cm
a **b** ADULT Pale cap, vinous-chestnut underparts, and maroon-brown mantle and wing-coverts with green-and-purple gloss. Tropical and subtropical forest and secondary growth. AN: nr, MH: nr

Oriental Turtle Dove *Streptopelia orientalis* 33 cm
a **b** ADULT *S. o. meena*; **c** **d** ADULT *S. o. erythrocephala* Stocky dove with rufous-scaled scapulars and wing-coverts, and black and bluish-grey barring on neck sides. Has dusky-grey underwing. Migrant race *meena* has white sides and tip to tail, and vinaceous-pink underparts. Resident race *erythrocephala* has grey sides and tip to tail, and reddish-brown head, neck and underparts. *See* Appendix for differences from European Turtle Dove. Open forest, especially near cultivation. AN: nr, GO: nr?, KA: nr, KE: v, LS: v, MH: nr, MV: v, TN: nw

Laughing Dove *Streptopelia senegalensis* 27 cm
a **b** ADULT Slim, small dove with fairly long tail. Brownish-pink head and underparts, uniform upperparts and black stippling on upper breast. Dry cultivation and scrub-covered hills. AN: cr, GO: v, KA: cr, KE: nr, MH: cr, TN: cr

Spotted Dove *Streptopelia chinensis* 30 cm
a **b** ADULT Spotted upperparts, and black-and-white-chequered patch on neck sides. Cultivation, habitation and open forest. AN: cr, GO: cr, KA: cr, KE: cr, MH: cr, MV: v, TN: cr

Red Collared Dove *Streptopelia tranquebarica* 23 cm
a MALE and **b** FEMALE Small, stocky dove, with shorter tail than Eurasian Collared. Male has blue-grey head, pinkish-maroon upperparts and pink underparts. Female similar to Eurasian Collared, but is more compact, with darker buffish-grey underparts, darker fawn-brown upperparts and greyer underwing-coverts. Light woodland and trees in open country. AN: nr, GO: v, KA: nr, MH: nr, TN: cr

Eurasian Collared Dove *Streptopelia decaocto* 32 cm
a **b** ADULT Sandy-brown with black half-collar. Larger and longer-tailed than Red Collared. Plumage similar to female Red Collared but with paler upperparts and underparts, and white underwing-coverts. Open dry country with cultivation and groves. AN: nr, GO: np, KA: cr, MH: nr, TN: cr

1 **Emerald Dove** *Chalcophaps indica* 27 cm
a MALE and b c FEMALE Stout and broad-winged dove, with very rapid flight. Upperparts green, with black-and-white banding on back. Male has grey crown and white shoulder-patch. Moist tropical and subtropical broadleaved forest. AN: nr, GO: nr?, KA: nr, KE: cr, MH: nr, TN: nr

2 **Orange-breasted Green Pigeon** *Treron bicincta* 29 cm
a MALE and b FEMALE Central tail feathers of both sexes are grey. Male has orange breast, bordered above by lilac band, grey hind-crown and nape, and green mantle. Female has yellow cast to breast and belly, and grey hind-crown and nape. Sal and riverine forest. AN: nr, GO: v, KA: nr, KE: nw, TN: nr

3 **Pompadour Green Pigeon** *Treron pompadora* 28 cm
a MALE and b FEMALE Male has maroon mantle and grey cap. Grey cap and tail pattern help separate female from female Orange-breasted. Sal and riverine forest. GO: nr, KA: nr, KE: cr, MH: nr, TN: cr

4 **Yellow-footed Green Pigeon** *Treron phoenicoptera* 33 cm
ADULT Large size, broad olive-yellow collar, pale greyish-green upperparts, mauve shoulder-patch, and yellow legs and feet. Deciduous forest and fruiting trees around villages and cultivation. AN: nr, GO: nr, KA: nr, KE: nr, MH: nr, TN: nr

5 **Green Imperial Pigeon** *Ducula aenea* 43–47 cm
a b ADULT Large size, metallic green upperparts and tail, and maroon undertail-coverts (darker than belly). Moist tropical broadleaved forest. AN: nr, GO: nr, KA: nr, KE: nr, MH: nr, TN: nr

6 **Mountain Imperial Pigeon** *Ducula badia* 43–51 cm
a b ADULT Large size, brownish upperparts, dark brown band across base of tail, and pale buff undertail-coverts. Dense broadleaved forest. GO: nr, KA: nr, KE: nr, MH: nr, TN: nr

1

Indian Bustard *Ardeotis nigriceps* 92–122 cm
[a] [b] MALE and [c] FEMALE Very large bustard. In all plumages, has greyish or white neck, black crown and crest, uniform brown upperparts and white-spotted black wing-coverts. Upperwing lacks extensive area of white. Male huge, with black breast-band, and with almost white neck only very finely vermiculated with dark grey. Female smaller; neck appears greyer owing to profuse dark grey vermiculations, and typically lacks black breast-band. Dry grassland with bushes. AN: nr, KA: xr, MH: nr, TN: nr

2

Lesser Florican *Sypheotides indica* 46–51 cm
[a] [b] MALE BREEDING, [c] MALE NON-BREEDING and [d] [e] FEMALE Small, slim, long-necked bustard. Breeding male has spatulate-tipped head plumes, black head/neck and underparts, and white collar across upper mantle; white wing-coverts show as patch on closed wing. Non-breeding male similar to female, but has white wing-coverts. Female and immature are sandy or cinnamon-buff, with heavily marked upperparts and rufous coloration to barred flight feathers. Grassland and cultivation. Globally threatened. AN: nr, KA: nr, KE: v, MH: nr, TN: nw

3

Sarus Crane *Grus antigone* 156 cm
[a] [b] ADULT and [c] IMMATURE Adult is grey, with bare red head and upper neck, and bare ashy-green crown. In flight, black primaries contrast with rest of wing. Immature has rusty-buff feathering to head and neck, and upperparts are marked with brown; older immatures are similar to adult but have dull red head and upper neck, and lack greenish crown of adult. Cultivation in well-watered country. Globally threatened. AN: nr, GO: v, MH: nr

4

Demoiselle Crane *Grus virgo* 90–100 cm
[a] [b] ADULT and [c] IMMATURE Small crane. Adult has black head and neck with white tuft behind eye, and grey crown; black neck feathers extend as a point beyond breast, and elongated tertials project as shallow arc beyond body, giving rise to distinctive shape. Immature similar to adult, but head and neck are dark grey, tuft behind eye is grey and less prominent, and has grey-brown cast to upperparts. In flight, Demoiselle is best separated at a distance from Common by black breast. Cultivation and large rivers. AN: v, KA: nw, MH: v, TN: v

5

Common Crane *Grus grus* 110–120 cm
[a] [b] ADULT and [c] IMMATURE Adult has mainly black head and foreneck, with white stripe behind eye extending down side of neck. Immature has brown markings on upperparts, with buff or grey head and neck. Adult head pattern apparent on some by first winter, and as adult by second winter. Cultivation, large rivers and marshes. AN: v, GO: v, MH: nw

Slaty-legged Crake *Rallina eurizonoides* 25 cm
a ADULT and **b** JUVENILE Adult has greenish or grey legs, olive-brown mantle contrasting with rufous neck and breast, white barring on underparts, and prominent white throat. Juvenile is largely dark olive-brown with white throat and white barring on underparts; leg colour as adult. Marshes in well-wooded country. GO: v, KA: nr, KE: nr?, MH: nr, TN: nr

Slaty-breasted Rail *Gallirallus striatus* 27 cm
a ADULT MALE and **b** JUVENILE Straightish, longish bill with red at base. Legs olive-grey. Adult has chestnut crown and nape, slate-grey foreneck and breast, white barring and spotting on upperparts, and barred flanks and undertail-coverts. Juvenile has rufous-brown crown and nape, and white barring on wing-coverts. Marshes, mangroves and paddy-fields. AN: nr, GO: nr?, KA: nr, KE: nr?, MH: nr, TN: nr

Water Rail *Rallus aquaticus* 23–28 cm
a ADULT MALE and **b** JUVENILE Slightly downcurved bill with red at base. Legs pinkish. Adult has streaked upperparts, greyish underparts and barring on flanks. Marshes and wet fields. AN: v, MH: v, TN: v

Brown Crake *Amaurornis akool* 28 cm
ADULT Olive-brown upperparts, grey underparts, and olive-brown flanks and undertail-coverts; underparts lack barring. Has greenish bill and pinkish-brown to purple legs. Juvenile similar to adult. Marshes and vegetation bordering watercourses. AN: nr, GO: nr?, KA: nr, MH: nr, TN: nr

White-breasted Waterhen *Amaurornis phoenicurus* 32 cm
a ADULT and **b** JUVENILE Adult has grey upperparts, and white face, foreneck and breast; undertail-coverts are rufous-cinnamon. Juvenile has greyish face, foreneck and breast, and olive-brown upperparts. Marshes and thick cover close to pools, lakes and ditches. AN: nr, GO: cr, KA: cr, KE: nr, LS: nr, MH: cr, MV: cr, TN: nr

Baillon's Crake *Porzana pusilla* 17–19 cm
a ADULT and **b** JUVENILE Adult has rufous-brown upperparts, extensively marked with white. Flanks are barred. Bill and legs are green. Juvenile is similar but has buff underparts. Marshes, reedy lake edges and wet fields. *See* Appendix for comparison with Little Crake. AN: nw, GO: nw, KA: nw, KE: nw, MH: cw

Ruddy-breasted Crake *Porzana fusca* 22 cm
a ADULT and **b** JUVENILE Red legs, chestnut underparts, and black-and-white barring on rear flanks and undertail-coverts (less extensive than in Slaty-legged Crake). Juvenile is dark olive-brown, with white-barred undertail-coverts and fine greyish-white mottling/barring on rest of underparts; legs are reddish. Leg colour is best feature separating it from Slaty-legged Crake in all plumages. Marshes and wet paddy-fields. AN: nr, GO: nw, KA: nr, KE: nr, MH: nr, TN: nr

Spotted Crake *Porzana porzana* 22–24 cm
a ADULT and **b** JUVENILE Profuse white spotting on head, neck and breast. Stout bill, barred flanks and unmarked buff undertail-coverts. Adult has yellowish bill with red at base, and grey head and breast. Juvenile has buffish-brown head and breast, and bill is brown. *See* Appendix for description of Corn Crake. Marshes and lakes. GO: v, KA: v, MH: nw

Watercock *Gallicrex cinerea* M 43 cm, F 36 cm

a MALE BREEDING, **b** JUVENILE MALE and **c** FEMALE Male is mainly greyish black, with yellow-tipped red bill and red shield and horn. Non-breeding male and female have buff underparts with fine barring, and buff fringes to dark brown upperparts. Juvenile has uniform rufous-buff underparts, and rufous-buff fringes to upperparts. Male is much larger than female. Marshes and flooded fields. AN: nr, GO: nw, KA: nr, KE: nr, MH: nr, MV: nr?, TN: nr

Purple Swamphen *Porphyrio porphyrio* 45–50 cm

a ADULT and **b** JUVENILE Large size, purplish-blue coloration, and huge red bill and red frontal shield. Juvenile greyer, with duller bill. Reedbeds and marshes. AN: nr, GO: nr, KA: cr, KE: nr, MH: nr, TN: nr

Common Moorhen *Gallinula chloropus* 32–35 cm

a ADULT and **b** JUVENILE White undertail-coverts and line along flanks. Adult has red bill with yellow tip and red shield. Juvenile has dull green bill and is mainly brown. Marshes and reed-edged pools. AN: cr, GO: nw, KA: cr, KE: nr?, MH: nr, MV: nr, TN: nr

Common Coot *Fulica atra* 36–38 cm

a ADULT and **b** JUVENILE Blackish, with white bill and shield. Reed-edged lakes and pools. AN: nr, GO: nr?, KA: cr, KE: nr, MH: nr, MV: v, TN: nr

Chestnut-bellied Sandgrouse *Pterocles exustus* 31–33 cm

a **b** MALE and **c** **d** FEMALE Both sexes have long, pointed central tail feathers, and blackish underwing with white trailing edge. Male has blackish-chestnut belly and black breast line; head and upperparts are comparatively uniform compared with male Painted Sandgrouse. Female has a broad buff breast-band, which is a feature separating it from female Painted (together with pintail and underwing pattern). Desert and sparse thorn scrub. *See* Appendix for comparison with Black-bellied Sandgrouse. AN: nr, KA: nr, MH: nr, TN: nr

Painted Sandgrouse *Pterocles indicus* 28 cm

a **b** MALE and **c** FEMALE Small, stocky and heavily barred. Lacks elongated central tail feathers. Underwing is grey. Male has black-and-white patterning on forehead, chestnut, buff and black breast-bands, unbarred orange-buff neck and inner wing-coverts, and heavily marked upperparts. Female heavily barred all over, with yellowish face and throat. Arid low hills. AN: nr, KA: nr, MH: nr, TN: nr

Eurasian Woodcock *Scolopax rusticola* 33–35 cm

a **b** ADULT Bulky, with broad, rounded wings. Head banded black and buff; lacks sharply defined mantle and scapular stripes. Crepuscular and nocturnal. Dense, moist forest. AN: v, KA: nw, KE: nw, MH: nw, TN: nw

Wood Snipe *Gallinago nemoricola* 28–32 cm

a **b** ADULT Large snipe, with heavy and direct flight and broad wings. Bill relatively short and broad-based. More boldly marked than Solitary, with buff and blackish head stripes, broad buff stripes on blackish mantle and scapulars, and warm buff neck and breast with brown streaking. Legs greenish. Forest marshes. Globally threatened. *See* Appendix for comparison with Great Snipe. AN: nw, KA: nw, KE: nw, MH: nw, TN: nw

Pintail Snipe *Gallinago stenura* 25–27 cm

a ADULT and **b** **c** IN FLIGHT More rounded wings than Common, and slower and more direct flight. Lacks white trailing edge to secondaries, and has densely barred underwing-coverts and pale (buff-scaled) upperwing-covert panel (more pronounced than shown). Feet project noticeably beyond tail in flight. Flight call is a rasping *tetch*. *See* Appendix for comparison with Great Snipe. Marshes and wet paddy-fields. AN: nw, GO: nw, KA: cw, KE: cw, MH: cw, MV: nw, TN: cw

Swinhoe's Snipe *Gallinago megala* 25–27 cm

a ADULT and **b** **c** IN FLIGHT Very similar to Pintail. In flight, is heavier, with longer bill and more pointed wings, and feet only just project beyond tail. Some birds quite dusky on neck, breast and flanks, unlike Pintail. Marshes. KA: v, KE: nw, MH: nw, MV: v, TN: nw

Common Snipe *Gallinago gallinago* 25–27 cm

a ADULT and **b** **c** IN FLIGHT Compared with Pintail, wings are more pointed and has faster and more erratic flight; shows prominent white trailing edge to wing and white banding on underwing-coverts. Flight call is a grating *scaaap*, higher-pitched and more anxious than that of Pintail. Marshes and wet paddy stubble. *See* Appendix for comparison with Great Snipe. AN: nw, GO: nw, KA: cw, KE: cw, MH: cw, MV: nw, TN: nw

Jack Snipe *Lymnocryptes minimus* 17–19 cm

a ADULT and **b** **c** IN FLIGHT Small, with short bill. Flight weaker and slower than that of Common, with rounded wing-tips. Has divided supercilium but lacks pale crown-stripe. Mantle and scapular stripes very prominent. If flushed, flies off silently and without zigzagging flight. Marshes and wet paddy stubble. AN: nw, GO: v, KA: nw, KE: nw, MH: nw, TN: nw

Greater Painted-snipe *Rostratula benghalensis* 25 cm

a ADULT MALE, **b** ADULT FEMALE and **c** JUVENILE Rail-like wader, with broad, rounded wings and longish, downcurved bill. White or buff 'spectacles' and 'braces'. Adult female has maroon head and neck, and dark greenish wing-coverts. Adult male and juvenile duller, and have buff spotting on wing-coverts. When flushed, rises heavily with legs trailing. Marshes, vegetated pools and stream banks. AN: nr, GO: nr?, KA: nr, KE: nr, MH: nr, TN: nr

1 Black-tailed Godwit *Limosa limosa* 36–44 cm

a MALE BREEDING, **b** NON-BREEDING, **c** JUVENILE and **d** IN FLIGHT White wing-bars and white tail-base with black tail-band. In breeding plumage, male has rufous-orange neck and breast, with blackish barring on underparts and white belly; breeding female is duller. In non-breeding plumage, is uniform grey on neck, upperparts and breast. Juvenile has cinnamon underparts and cinnamon fringes to dark-centred upperparts. Banks and shallow waters of lakes and rivers. AN: nw, GO: nw, KA: nw, KE: nw, LS: v, MH: nw, MV: v, TN: nw

2 Bar-tailed Godwit *Limosa lapponica* 37–41 cm

a MALE BREEDING, **b** NON-BREEDING, **c** JUVENILE and **d** IN FLIGHT Lacks wing-bar, has barred tail and white V on back. Breeding male has chestnut-red underparts. Breeding female has pale chestnut or cinnamon underparts, although many same as non-breeding. Non-breeding has dark streaking on breast and streaked appearance to upperparts. Juvenile similar to non-breeding, but with buff wash to underparts and buff edges to mantle/scapulars. *See* plate 28 for comparison with Asian Dowitcher. Estuaries and lagoons. AN: v, GO: np, KE: nw, LS: v, MH: nw, MV: nw, TN: nw

3 Whimbrel *Numenius phaeopus* 40–46 cm

a **b** ADULT Smaller than Eurasian Curlew, with shorter bill. Distinctive head pattern, with whitish supercilium and crown-stripe, dark eye-stripe and dark sides of crown. Flight call distinctive, *he-he-he-he-he-he-he*. Banks of rivers and lakes, grassy areas. AN: nw, GO: nw, KA: nw, KE: nw, LS: nw, MH: lcw, MV: nw, TN: nw

4 Eurasian Curlew *Numenius arquata* 50–60 cm

a **b** ADULT Large size and long, curved bill. Rather plain head. Has distinctive mournful *cur-lew* call. Banks of rivers and lakes, grassy areas. AN: nw, GO: nw, KA: nw, KE: nw, LS: nw, MH: nw, MV: nw, TN: nw

5 Spotted Redshank *Tringa erythropus* 29–32 cm

a ADULT BREEDING, **b** **c** ADULT NON-BREEDING and **d** JUVENILE Red at base of bill, and red legs. Longer bill and legs than Common Redshank, and upperwing uniform. Non-breeding plumage is paler grey above and whiter below than Common. Underparts mainly black in breeding plumage. Juvenile has grey barring on underparts. Has distinctive *tu-ick* flight call. Banks and shallow waters of rivers and lakes. AN: nw, GO: nwp, KA: nw, MH: nw, MV: v, TN: nw

6 Common Redshank *Tringa totanus* 27–29 cm

a ADULT BREEDING, **b** **c** ADULT NON-BREEDING and **d** JUVENILE Orange-red at base of bill, and orange-red legs. Shorter bill and legs than Spotted Redshank, and with broad white trailing edge to wing. Non-breeding plumage is grey-brown above, with grey breast. Neck and underparts heavily streaked in breeding plumage. Juvenile has brown upperparts with buff spotting. Call is an anxious *teu-hu-hu*. Banks of rivers and lakes, marshes. AN: nw, GO: cw, KA: nw, KE: nw, LS: v, MH: cw, MV: nw, TN: nw

7 Marsh Sandpiper *Tringa stagnatilis* 22–25 cm

a ADULT BREEDING and **b** **c** ADULT NON-BREEDING Smaller and daintier than Common Greenshank, with proportionately longer legs and finer bill. Legs greenish or yellowish. Upperparts are grey and foreneck and underparts white in non-breeding plumage. In breeding plumage, foreneck and breast streaked and upperparts blotched and barred. Juvenile has dark-streaked upperparts with buff fringes. Has an abrupt, dull *yup* flight call. Banks of rivers and lakes, marshes. AN: nw, GO: nw, KA: lcw, KE: nw, MH: nw, MV: nw, TN: nw

8 Common Greenshank *Tringa nebularia* 30–34 cm

a ADULT BREEDING and **b** **c** ADULT NON-BREEDING Stocky, with long, stout bill and long, stout greenish legs. Upperparts are grey and foreneck and underparts white in non-breeding plumage. In breeding plumage, foreneck and breast streaked and upperparts untidily streaked. Juvenile has dark-streaked upperparts with fine buff or whitish fringes. Call is a loud, ringing and very distinctive *tu-tu-tu*. Wetlands. AN: nw, GO: cw, KA: cw, KE: nw, LS: nw, MH: nw, MV: nw, TN: nw

√1 **Green Sandpiper** *Tringa ochropus* 21–24 cm
a **b** **c** ADULT NON-BREEDING Greenish legs. White rump; dark upperwing and underwing. Compared with Wood, has indistinct (or non-existent) supercilium behind eye and darker upperparts. *Tluee-tueet* flight call. Wetlands. AN: nw, GO: nw, KA: cw, KE: nw, LS: v, MH: cw, TN: nw

√2 **Wood Sandpiper** *Tringa glareola* 18–21 cm
a **b** **c** ADULT NON-BREEDING and **d** JUVENILE Yellowish legs. White rump, and upperwing lacks wing-bar. Compared with Green, shows prominent supercilium, more heavily spotted upperparts and paler underwing. Flight call is a soft *chiff-if-if*. Banks of rivers and lakes, marshes. AN: cw, GO: cw, KA: cw, KE: nw, LS: v, MH: nw, MV: nw, TN: cw

3 **Terek Sandpiper** *Xenus cinereus* 22–25 cm
a **b** ADULT BREEDING, **c** ADULT NON-BREEDING and **d** JUVENILE Longish, upturned bill and short, yellowish legs. In flight, shows prominent white trailing edge to secondaries and grey rump and tail. Adult breeding has blackish scapular lines. Flight call is pleasant *hu-hu-hu*. Mainly coastal wetlands. AN: v, GO: nw, KA: nw, KE: nw, LS: v, MH: nw, MV: nw, TN: nw

√4 **Common Sandpiper** *Actitis hypoleucos* 19–21 cm
a **b** ADULT and **c** **d** JUVENILE Horizontal stance and constant bobbing action. In flight, rapid shallow wing-beats are interspersed with short glides. Juvenile has buff fringes to upperparts. Flight call is an anxious *wee-wee-wee*. Wetlands. AN: nw, GO: cw, KA: cw, KE: cw, LS: nw, MH: cw, MV: nw, TN: cw

√5 **Ruddy Turnstone** *Arenaria interpres* 23 cm
a ADULT, **b** **c** ADULT NON-BREEDING and **d** JUVENILE Short bill and orange legs. In flight, shows white stripes on wings and back and black tail. In breeding plumage, has complex black-and-white neck and breast pattern and much chestnut-red on upperparts; duller and less strikingly patterned in non-breeding and juvenile plumages. Rocky coasts and tidal mudflats. AN: v, GO: np, KA: np, LS: cw, MH: nw, MV: cw, TN: nw

6 **Asian Dowitcher** *Limnodromus semipalmatus* 34–36 cm
a ADULT BREEDING, **b** **c** ADULT NON-BREEDING and **d** JUVENILE Slightly smaller than Bar-tailed Godwit. Broad-based black bill with swollen tip, and square-shaped head. Shows diffuse pale wing-bar and grey tail in flight. Underparts brick-red in breeding plumage. Upperparts and underparts heavily streaked in non-breeding plumage. Juvenile has buff fringes to upperparts and buff wash to breast. Intertidal mudflats and mud banks. TN: nw

7 **Great Knot** *Calidris tenuirostris* 26–28 cm
a ADULT BREEDING, **b** **c** ADULT NON-BREEDING and **d** JUVENILE Larger than Red Knot, and often with slightly downcurved bill. Adult breeding heavily marked with black on breast and flanks, with chestnut patterning to scapulars. Adult non-breeding typically more heavily streaked on upperparts and breast than Red Knot, and juvenile is more strongly patterned than that species. Intertidal flats and tidal creeks. AN: v, GO: nwp, KA: v, KE: nw, LS: v, MH: nw, TN: nw

8 **Red Knot** *Calidris canutus* 23–25 cm
a ADULT BREEDING, **b** **c** ADULT NON-BREEDING and **d** JUVENILE Stocky, with short, straight bill. Adult breeding is brick-red on underparts. Adult non-breeding whitish on underparts and uniform grey on upperparts. Juvenile has buff fringes and dark subterminal crescents to upperparts. Mainly intertidal mudflats. AN: v, TN: nw

1 Sanderling *Calidris alba* 20 cm

a **b** ADULT BREEDING, **c** **d** ADULT NON-BREEDING and **e** JUVENILE Stocky, with short bill. Very broad white wing-bar. Adult breeding usually shows some rufous on sides of head, breast and upperparts. Non-breeding is pale grey above and very white below. Juvenile chequered black-and-white above. Sandy beaches. AN: v, GO: nwp, KA: nw, KE: v, LS: v, MH: nw, MV: nw, TN: nw

2 Little Stint *Calidris minuta* 13–15 cm

a ADULT BREEDING FRESH and **b** WORN, **c** **d** ADULT NON-BREEDING and **e** **f** JUVE-NILE More rotund than Temminck's, and with dark legs. Grey sides to tail. Adult breeding has pale mantle V, rufous wash to face, neck sides and breast, and rufous fringes to upperpart feathers. Non-breeding has untidy, mottled/streaked appearance, with grey breast sides. Juvenile has whitish mantle V, greyish nape and rufous fringes to upperparts, with some variation in warmth of plumage coloration. Flight call is a weak *pi-pi-pi*. Muddy edges of lakes, streams and rivers. AN: cw, GO: nw, KA: cw, KE: nw, LS: nw, MH: cw, MV: nw, TN: cw

3 Red-necked Stint *Calidris ruficollis* 13–16 cm

a ADULT BREEDING FRESH and **b** WORN, **c** **d** ADULT NON-BREEDING and **e** **f** JUVE-NILE Very similar to Little. Adult breeding typically has unstreaked rufous-orange throat, foreneck and breast, white sides of lower breast with dark streaking, and greyish-centred tertials and wing-coverts (with greyish-white fringes); lacks prominent mantle V. Juvenile lacks prominent mantle V; has different coloration and patterning to lower scapulars (grey with dark subterminal marks and whitish or buffish fringes; typically blackish with rufous fringes in Little), and grey-centred, whitish- or buffish-edged tertials (usually blackish with rufous edges in Little); supercilium does not usually split in front of eye. Call much as Little. Mainly coastal. GO: v, TN: nw

4 Temminck's Stint *Calidris temminckii* 13–15 cm

a **b** ADULT BREEDING, **c** ADULT NON-BREEDING and **d** JUVENILE More elongated and horizontal than Little. White sides to tail in flight. Legs yellowish. In all plumages, lacks mantle V and is usually rather uniform, with complete breast-band and indistinct supercilium. Flight call is a purring trill. Wetlands. AN: nw, GO: nw, KA: nw, KE: nw, MH: cw, MV: np, TN: cw

5 Long-toed Stint *Calidris subminuta* 13–15 cm

a ADULT BREEDING, **b** **c** ADULT NON-BREEDING and **d** JUVENILE Long and yellowish legs, longish neck and upright stance. In all plumages, has prominent supercilium and heavily streaked foreneck and breast. Adult breeding and juvenile have prominent rufous fringes to upperparts; juvenile has very striking mantle V. In winter, upperparts more heavily marked than that of Little. Call is a soft *prit* or *chirrup*. Freshwater and coastal wetlands. AN: v, GO: np, MV: nw, TN: nw

1 Dunlin *Calidris alpina* 16–22 cm

a **b** ADULT BREEDING, **c** **d** ADULT NON-BREEDING and **e** JUVENILE Dark centre to rump. Adult breeding has black belly. Adult non-breeding darker grey-brown than Curlew Sandpiper, with less distinct supercilium. Juvenile has streaked belly, rufous fringes to mantle and buff mantle V. Flight call is a slurred *screet*. Banks of rivers and lakes. AN: v, GO: nw, KA: nw, KE: nw, MH: nw, MV: nw, TN: nw

2 Curlew Sandpiper *Calidris ferruginea* 18–23 cm

a ADULT BREEDING, **b** **c** ADULT NON-BREEDING and **d** JUVENILE White rump. More elegant than Dunlin, with longer and more downcurved bill. Adult breeding has chestnut-red underparts. Adult non-breeding paler grey than Dunlin, with more distinct supercilium. Juvenile has strong supercilium, buff wash to breast, and buff fringes to upperparts. Flight call is a purring *prrriit*. River banks. AN: v, GO: nw, KA: nw, KE: nw, MH: nw, MV: cw, TN: nw

3 Spoon-billed Sandpiper *Calidris pygmea* 14–16 cm

a ADULT BREEDING, **b** **c** ADULT NON-BREEDING and **d** JUVENILE Stint-sized. Spatulate tip to bill. Adult winter has paler grey upperparts than Little Stint, with more pronounced white supercilium, forehead and cheeks; underparts appear cleaner and whiter. Adult breeding more uniform rufous-orange on face and breast compared with Little Stint (recalling Red-necked Stint). Juvenile very similar to Little Stint, but shows more white on face and darker eye-stripe and ear-coverts (masked appearance). Flight call is a quiet *preep*. Intertidal mudflats. KE: v, MH: v, TN: nw

4 Broad-billed Sandpiper *Limicola falcinellus* 16–18 cm

a ADULT BREEDING, **b** **c** ADULT NON-BREEDING and **d** JUVENILE Distinctive shape: stockier than Dunlin, with legs set well back and downward-kinked bill. In all plumages, has more prominent supercilium than Dunlin, with 'split' before eye and contrasting with dark eye-stripe. Adult breeding has bold streaking on neck and breast contrasting with white belly. Non-breeding has dark patch at bend of wing (sometimes obscured by breast feathers) and strong streaking on breast; dark inner wing-coverts show as dark leading edge to wing in flight. Juvenile has buff mantle/scapular lines and streaked breast. Flight call is a buzzing *chrrreet*. Intertidal mudflats and tidal creeks. GO: nw, KA: nw, KE: v, MH: nw, TN: nw

5 Ruff *Philomachus pugnax* M 26–32 cm, F 20–25 cm

a **b** **c** MALE BREEDING, **d** **e** NON-BREEDING and **f** JUVENILE Males larger than females. Non-breeding and juvenile have neatly fringed upperparts. Breeding male has variable ruff. (*See* Appendix for comparison with Buff-breasted Sandpiper.) Marshes, wet fields, and banks of rivers and lakes. AN: nw, GO: nw, KA: nw, KE: v, MH: nw, MV: v, TN: nw

6 Red-necked Phalarope *Phalaropus lobatus* 18–19 cm

a ADULT BREEDING, **b** **c** ADULT NON-BREEDING and **d** JUVENILE Typically seen swimming. Delicately built, with fine bill. Adult breeding has white throat and red stripe down side of grey neck. Adult non-breeding has dark grey upperparts, with white edges to mantle and scapular feathers, forming fairly distinct lines (poorly depicted in plate). Juvenile has dark grey upperparts with orange-buff mantle and scapular lines. Winters at sea. AN: v, GO: v, KA: v, LS: v, MV: v, TN: nw

Pheasant-tailed Jacana *Hydrophasianus chirurgus* 31 cm

a **b** ADULT BREEDING and **c** ADULT NON-BREEDING Extensive white on upperwing, and white underwing. Yellowish patch on sides of neck. Adult breeding has brown underparts and long tail. Adult non-breeding and juvenile have white underparts, with dark line down side of neck and dark breast-band (which are too distinct in plate). Marshes, lakes and ponds with floating vegetation. AN: nr, GO: nr, KA: lcr, KE: nr, MH: cr, TN: nr

Bronze-winged Jacana *Metopidius indicus* 28–31 cm

a **b** ADULT and **c** IMMATURE Dark upperwing and underwing. Adult has white supercilium, bronze-green upperparts and blackish underparts. Juvenile has orange-buff wash on breast, short white supercilium, and yellowish bill. Marshes, pools and lakes with floating vegetation. AN: nr, GO: nr, KA: nr, KE: nr, MH: cr, TN: nr

Eurasian Thick-knee *Burhinus oedicnemus* 40–44 cm

a **b** ADULT Sandy-brown and streaked. Short yellow-and-black bill, striking yellow eye and long yellow legs. Call is a loud *cur-lee*. Mainly active at dusk and during the night; spends the day sitting in shade. Desert, stony hills, open dry forest and fields. AN: nr, GO: v, KA: nr, KE: nr, LS: v, MH: nr, TN: nr

Great Thick-knee *Esacus recurvirostris* 49–54 cm

a **b** ADULT Upturned black-and-yellow bill, white forehead and 'spectacles', and dark mask. Dark bar across coverts very prominent at rest. In flight, shows grey mid-wing panel and white patches in primaries. Mainly active at dusk and during the night, but often observable during the day, especially when disturbed. Stony banks of larger rivers and lakes. AN: nr, GO: v, KA: nr, KE: v, MH: nr, TN: nr

Eurasian Oystercatcher *Haematopus ostralegus* 40–46 cm

a **b** ADULT BREEDING and **c** ADULT NON-BREEDING Black and white, with broad white wing-bar. Bill reddish. White collar in non-breeding plumage. Sandy and rocky coasts, and coral reefs. AN: v, GO: nw, KA: nw, KE: nw, MH: nw, MV: v, TN: nw

Black-winged Stilt *Himantopus himantopus* 35–40 cm

a **b** ADULT and **c** IMMATURE Black and white, with slender appearance, long pinkish legs and fine straight bill. Upperwing is black and legs extend a long way behind tail in flight. Juvenile has browner upperparts with buff fringes. Shallow waters in marshes, pools and lakes. AN: cr, GO: nr, KA: nr, KE: nw, LS: v, MH: cr, MV: v, TN: nr

Pied Avocet *Recurvirostra avosetta* 42–45 cm

a **b** ADULT Upward kink to black bill. Distinctive black-and-white patterning. Juvenile has brown-and-buff mottling on mantle and scapulars. Marshes and banks of rivers and lakes. AN: v, KA: v, KE: nw, LS: v, MH: nw, TN: nw

Crab-plover *Dromas ardeola* 38–41 cm

a **b** ADULT and **c** JUVENILE Black-and-white plumage, with stout black bill and very long blue-grey legs. Juvenile is like a washed-out version of adult. Intertidal mudflats, coral reefs and coastal rocks. AN: v, GO: nw, KA: nw, KE: nw, LS: nr?, MH: nw, MV: cr?, TN: v

Pacific Golden Plover *Pluvialis fulva* 23–26 cm

a **b** ADULT BREEDING and **c** **d** ADULT NON-BREEDING A slim-bodied, long-necked and long-legged plover. In all plumages, has golden-yellow markings on upperparts, and dusky grey underwing-coverts and axillaries. In flight, shows narrower white wing-bar and dark rump. In non-breeding plumage, usually shows prominent pale supercilium and dark patch at rear of ear-coverts (not depicted well in plate). Black underparts with white border striking in breeding plumage. Call is a plaintive *tu-weep*. Mud banks of wetlands, ploughed fields and grassland. AN: nw, GO: nw, KA: nw, KE: cw, LS: nw, MH: nw, MV: cw, TN: lcw

Grey Plover *Pluvialis squatarola* 27–30 cm

a ADULT BREEDING and **b** **c** **d** ADULT NON-BREEDING White underwing and black axillaries. Stockier, with stouter bill and shorter legs, than Pacific Golden. Whitish rump and prominent white wing-bar. Has extensive white spangling to upperparts in breeding plumage; upperparts mainly grey in non-breeding (in all plumages these lack golden spangling of Pacific Golden). Call is a mournful *chee-woo-ee*. Sandy shores, mudflats and tidal creeks. AN: nw, GO: nw, KA: nw, KE: nw, LS: nw, MH: nw, MV: cw, TN: nw

Common Ringed Plover *Charadrius hiaticula* 18–20 cm

a ADULT BREEDING and **b** **c** ADULT NON-BREEDING Prominent breast-band and white hind-collar, and prominent wing-bar in flight. Adult breeding has orange legs and bill-base (duller in non-breeding; more olive-yellow in juvenile). Non-breeding and juvenile have prominent whitish supercilium and forehead compared with Little Ringed. Flight call is a soft *too-li*, or *too weep* when alarmed. Mud banks of freshwater and coastal wetlands. AN: v, GO: nw, KA: v, MV: nw, TN: nw

Little Ringed Plover *Charadrius dubius* 14–17 cm

a ADULT BREEDING and **b** **c** ADULT NON-BREEDING Small size, elongated and small-headed appearance, and uniform upperwing with only a narrow wing-bar. Legs yellowish or pinkish. Adult breeding has striking yellow eye-ring. Adult non-breeding and juvenile have less distinct head pattern. Flight call is a clear *peeu*. Shingle and mud banks of rivers, pools and lakes. AN: nr, GO: lcr, KA: lcr, KE: nr, MH: lcr, MV: nw, TN: nr

Kentish Plover *Charadrius alexandrinus* 15–17 cm

a ADULT MALE BREEDING and **b** **c** ADULT MALE NON-BREEDING *C. a. alexandrinus*; **d** ADULT MALE BREEDING *C. a. seebohmi* Small size and stocky appearance. White hind-collar and usually small, well-defined patches on sides of breast. Breeding male has rufous cap, black ear-coverts and band across forehead. Breeding male *C. a. seebohmi* of the peninsula has less striking head pattern. Flight call is a soft *pi...pi...pi*, or a rattling trill. Banks of rivers and lakes. AN: nw, GO: lcw, KA: nw, KE: nw, LS: nw, MH: nr, MV: nw, TN: nw

Lesser Sand Plover *Charadrius mongolus* 19–21 cm

a MALE BREEDING, **b** FEMALE BREEDING and **c** **d** ADULT NON-BREEDING Larger and longer-legged than Kentish, lacking white hind-collar. Very difficult to distinguish from Greater Sand, although it is smaller and has a stouter bill (with blunt tip), and shorter dark grey or dark greenish legs. In flight, feet do not usually extend beyond tail and white wing-bar is narrower across primaries. Breeding male typically shows full black mask and forehead, and more extensive rufous on breast compared with Greater Sand (although variation exists in these characters). Flight call is a hard *chitik* or *chi-chi-chi*. Banks of rivers and lakes. AN: nw, GO: nw, KA: nw, KE: nw, LS: cw, MH: lcw, MV: cw, TN: nw

Greater Sand Plover *Charadrius leschenaultii* 22–25 cm

a MALE BREEDING, **b** FEMALE BREEDING and **c** **d** ADULT NON-BREEDING Larger and lankier than Lesser Sand, with longer and larger bill, usually with pronounced gonys and more pointed tip. Longer legs are paler, with distinct yellowish or greenish tinge. In flight, feet project beyond tail and it has a broader white wing-bar across primaries. Flight call is a trilling *prrrirt*, softer than that of Lesser. Coastal wetlands. *See* Appendix for comparison with Caspian Plover. AN: v, GO: nw, KA: nw, KE: nw, LS: nw, MH: lcw, MV: nw, TN: nw

Yellow-wattled Lapwing *Vanellus malarbaricus* 26–28 cm

a **b** ADULT Yellow wattles and legs. White supercilium, dark cap and brown breast-band. Wing and tail pattern much as Red-wattled. Call is a strident *chee-eet* and a hard *tit-tit-tit*. Dry river beds and open dry country. AN: cr, GO: nr, KA: cr, KE: nr, MH: nr, TN: cr

River Lapwing *Vanellus duvaucelii* 29–32 cm

a **b** ADULT Black cap and throat, grey sides to neck, and black bill and legs. Black patch on belly. Call is a high-pitched *did, did, did*. Sand and shingle banks of rivers. AN: nr, MH: nr

Red-wattled Lapwing *Vanellus indicus* 32–35 cm

ADULT Black cap and breast, red bill with black tip, and yellow legs. Wing and tail pattern much as Yellow-wattled. Call is an agitated *did he do it, did he do it*. Open flat ground near water. AN: cr, GO: cr, KA: cr, KE: cr, MH: cr, TN: cr

Sociable Lapwing *Vanellus gregarius* 27–30 cm

a **b** ADULT BREEDING and **c** ADULT NON-BREEDING Dark cap, with white supercilia that join at nape. Adult breeding has yellow wash to sides of head, and black-and-maroon patch on belly. Non-breeding and immature have duller head pattern, white belly and streaked breast. Dry fallow fields and scrub desert. AN: v, KA: v, KE: v, MH: nw, MV: v

White-tailed Lapwing *Vanellus leucurus* 26–29 cm

a **b** ADULT and **c** JUVENILE Blackish bill, and very long yellow legs. Plain head. Tail all white, lacking black band of other lapwings. Freshwater marshes and marshy lake edges. GO: v, KA: v, MH: nw

Jerdon's Courser *Rhinoptilus bitorquatus* 27 cm

a **b** ADULT Huge eye, and short yellow bill with black tip. Broad supercilium, and brown and white bands across breast. Thin scrub forest in rocky foothills. AN: nr

Indian Courser *Cursorius coromandelicus* 23 cm

a **b** ADULT Grey-brown upperparts and orange underparts, with dark belly. Has chestnut crown, prominent white supercilium and dark eye-stripe. In flight, shows white band across upper-tail-coverts; underwing very dark, and wings broad with rounded wing-tips. Juvenile has brown barring on chestnut-brown underparts. Open dry country and dry river beds. AN: nr, KA: nr, KE: nr, MH: nr, TN: nr

Oriental Pratincole *Glareola maldivarum* 23–24 cm

a **b** **c** ADULT BREEDING, **d** ADULT NON-BREEDING and **e** JUVENILE Adult breeding has black-bordered creamy-yellow throat and peachy-orange wash to underparts (patterning much reduced in non-breeding plumage). Shows red underwing-coverts in flight. Very grace-ful, feeding mainly by hawking insects on the wing in tern-like manner. Dry bare ground near wetlands. *See* Appendix for comparison with Collared Pratincole. AN: np, GO: np, KE: ns, MH: np, MV: cw, TN: nw

Small Pratincole *Glareola lactea* 16–19 cm

a **b** **c** ADULT BREEDING and **d** ADULT NON-BREEDING Small size, with sandy-grey col-oration, and shallow fork to tail. In flight, shows white panel across secondaries, blackish under-wing-coverts and black tail-band. Also hawks insects on the wing, often in large groups. Large rivers and lakes with sand or shingle banks. AN: nr, GO: nr?, KA: nr, KE: nr?, MH: nr, TN: nr

1 Pomarine Jaeger *Stercorarius pomarinus*   56 cm

a ADULT DARK MORPH BREEDING, **b** ADULT PALE MORPH BREEDING, **c** ADULT PALE MORPH NON-BREEDING, **d** JUVENILE PALE MORPH and **e** JUVENILE DARK MORPH Larger and stockier than Parasitic Jaeger, with heavier bill and broader-based wings. Adult breeding has long, broad central tail feathers twisted at end to form swollen tip (although tips can be broken off) which is the best feature from adult breeding Parasitic. Occurs in both pale and dark morphs. Adult non-breeding as Parasitic but with broader round-tipped central tail feathers. Juvenile variable, typically dark brown (with broader pale barring on uppertail- and undertail-coverts and underwing-coverts than in Parasitic); head, neck and underparts never appear rufous-coloured as on some juvenile Parasitic (although others appear virtually identical to Pomarine); further slight differences are a second pale crescent at base of primary coverts on underwing on most birds (in addition to pale base to underside of primaries), diffuse vermiculations (never streaking) on nape and neck, and blunt-tipped or almost non-existent projection of central tail feathers (more prominent and pointed in juvenile Parasitic). Coastal waters. GO: np, KE: v, LS: v, MH: v, MV: np

2 Parasitic Jaeger *Stercorarius parasiticus*   45 cm

a ADULT DARK MORPH BREEDING, **b** ADULT PALE MORPH BREEDING, **c** ADULT PALE MORPH NON-BREEDING, **d** JUVENILE PALE MORPH, **e** JUVENILE INTERMEDIATE MORPH and **f** JUVENILE DARK MORPH Smaller and more lightly built than Pomarine Jaeger, with slimmer bill and narrower-based wings. Adult breeding has pointed tip to elongated central tail feathers. Occurs in both pale and dark morphs. Adult non-breeding is as Pomarine but has more pointed tail-tip. Juvenile more variable than juvenile Pomarine, ranging from grey and buff with heavy barring to completely blackish brown, and many have rusty-orange to cinnamon-brown cast to head and nape (not found on Pomarine); except for all-dark juveniles, further distinctions from Pomarine are dark streaking on head and neck, and pale tips to primaries. Coastal waters. GO: np, KA: np, KE: np, LS: v, MH: np

3 Sooty Gull *Larus hemprichii*   45 cm

a ADULT BREEDING, **b** 1ST-WINTER and **c** 2ND-WINTER Dark upperwing and underwing. Heavy, long, two-toned bill. Adult has brown hood, and greyish-brown mantle and upperwing; bill yellow with black-and-red tip. First-winter and second-winter have rather uniform brownish head and breast, and dark tail-band; bill initially greyish with black tip, becoming similar to adult during second winter. *See* Appendix for comparison with White-eyed Gull. Coasts. MH: v, MV: nw

4 Heuglin's Gull *Larus heuglini*   58–65 cm

a ADULT NON-BREEDING, **b** 1ST-WINTER and **c** 2ND-WINTER Darkest large gull of region. Adult has darker grey upperparts than Caspian. First-winter distinguished from Caspian by dark inner primaries and darker underwing-coverts, and usually broader dark tail-band. Second-year has darker grey mantle and darker upperwing and underwing than second-year Caspian. Lakes and large rivers. GO: nw, KA: nw, KE: v, LS: v, MH: nw, MV: v, TN: nw

5 Caspian Gull *Larus cachinnans*   55–65 cm

a ADULT NON-BREEDING, **b** 1ST-WINTER and **c** 2ND-WINTER Adult has paler grey upperparts than Heuglin's. Adult may show faint streaking on head in non-breeding plumage, but head is generally less heavily marked than in non-breeding Heuglin's. First-winter separable from Heuglin's by paler inner primaries, and much paler underwing-coverts with dark barring; brown mottling on mantle best distinction from first-winter Pallas's. Second-year has paler grey mantle than second-year Heuglin's; diffusely barred tail, dark greater-covert bar and lack of distinct mask help separate it from first-year Pallas's. *See* Appendix for comparison with Mew Gull. Lakes and large rivers. AN: nw, GO: nw, KA: nw, KE: ?, LS: v, MH: nw, MV: v, TN: nw

6 Pallas's Gull *Larus ichthyaetus*   69 cm

a ADULT BREEDING, **b** ADULT NON-BREEDING, **c** 1ST-WINTER and **d** 2ND-WINTER Angular head with gently sloping forehead, crown peaking behind eye. Bill large, 'dark-tipped', with bulging gonys. Adult breeding has black hood with bold white eye-crescents, and distinctive wing pattern. Adult non-breeding has largely white head with variable black mask. First-winter has grey mantle and scapulars; told from second-winter Caspian by head pattern (as adult non-breeding), absence of dark greater-covert bar, and more pronounced dark tail-band. Second-winter has largely grey upperwing, with dark lesser-covert bar and extensive black on primaries and primary coverts. Lakes and large rivers. AN: nw, GO: nw, KA: nw, KE: nw, MH: nw, MV: v, TN: nw

1

Brown-headed Gull *Larus brunnicephalus* 42 cm
a ADULT BREEDING, **b** ADULT NON-BREEDING and **c** 1ST-WINTER Larger than Black-headed, with more rounded wing-tips and broader bill. Adult has broad black wing-tips (broken by white 'mirrors') and white patch on outer wing; underside to primaries largely black; iris pale yellow (rather than brown as in adult Black-headed). In breeding plumage, hood paler brown than that of Black-headed. First-winter has broad black wing-tips. Lakes and rivers. AN: nw, GO: cw, KA: nw, KE: nw, MH: cw, MV: v, TN: nw

2

Black-headed Gull *Larus ridibundus* 38 cm
a ADULT BREEDING, **b** ADULT NON-BREEDING and **c** 1ST-WINTER White 'flash' on primaries of upperwing. In non-breeding and first-winter, bill tipped black and head largely white with dark ear-covert patch. Lakes and rivers. AN: nw, GO: nw, KA: nw, KE: nw, MH: lcw, MV: v, TN: nw

3

Slender-billed Gull *Larus genei* 43 cm
a ADULT BREEDING, **b** ADULT NON-BREEDING and **c** 1ST-WINTER Head white throughout year, although may show grey ear-covert spot in winter. Gently sloping forehead and longish neck. Iris pale, except in juvenile. Adult has variable pink flush on underparts. Large rivers. AN: v, GO: nw, KA: nw, MH: nw, TN: v

4

Indian Skimmer *Rynchops albicollis* 40 cm
a ADULT and **b** JUVENILE Large, drooping, orange-red bill. Juvenile has whitish fringes to upperparts. Large rivers. Globally threatened. AN: nr, GO: v, KA: v, MH: nr, TN: nr

1

Gull-billed Tern *Gelochelidon nilotica* 35–38 cm
a b ADULT BREEDING and **c** ADULT NON-BREEDING Stout, gull-like black bill and gull-like appearance. Grey rump and tail concolorous with back. Black half-mask in non-breeding and immature plumages. Juvenile has brown markings to upperparts, but by first winter plumage is much as in adult non-breeding. Lakes and large rivers. AN: v, GO: cw, KA: nw, KE: nw, LS: v, MH: nw, MV: nr, TN: nw

2

Caspian Tern *Sterna caspia* 47–54 cm
a ADULT BREEDING, **b** ADULT NON-BREEDING and **c** JUVENILE Large size with huge red bill. Lakes and large rivers. AN: v, GO: nw, KA: nw, KE: nw, MH: nw, MV: nwp, TN: nw

3

River Tern *Sterna aurantia* 38–46 cm
a b ADULT BREEDING, **c** ADULT NON-BREEDING, and **d** JUVENILE Adult breeding has orange-yellow bill, black cap, greyish-white underparts, and long tail. Large size, stocky appearance and stout yellow bill (with dark tip) help separate adult non-breeding and immature from Black-bellied. Marshes, streams and rivers. AN: nr, GO: nr?, KA: nr, KE: nr, MH: nr, TN: nr

4

Lesser Crested Tern *Sterna bengalensis* 35–37 cm
a b ADULT BREEDING, **c** ADULT NON-BREEDING, **d** 1ST-WINTER and **e** JUVENILE Orange to orange-yellow bill, smaller and slimmer than that of Great Crested, with paler grey upperparts (adult) and usually less boldly patterned upperwing (immatures). Mainly offshore waters; also tidal creeks and harbours. GO: nw, KA: nw, KE: nw, LS: nr?, MH: nw, MV: nr, TN: nw

√*5*

Great Crested Tern *Sterna bergii* 46–49 cm
a b ADULT BREEDING, **c** ADULT NON-BREEDING, **d** 1ST-WINTER and **e** JUVENILE Lime-green to cold-yellow bill. Larger and stockier than Lesser Crested, with darker grey upperparts (adult) or darker and usually more strongly patterned upperwing (immatures). Mainly offshore waters; also tidal channels. GO: nw, KA: nw, KE: nw, LS: nr, MH: nr, MV: nr, TN: nr

6

Sandwich Tern *Sterna sandvicensis* 36–41 cm
a b ADULT BREEDING, **c** ADULT NON-BREEDING and **d** 1ST-WINTER Slim black bill with yellow tip, and more rakish appearance than Gull-billed. White rump and tail contrast with greyer back. U-shaped black crest in non-breeding and first-winter/first-summer plumages. Juvenile more heavily marked than juvenile Gull-billed, and has black rear-crown and nape. Coasts, tidal creeks and open sea. GO: nw, KA: nw, KE: nw, MH: nw, TN: nw

1 Roseate Tern *Sterna dougallii* 33–38 cm

a **b** ADULT BREEDING, **c** ADULT NON-BREEDING, **d** 1ST-SUMMER and **e** JUVENILE
Pale grey upperparts and rump concolorous with back, long tail with white outer feathers, broad white trailing edge to wing, and rather stiff and rapid flight action. In breeding plumage, has more black at bill-tip than Common Tern, and pink flush to underparts. Juvenile has black bill and legs, black subterminal marks to upperpart feathers, and largely black crown. Flight call is different from those of Common and Black-naped, a disyllabic *chu-vee*. Coastal waters and offshore islands. GO: np, KA: np, MH: ns, MV: nr, TN: ns

2 Black-naped Tern *Sterna sumatrana* 35 cm

a ADULT BREEDING, **b** ADULT NON-BREEDING and **c** JUVENILE Adult very pale greyish white, with black bill and legs, and black mask and nape-band. Black nape-band not so clear-cut in non-breeding plumage. Juvenile has black subterminal marks to upperpart feathers, and head pattern similar to adult but with black streaking on crown; shows less black on crown than juvenile Roseate but is otherwise very similar in plumage. Inshore waters around islands and lagoons. KE: v, MV: cr

3 Common Tern *Sterna hirundo* 31–35 cm

a **b** ADULT BREEDING, **c** ADULT NON-BREEDING and **d** JUVENILE Grey mantle contrasts with white rump and uppertail-coverts (compare with Roseate and White-cheeked), although contrast may be less apparent in non-breeding birds. In breeding plumage, compared with Roseate, has orange-red bill with less black at tip, pale grey wash to underparts, dark trailing edge to underside of primaries and dark outer wedge to upperside, and shorter tail streamers that do not extend beyond tail at rest. Non-breeding and first-winter have darker grey upperparts, shorter tail with grey outer webs to feathers, and narrower white trailing edge to wing compared with Roseate. Juvenile has orange legs and bill-base. Lakes and large rivers. AN: v, GO: nwp, KA: np, KE: v, MH: nwp, MV: nw, TN: nw

4 Little Tern *Sterna albifrons* 22–24 cm

a **b** ADULT BREEDING, **c** ADULT NON-BREEDING and **d** JUVENILE; **e** ADULT BREEDING *S. a. sinensis* Fast flight with rapid wing beats from narrow-based wings. Adult breeding has white forehead and black-tipped yellow bill. Adult non-breeding has blackish bill, black mask and nape-band, and dark lesser-covert bar. Juvenile has dark subterminal marks to upperpart feathers. *Sterna albifrons sinensis*, of western coast of peninsula, has longer tail and white primary shafts. Lakes and rivers. AN: nw, GO: nw, KA: nw, KE: nw, LS: v, MH: nr, MV: v, TN: nw

5 Saunders's Tern *Sterna saundersi* 23 cm

a **b** ADULT BREEDING and **c** 1ST-WINTER Adult breeding as Little Tern, but more rounded white forehead patch (lacking short white supercilium), shorter reddish-brown to brown legs (orange on Little), broader black outer edge to primaries, and grey rump and centre of tail (can be grey on some Little, e.g. *S. a. sinensis*). There are no sure features for separating the species in other plumages, although darker grey upperparts, including rump and dark bar on secondaries in Saunders's, may be useful. Coastal waters. KE: v, MH: nw, MV: cr, TN: nr

6 White-cheeked Tern *Sterna repressa* 32–34 cm

a **b** ADULT BREEDING, **c** ADULT NON-BREEDING and **d** JUVENILE Smaller than Common, with darker grey upperparts, and uniform grey rump and tail concolorous with back; underwing has darker trailing edge and pale central panel. In breeding plumage, darker grey on underparts than Common, and with white cheeks; separable from adult breeding Whiskered by longer bill, paler grey underparts and longer tail streamers. Offshore waters. GO: cp, KE: v, LS: v, MH: ns xp, MV: v, TN: v

7 Black-bellied Tern *Sterna acuticauda* 33 cm

a **b** ADULT BREEDING, **c** ADULT NON-BREEDING and **d** JUVENILE Much smaller than River Tern, with orange bill (with variable black tip) in all plumages. Adult breeding has black belly and vent. Adult non-breeding and juvenile have white underparts, and black mask and streaking on crown. Marshes, lakes and rivers. AN: nr, GO: v, KA: nr, KE: nr?, MH: nr, TN: nr

1

White Tern *Gygis alba* 30 cm

a **b** ADULT and **c** JUVENILE Adult all white, with beady black eye and upturned bill. Juvenile has buff and brown barring and spotting on upperparts. Pelagic, except when breeding. MV: lcr

2

Bridled Tern *Sterna anaethetus* 30–32 cm

a **b** ADULT BREEDING, **c** ADULT NON-BREEDING and **d** **e** JUVENILE Smaller and more elegant than Sooty Tern. In breeding plumage, white forehead patch extends over eye as broad white supercilium, and has brownish-grey mantle and wings. Juvenile has greyish-white crown, dark mask and white forehead and supercilium (shadow-pattern of adult), buffish fringes to mantle and wing-coverts, and brownish patch on side of breast. Mainly offshore waters. GO: cp, KA: v, KE: v, LS: ns, MH: ns, MV: ns, TN: v

3

Sooty Tern *Sterna fuscata* 33–36 cm

a **b** ADULT, **c** 1ST-SUMMER and **d** **e** JUVENILE Larger and more powerful than Bridled Tern, with blacker upperparts, more extensive blackish underside to primaries (contrasting with white underwing-coverts), and white forehead patch not extending over eye. Juvenile has sooty-black head and breast contrasting with whitish lower belly, bold white spotting on mantle, scapulars and upperwing-coverts, and pale underwing-coverts. Pelagic, except when breeding. GO: np, KE: v, LS: cs, MH: ns, MV: ns, TN: v

4

Whiskered Tern *Chlidonias hybridus* 23–25 cm

a **b** ADULT BREEDING, **c** ADULT NON-BREEDING and **d** JUVENILE In breeding plumage, white cheeks contrast with grey underparts; lacks greatly elongated outer tail feathers. In non-breeding and juvenile, distinguished from White-winged by larger bill, grey rump concolorous with back and tail, and different patterning of black on head. *See* Appendix for comparison with Black Tern. Marshes, lakes and rivers. AN: nw, GO: nw, KA: nw, KE: nw, MH: nr, MV: v, TN: nw

5

White-winged Tern *Chlidonias leucopterus* 20–23 cm

a ADULT BREEDING, **b** **c** ADULT NON-BREEDING and **d** JUVENILE In breeding plumage, black head and body contrast with pale upperwing-coverts, and has black underwing-coverts. In non-breeding and juvenile, smaller bill, whitish rump contrasting with grey tail, and different patterning of black on head are distinctions from Whiskered. *See* Appendix for comparison with Black Tern. Marshes, lakes and rivers. GO: nwp, KA: v, MH: v, MV: nw, TN: nw

6

Brown Noddy *Anous stolidus* 42 cm

a **b** ADULT and **c** **d** JUVENILE Brown, with coverts that are paler than flight feathers, and pale panel across upperwing-coverts. Bill stouter, proportionately shorter and noticeably downcurved compared with Lesser. Juvenile has browner forehead and crown. Pelagic, except when breeding. GO: v, KE: v, LS: cs, MH: v, MV: cr, TN: v

7

Lesser Noddy *Anous tenuirostris* 32 cm

a **b** ADULT Long, slim bill. Pale greyish lores contrasting with black patch in front of eye. Upperwing-coverts slightly paler than remiges, underwing-coverts concolorous with remiges, and paler and greyer tail centre contrasting with darker upperparts. Pelagic, except when breeding. LS: v, MV: cr

Osprey *Pandion haliaetus* 55–58 cm
a b ADULT Long wings, typically angled at carpals, and short tail. Has whitish head with black stripe through eye, white underbody and underwing-coverts, and black carpal patches. Frequently hovers over water when fishing. Lakes and rivers. AN: nw, GO: nw, KA: nw, KE: nw, LS: v, MH: nw, MV: v, TN: nw

Jerdon's Baza *Aviceda jerdoni* 46 cm
a b ADULT and c JUVENILE Long and erect, white-tipped crest. Long, broad wings (pinched in at base) and fairly long tail. Adult has pale rufous head, indistinct gular stripe, rufous-barred underparts and underwing-coverts, and broad barring across primary tips. At rest, closed wings extend well down tail. Juvenile has whitish head and narrower dark barring on tail. Broadleaved evergreen forest. AN: v, KA: nr, KE: x?r, TN: nr

Black Baza *Aviceda leuphotes* 33 cm
a b c ADULT Largely black, with long crest, white breast-band, and greyish underside to primaries contrasting with black underwing-coverts. Broadleaved evergreen forest. AN: v, GO: v, KA: v, KE: nr, MH: v, TN: nw

Black-shouldered Kite *Elanus caeruleus* 31–35 cm
a b ADULT and c JUVENILE Small size. Grey and white with black 'shoulders'. Flight buoyant, with much hovering. Juvenile has brownish-grey upperparts with pale fringes, and less distinct shoulder-patch. Grassland with cultivation and open scrub. AN: cr, GO: nr, KA: cr, KE: nw, LS: v, MH: nr, TN: nr

Black Kite *Milvus migrans* 55–68.5 cm
a b c ADULT and d e JUVENILE Shallow tail-fork. Much manoeuvring of arched wings and twisting of tail in flight. Dark rufous-brown, with variable whitish crescent at primary bases on underwing and pale band across median coverts on upperwing. Juvenile has broad whitish or buffish streaking on head and underparts. Mainly around habitation, also mountains. AN: cr, GO: cr, KA: cr, KE: cr, LS: nw, MH: cr, TN: cr

Brahminy Kite *Haliastur indus* 48 cm
a b ADULT and c d JUVENILE Small size and kite-like flight. Wings usually angled at carpals. Tail rounded. Adult mainly chestnut, with white head, neck and breast. Juvenile mainly brown, with pale streaking on head, mantle and breast, large whitish patches at bases of primaries on underwing, and cinnamon-brown tail. Wetlands. AN: nr, GO: cr, KA: lcr, KE: cr, MH: nr, MV: v, TN: cr

1

White-bellied Sea Eagle *Haliaeetus leucogaster* 66–71 cm

a **b** ADULT and **c** **d** JUVENILE Soars and glides with wings pressed forward and in pronounced V. Distinctive shape, with slim head, bulging secondaries and short wedge-shaped tail. Adult has white head and underparts, grey upperparts, white underwing-coverts contrasting with black remiges, and mainly white tail. Juvenile has pale head, whitish tail with brownish subterminal band, and pale wedge on inner primaries. Immatures show mixture of juvenile and adult features. Mainly coastal habitats. AN: nr, GO: nr, KA: nr, KE: nr, LS: v, MH: nr, TN: nr

2

Pallas's Fish Eagle *Haliaeetus leucoryphus* 76–84 cm

a **b** ADULT and **c** **d** JUVENILE Soars and glides with wings flat. Long, broad wings and protruding head and neck. Adult has pale head and neck, dark brown upperwing and underwing, and mainly white tail with broad black terminal band. Juvenile less bulky than juvenile White-tailed Eagle (*see* Appendix), with dark mask, pale band across underwing-coverts, pale patch on underside of inner primaries, all-dark tail and pale crescent on uppertail-coverts. Large rivers and lakes. Globally threatened. KA: v, MH: v

√*3*

Grey-headed Fish Eagle *Ichthyophaga ichthyaetus* 69–74 cm

a **b** ADULT and **c** **d** JUVENILE Adult has largely white tail with broad black subterminal band, dark brown upperparts and rufous-brown breast. Juvenile has pale supercilium, boldly streaked head and underparts, diffuse brown tail barring, and whitish underwing with pronounced dark trailing edge. Spends most of the day perched in regularly used trees above the water. Very noisy during the breeding season, a far-carrying *tiu-weeeu*. *See* Appendix for comparison with Lesser Fish Eagle. Slow-running waters and lakes in wooded country. AN: nr, GO: v?, KA: nr?, KE: nr, MH: nr?, TN: nr

4

Egyptian Vulture *Neophron percnopterus* 60–70 cm

a **b** **c** ADULT, **d** **e** IMMATURE and **f** JUVENILE Small vulture with long, pointed wings, small and pointed head, and wedge-shaped tail. Adult mainly dirty white, with bare yellowish face and black flight feathers. Juvenile blackish brown with bare grey face. With maturity, tail, body and wing-coverts become whiter and face becomes yellower. Open country around habitation. AN: cr, GO: v, KA: cr, KE: nr, MH: nr, TN: lcr

1 White-rumped Vulture *Gyps bengalensis* 75–85 cm

a **b** **c** ADULT and **d** **e** **f** JUVENILE Smallest of the *Gyps* vultures. Adult mainly black-ish, with white rump and back, and white underwing-coverts. Key features of juvenile are dark brown coloration, streaking on underparts and upperwing-coverts, dark rump and back, whitish head and neck, and all-dark bill; in flight, underbody and lesser underwing-coverts distinctly dark-er than on Indian. Around habitation. AN: nr, GO: nr, KA: nr, KE: nr, MH: nr, TN: nr

2 Indian Vulture *Gyps indicus* 80–95 cm

a **b** ADULT and **c** JUVENILE Adult has sandy-brown body and upperwing-coverts, black-ish head and neck with sparse white down on hind-neck, white downy ruff and yellowish bill and cere, and lacks pale streaking on underparts; in flight, lacks broad whitish band across medi-an underwing-coverts shown by Eurasian Griffon, and has whiter rump and back. Juvenile has feathery buff neck-ruff, dark bill and cere with a pale culmen, and the head and neck have whitish down; distinguished from juvenile Eurasian Griffon by pale culmen, darker brown upperparts with more pronounced pale streaking, and paler and less rufescent coloration to streaked under-parts; best distinctions from juvenile White-rumped are paler and less clearly streaked under-parts, paler upper- and underwing-coverts, and whitish rump and back. Around habitation. AN: nr, GO: nr, KA: nr, KE: nr, MH: nr, TN: nr

3 Eurasian Griffon *Gyps fulvus* 95–105 cm

a **b** **c** ADULT and **d** **e** **f** JUVENILE Larger than Indian Vulture, with stouter bill. Key features of adult are yellowish bill with blackish cere, whitish head and neck, fluffy white ruff, rufescent-buff upperparts, rufous-brown underparts and thighs with prominent pale streaking, and dark grey legs and feet; rufous-brown underwing-coverts usually show prominent whitish banding (especially across medians). Immature richer rufous-brown on upperparts and upper-wing-coverts (with prominent pale streaking) than adult; has rufous-brown feathered neck-ruff, more whitish down covering grey head and neck, blackish bill and dark iris (pale yellowish brown in adult). *See* Appendix for comparison with Himalayan Griffon. Open country. AN: v, GO: v?, KA: v, KE: v, MH: v, TN: v

4 Red-headed Vulture *Sarcogyps calvus* 85 cm

a **b** **c** ADULT and **d** **e** **f** IMMATURE Comparatively slim and pointed wings. Adult has bare reddish head and cere, white patches at base of neck and upper thighs, and reddish legs and feet; in flight, greyish-white bases to secondaries show as broad panel. Juvenile has white down on head; pinkish coloration to head and feet, white patch on upper thighs and whitish undertail-coverts are best features. Open country near habitation, and well-wooded hills. AN: nr, GO: nr, KA: nr, KE: nr, MH: nr, TN: nr

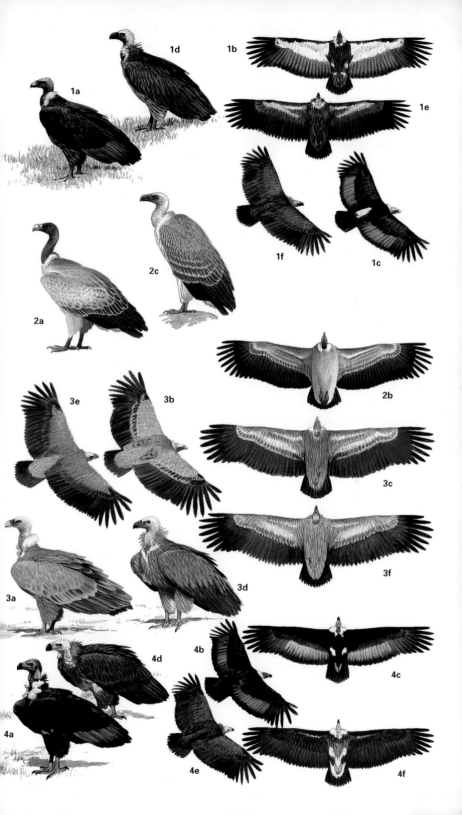

Black Eagle *Ictinaetus malayensis*   69–81 cm
a b ADULT and c d JUVENILE In flight has distinctive wing shape and long tail. Flies with wings raised in V, with primaries upturned. At rest, long wings extend to tip of tail. Adult dark brownish black, with striking yellow cere and feet; in flight, shows whitish barring on uppertail-coverts, and faint greyish barring on tail and underside of remiges. Juvenile has dark-streaked buffish head, underparts and underwing-coverts. Hunts by sailing buoyantly and slowly over the canopy, sometimes weaving in and out of tree-tops. Broadleaved forest in hills and mountains. AN: nr, GO: nr, KA: nr, KE: cr, MH: nr, TN: nr

Short-toed Snake Eagle *Circaetus gallicus*   62–67 cm
a b c PALE PHASE and d DARK PHASE Long and broad wings, pinched in at base, and rather long tail. Head broad and rounded. Soars with wings flat or slightly raised; frequently hovers. Pattern variable, often with dark head and breast, barred underbody, dark trailing edge to underwing, and broad subterminal tail-band; can be very pale on underbody and underwing. Open dry country. AN: nr, GO: nw, KA: nr, KE: cr, MH: nr, TN: nr

Crested Serpent Eagle *Spilornis cheela*   56–74 cm
a b ADULT and c JUVENILE Broad, rounded wings. Soars with wings held forward and in pronounced V. Adult has broad white bands across wings and tail; hooded appearance at rest, with yellow cere and lores, and white spotting on brown underparts. Juvenile has blackish ear-coverts, yellow cere and lores, whitish head and underparts, narrower barring on tail than adult, and largely white underwing with fine dark barring and dark trailing edge. Frequently soars above forest, often in pairs, uttering loud whistling cry. Forest and well-wooded country. AN: nr, GO: nr?, KA: nr, KE: nr, MH: nr, TN: nr

Eurasian Marsh Harrier *Circus aeruginosus*   48–58 cm
a b c ADULT MALE, d e f ADULT FEMALE and g JUVENILE Broad-winged and stocky. As with other harriers, glides and soars with wings in noticeable V, quartering the ground a few metres above it, occasionally dropping to catch prey. Male has head, brown mantle and upperwing-coverts contrasting with grey secondaries/inner primaries; female mainly dark brown, except for cream on head and on leading edge of wing. Juvenile may be entirely dark. Marshes, lakes and grasslands. AN: cw, GO: cw, KA: nw, KE: cw, LS: v, MH: nw, MV: nw, TN: lcw

1 **Pied Harrier** *Circus melanoleucos* 41–46.5 cm

a **b** **c** ADULT MALE, **d** **e** **f** ADULT FEMALE and **g** **h** **i** JUVENILE Male has black head, upperparts and breast, white underbody and forewing, and black median-covert bar. Female has white uppertail-covert patch, dark-barred greyish remiges and rectrices, pale leading edge to wing, pale underwing and whitish belly. Juvenile has pale markings on head, rufous-brown underbody, white uppertail-covert patch, and dark underwing with pale patch on primaries. Open grassland and cultivation. AN: v, GO: v, KA: nw, KE: nw, MH: nw, TN: nw

2 **Hen Harrier** *Circus cyaneus* 44–52 cm

a **b** **c** ADULT MALE and **d** **e** **f** ADULT FEMALE Comparatively broad-winged and stocky. Male has dark grey upperparts, extensive black wing-tips and lacks black secondary bars. Female has broad white band across uppertail-coverts and rather plain head pattern (usually lacking dark ear-covert patch). Juvenile has streaked underparts as female, but with rufous-brown coloration. Open country. AN: v, KA: nw, KE: v, MH: nw

3 **Pallid Harrier** *Circus macrourus* 40–48 cm

a **b** **c** ADULT MALE, **d** **e** **f** ADULT FEMALE and **g** **h** JUVENILE Slim-winged and fine-bodied, with buoyant flight. Folded wings fall short of tail-tip, and legs longer than on Montagu's. Male has pale grey upperparts, dark wedge on primaries, very pale grey head and underbody, and lacks black secondary bars. Female has distinctive underwing pattern: pale primaries, irregularly barred and lacking dark trailing edge, contrast with darker secondaries, which have pale bands narrower than on female Montagu's and tapering towards body (although first-summer Montagu's more similar in this respect), and lacks prominent barring on axillaries. Typically, female has stronger head pattern than Montagu's, with more pronounced pale collar, dark ear-coverts and dark eye-stripe, and upperside of flight feathers darker and lacking banding; told from female Hen by narrower wings with more pointed hand, stronger head pattern, and patterning of underside of primaries. Juvenile has primaries evenly barred (lacking pronounced dark fingers), without dark trailing edge, and usually with pale crescent at base; head pattern more pronounced than Montagu's, with narrower white supercilium, more extensive dark ear-covert patch, and broader pale collar contrasting strongly with dark neck sides. Open country. AN: nw, GO: nw, KA: nw, KE: nw, LS: v, MH: nw, MV: nw, TN: nw

4 **Montagu's Harrier** *Circus pygargus* 43–47 cm

a **b** **c** ADULT MALE, **d** **e** **f** ADULT FEMALE and **g** **h** JUVENILE Folded wings reach tail-tip, and legs shorter than on Pallid. Male has black band across secondaries, extensive black on underside of primaries, and rufous streaking on belly and underwing-coverts. Female differs from female Pallid in distinctly and evenly barred underside to primaries with dark trailing edge, broader and more pronounced pale bands across secondaries, barring on axillaries, less pronounced head pattern, and distinct dark banding on upperside of remiges. Juvenile has unstreaked rufous underparts and underwing-coverts, and darker secondaries than female; differs from juvenile Pallid in having broad dark fingers and dark trailing edge to hand on underwing, and paler face with smaller dark ear-covert patch and less distinct collar. Open country. AN: nw, GO: v, KA: nw, KE: nw, LS: v, MH: nw, MV: nw, TN: nw

Crested Goshawk *Accipiter trivirgatus* 30–46 cm

a **b** ADULT MALE and **c** JUVENILE Larger size and crest are best distinctions from Besra. Short and broad wings, pinched in at base. Wing-tips barely extend beyond tail-base at rest. Male has dark grey crown and paler grey ear-coverts, black submoustachial and gular stripes, rufous-brown streaking on breast, and barring on belly and flanks. Female has browner crown and ear-coverts, and browner streaking and barring on underparts. Juvenile has rufous or buffish fringes to crown, crest and nape feathers, streaked ear-coverts and buff/rufous wash to streaked underparts (barring restricted to lower flanks and thighs). Mainly forest; also hunts above the treeline. AN: nr, GO: nr?, KA: nr, KE: nr, MH: nr, TN: nr

Shikra *Accipiter badius* 30–36 cm

a ADULT MALE, **b** **c** ADULT FEMALE and **d** **e** JUVENILE *A. b. dussumier*; **f** ADULT MALE and **g** **h** ADULT FEMALE *A. b. badius* Adults paler than Besra and Eurasian Sparrowhawk. Underwing pale, with fine barring on remiges, and slightly darker wing-tips. Male has pale blue-grey upperparts, indistinct grey gular stripe, fine brownish-orange barring on underparts, unbarred white thighs, and unbarred or only lightly barred central tail feathers. Upperparts of female are more brownish grey. Juvenile has pale brown upperparts, more prominent gular stripe, and streaked underparts; distinguished from juvenile Besra by paler upperparts and narrower tail barring, and from Eurasian Sparrowhawk by streaked underparts. The subspecies *A. b. badius,* which occurs in Kerala, is darker grey above, and underparts are more heavily barred with rufous, and is therefore more similar in appearance to Besra (less pronounced gular stripe, absence of streaking on breast, plainer upper tail, and less heavily barred underwing are still useful features separating it from that species). Open woods and groves. AN: cr, GO: cr, KA: cr, KE: cr, LS: v, MH: cr, MV: v, TN: lcr

Besra *Accipiter virgatus* 29–36 cm

a ADULT MALE, **b** **c** ADULT FEMALE and **d** **e** JUVENILE Small. Upperparts darker than Shikra, with streaked breast and more strongly barred underwing. In all plumages, resembles Crested Goshawk, but considerably smaller, lacks crest, and has longer and finer legs. Male has dark slate-grey upperparts, broad blackish gular stripe, and bold rufous streaking on breast and barring on belly. Female browner on upperparts, with blackish crown and nape. Juvenile told from juvenile Shikra by darker, richer brown upperparts, broader gular stripe and broader tail barring. *See* Appendix for comparison with Japanese Sparrowhawk. Breeds in dense broadleaved forest; also open country in winter. AN: nr, GO: nr, KA: nr, KE: nr, MH: nr, TN: nr

Eurasian Sparrowhawk *Accipiter nisus* 31–36 cm

a **b** ADULT MALE, **c** **d** ADULT FEMALE and **e** JUVENILE Upperparts of adult darker than Shikra, with prominent tail barring and strongly barred underwing. Uniform barring on underparts and absence of prominent gular stripe should separate it from Besra. Male has dark slate-grey upperparts and reddish-orange barring on underparts. Female is dark brown on upperparts, with dark brown barring on underparts. Juvenile has dark brown upperparts and barred underparts. Well-wooded country and open forest. AN: nw, GO: v, KA: nw, KE: v, MH: nw, TN: nw

Oriental Honey-buzzard *Pernis ptilorhyncus* 57–60 cm

a b c ADULT MALE, **d** ADULT FEMALE and **e** JUVENILE Long and broad wings and tail, narrow neck and small head with small crest. Soars with wings flat. Very variable in plumage; often shows dark moustachial stripe and gular stripe, and gorget of streaking across lower throat. Lacks dark carpal patch. Male has grey face, greyish-brown upperparts, two black tail-bands, usually three black bands across underside of remiges, and dark brown iris. Female has browner face and upperparts, three black tail-bands, four narrower black bands across remiges, and yellow iris. Well-wooded country, usually of broadleaved species. AN: nr, GO: nr?, KA: lcr, KE: nw, MH: nr, MV: nw, TN: nr

White-eyed Buzzard *Butastur teesa* 43 cm

a b c ADULT and **d e** JUVENILE Longish, rather slim wings, long tail, and buzzard-like head. Pale median-covert panel. Adult has black gular stripe, white nape-patch, barred underparts, dark wing-tips and rufous tail; iris yellow. Juvenile has buffish head and breast streaked with dark brown, with moustachial and throat stripes indistinct or absent; rufous uppertail more strongly barred; iris brown. Dry open country, scrub and open dry forest. AN: nr, GO: nr?, KA: nr, KE: nr, MH: nr, TN: nr

Common Buzzard *Buteo buteo* 51–56 cm

a b c d ADULT *B. b. japonicus*; **e f** ADULT *B. b. refectus* Stocky, with broad wings and moderate-length tail. Soars with wings held in V shape. Variable; some very similar to Long-legged. *B. b. japonicus* typically has rather pale head and underparts, with variable dark streaking on breast and brown patch on belly/thighs; tail dark-barred grey-brown. *B. b. refectus* is dark brown to rufous-brown, with variable amounts of white on underparts; tail dull brown with some dark barring, or uniform sandy-brown. Open country. AN: v, GO: nw, KA: nw, KE: nw, MH: nw, TN: nw

Long-legged Buzzard *Buteo rufinus* 61 cm

a b c d ADULT and **e f** JUVENILE Larger and longer-necked than Common, with longer wings and tail (appears more eagle-like); soars with wings in deeper V. Variable in plumage. Most differ from Common in having combination of paler head and upper breast, rufous-brown lower breast and belly, more uniform rufous underwing-coverts, more extensive black carpal patches, larger pale primary patch on upperwing, and unbarred pale orange uppertail. Rufous and black morphs are similar to some plumages of Common. Open country. AN: v, GO: v, KA: v, KE: v, MH: nw, TN: v

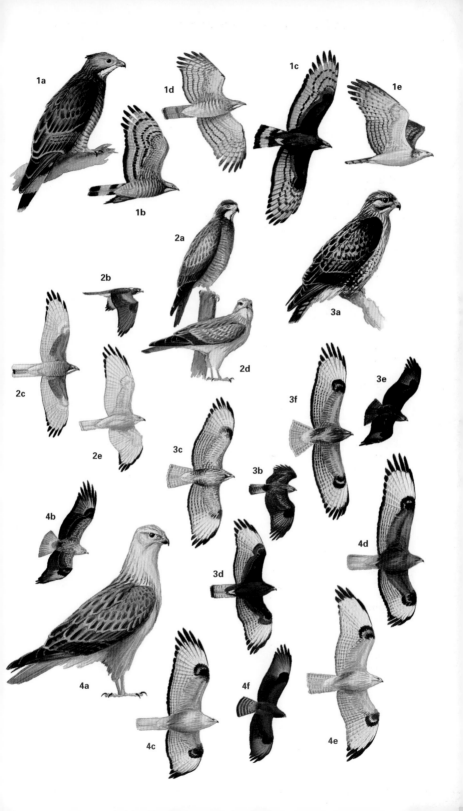

Indian Spotted Eagle *Aquila hastata* 60–65 cm

a **b** **c** ADULT and **d** **e** **f** JUVENILE A stocky, medium-sized eagle with rather short and broad wings, buzzard-like head with comparatively fine bill, and rather short tail. The wings are angled down at carpals when gliding and soaring. Adult is similar in overall appearance to Greater Spotted, and field characters are poorly understood. Has a wider gape than Greater Spotted, with thick 'lips', and gape-line extending well behind eye (reaching to below centre of eye in Greater Spotted). A possible additional feature of adult in the field is the paler brown lesser underwing-coverts, which contrast with rest of underwing (Greater Spotted typically has uniform dark underwing-coverts). Juvenile is more distinct from juvenile Greater Spotted; spotting on upperwing-coverts is less prominent, tertials are pale brown with diffuse white tips (dark with bold white tips in Greater Spotted), uppertail-coverts are pale brown with white barring (white in Greater Spotted), and underparts are paler light yellowish brown with dark streaking. In some plumages can resemble Steppe Eagle – differences mentioned below for Greater Spotted are likely to be helpful for separation (although gape-line is also long in Steppe). Wooded areas in plains to the edge of the hills. AN: v, GO: v, KA: v, KE: v, MH: nr, TN: v

Greater Spotted Eagle *Aquila clanga* 65–72 cm

a **b** **c** ADULT, **d** **e** **f** JUVENILE; **g** **h** JUVENILE '*fulvescens*' Medium-sized eagle with rather short and broad wings, stocky head and short tail. Wings distinctly angled down at carpals when gliding, almost flat when soaring. *See* account for Indian Spotted, for differences from that species. Compared with Steppe Eagle, has less protruding head in flight, with shorter wings and less-deep-fingered wing-tips; at rest, trousers less baggy, and bill smaller with rounded (rather than elongated) nostril and shorter gape; lacks adult Steppe's Pale variant '*fulvescens*' distinguished from juvenile Imperial Eagle (*see* Appendix) by structural difparts. Juvenile has bold whitish tips to dark brown coverts. Large rivers and lakes; prefers wooded areas near water. Globally threatened (Vulnerable). AN: nw, GO: nw, KA: nw, KE: v, MH: nw, TN: nw

Tawny Eagle *Aquila rapax* 63–71 cm

a **b** **c** **d** **e** ADULT, **f** **g** JUVENILE and **h** SUB-ADULT Compared with Steppe, hand of wing does not appear so long and broad, tail slightly shorter, and looks smaller and weaker at rest; gape-line ends level with centre of eye (extends to rear of eye in Steppe) and adult has yellowish iris. Differs from the spotted eagles in more protruding head and neck in flight, baggy trousers, yellow iris, and oval nostril. Adult extremely variable, from dark brown through rufous to pale cream, and unstreaked or streaked with rufous or dark brown. Dark morph very similar to adult Steppe (which shows much less variation); distinctions include less pronounced barring and dark trailing edge on underwing, dark nape and dark chin. Rufous to pale cream Tawny is uniformly pale from uppertail-coverts to back, with undertail-coverts same colour as belly (contrast often apparent on similar species). Pale adults also lack prominent whitish trailing edge to wing, tip to tail and greater-covert bar (present on immatures of similar species). Characteristic, if present, is distinct pale inner-primary wedge on underwing. Juvenile also variable, with narrow white tips to unbarred secondaries; otherwise as similar-plumaged adult. Many (possibly all) non-dark Tawny have distinctive immature/sub-adult plumage: dark throat and breast contrasting with pale belly, and can show dark banding across underwing-coverts; whole head and breast may be dark. Cultivation and open wooded country. AN: nr, GO: nw, KA: nr, MH: nr, TN: nr

Steppe Eagle *Aquila nipalensis* 76–80 cm

a **b** **c** ADULT, **d** **e** **f** JUVENILE and **g** **h** IMMATURE Broader and longer wings than Greater and Indian Spotted, with more pronounced and spread fingers, and more protruding head and neck; wings flatter when soaring and, less distinctly angled down at carpals when gliding. When perched, clearly bigger and heavier, with heavier bill and baggy trousers. Adult separated from adult spotted eagles by underwing pattern (dark trailing edge, distinct barring on remiges, indistinct/non-existent pale crescents in carpal region), pale rufous nape-patch and pale chin. Juvenile has broad white bar across underwing, double white bar on upperwing and white crescent across uppertail-coverts; prominence of bars on upperwing and underwing much reduced on older immatures. Wooded hills, open country and lakes. AN: v, GO: nw, KE: v, MH: nw, TN: v

Bonelli's Eagle *Hieraaetus fasciatus* 65–72 cm

a **b** **c** ADULT and **d** **e** **f** JUVENILE Medium-sized eagle with long and broad wings, distinctly protruding head and long, square-ended tail. Soars with wings flat. Adult has pale underbody and forewing, blackish band along underwing-coverts, whitish patch on mantle, and pale greyish tail with broad dark terminal band. Juvenile has ginger-buff to reddish-brown underbody and underwing-coverts (with variable dark band along greater underwing-coverts), uniform upperwing, and pale crescent on uppertail-coverts and patch on back. Well-wooded country. AN: nr, GO: v, KA: nr, KE: nr, MH: nr, TN: nr

Booted Eagle *Hieraaetus pennatus* 45–53 cm

a **b** **c** PALE MORPH and **d** **e** DARK MORPH Smallish eagle with long wings and long square-ended tail. Glides and soars with wings flat or slightly angled down at carpal. Always shows white shoulder-patches, pale median-covert panel, pale wedge on inner primaries, white crescent on uppertail-coverts, and greyish undertail with darker centre and tip. Head, body and wing-coverts whitish, brown or rufous respectively in pale, dark and rufous morphs. Well-wooded country. AN: nw, GO: nw, KA: nw, KE: nw, MH: nw, TN: nw

Rufous-bellied Eagle *Hieraaetus kienerii* 53–61 cm

a **b** ADULT and **c** **d** JUVENILE Smallish, with buzzard-shaped wings and tail. At rest, wing-tips extend well down tail. Glides and soars with wings flat. Adult has blackish hood and upperparts, white throat and breast, and (black-streaked) rufous rest of underparts. Juvenile has white underparts and underwing-coverts, dark mask and white supercilium, and dark patches on breast and flanks. Moist broadleaved forest. AN: v, GO: nr?, KA: nr, KE: nr, MH: v, TN: nr

Changeable Hawk Eagle *Spizaetus cirrhatus* 61–72 cm

a **b** ADULT and **c** **d** JUVENILE Narrower, more parallel-edged wings than Mountain Hawk Eagle. Soars with wings flat (except in display, when both wings and tail raised). Adult distinguished from Mountain by more pronounced throat stripe, boldly-streaked breast, dark brown thighs, vent and undertail-coverts, and more strongly-marked underwing-coverts. Juvenile generally whiter on head than juvenile Mountain; underparts are whiter with narrow and diffuse rufous barring on flanks (some, perhaps older birds, have sparse dark streaking on breast). Broadleaved forest and well-wooded country. AN: nr, GO: nr?, KA: nr, KE: nr, MH: nr, TN: nr

Mountain Hawk Eagle *Spizaetus nipalensis* 70–72 cm

a **b** ADULT and **c** **d** JUVENILE Prominent crest. Wings broader than on Changeable, with more pronounced curve to trailing edge. Soars with wings in shallow V. Distinguished from Changeable by indistinct throat stripe, rufous barring across entire underparts (with sparse darker streaking across upper breast) and almost unmarked buff underwing-coverts. Juvenile generally more heavily marked on head than juvenile Changeable; with broad and diffuse pale rufous barring on underparts (barring less pronounced than adult), and darker and more uniform upperparts. Forested hills and mountains. KA: nr, KE: nr, TN: nr

Lesser Kestrel *Falco naumanni* 29–32 cm

a **b** **c** ADULT MALE, **d** **e** IMMATURE MALE and **f** **g** **h** ADULT FEMALE Slightly smaller and slimmer than Common Kestrel. Flapping shallower and stiffer. Claws whitish (black on Common). Compared with Common, male lacks dark moustachial stripe, has unmarked upper-parts, blue-grey greater coverts and plainer orange-buff underparts. In flight, underwing whiter with more clearly pronounced darker tips to primaries; tail often looks more wedge-shaped. First-year male more like Common, but has unmarked rufous mantle and scapulars. Female and juvenile have less distinct moustachial stripe than Common, and lack any suggestion of dark eye-stripe; underwing tends to be cleaner and whiter, with primary bases unbarred (or only lightly barred) and coverts less heavily spotted, and dark primary tips more pronounced. Open grass-land and cultivation. Globally threatened. AN: v, KA: np, KE: np, MH: np, MV: np, TN: v

Common Kestrel *Falco tinnunculus* 32–35 cm

a **b** **c** ADULT MALE and **d** **e** **f** ADULT FEMALE Long, rather broad tail; wing-tips more rounded than on most falcons. Frequently hovers. Male has grey head and tail, and rufous upperparts heavily marked with black. Female and juvenile have rufous crown and nape streaked with black, diffuse and narrow dark moustachial stripe, rufous upperparts heavily marked with black, and dark barring on rufous tail. Open country. AN: cw, GO: nw, KA: cw, KE: nr, LS: nw, MH: nr, MV: nw, TN: lcr

Red-necked Falcon *Falco chicquera* 31–36 cm

a **b** **c** ADULT and **d** JUVENILE Powerful falcon with pointed wings and longish tail. Flight usually fast and dashing. Has rufous crown and nape, pale blue-grey upperparts, white underparts finely barred with black, and grey tail with broad black subterminal band. Open country. AN: nr, GO: v, KA: nr, KE: nr, MH: nr, TN: nw

Amur Falcon *Falco amurensis* 28–31 cm

a **b** ADULT MALE, **c** **d** ADULT FEMALE, **e** **f** IMMATURE MALE and **g** JUVENILE In all plumages, has red to pale orange cere, eye-ring, legs and feet. Frequently hovers. Male dark grey, with rufous undertail-coverts and white underwing-coverts. Female has dark grey upperparts, short moustachial stripe, whitish underparts with some dark barring and spotting, and orange-buff thighs and undertail-coverts; uppertail barred; underwing white with strong dark barring. Juvenile has rufous-buff fringes to upperparts, rufous-buff streaking on crown, and boldly streaked underparts. Open country. AN: v, GO: np, KA: np, KE: np, MH: v, MV: np, TN: v

1 **Eurasian Hobby** *Falco subbuteo* 30–36 cm

  a **b** ADULT and **c** JUVENILE Slim, with long pointed wings and medium-length tail. Hunting flight swift and powerful, with stiff beats interspersed with short glides. Adult has broad black moustachial stripe, cream underparts with bold blackish streaking, and rufous thighs and undertail-coverts. Juvenile has dark brown upperparts with buffish fringes, pale buffish underparts that are more heavily streaked, and lacks rufous thighs and undertail-coverts. Well-wooded areas; also open country in winter. AN: v, GO: v, KA: nw, MH: nw, MV: nw, TN: nw

2 **Oriental Hobby** *Falco severus* 27–30 cm

  a **b** ADULT and **c** IMMATURE Similar to Eurasian Hobby in structure and flight action. Adult has complete blackish hood, bluish-black upperparts and unmarked rufous underparts. Juvenile has browner upperparts and heavily streaked rufous-buff underparts. Open wooded hills. KA: v, KE: nw

3 **Laggar Falcon** *Falco jugger* 43–46 cm

  a **b** ADULT and **c** **d** JUVENILE Large falcon, although smaller, slimmer-winged and less powerful than Saker. Adult has rufous crown, fine but prominent dark moustachial stripe, dark brown upperparts, and rather uniform uppertail; underparts and underwing-coverts vary in extent of streaking, but lower flanks and thighs usually wholly dark brown; may show dark panel across underwing-coverts. Juvenile similar to adult, but crown duller and underparts very heavily streaked, and has greyish bare parts; differs from juvenile Peregrine in paler crown, finer moustachial stripe and unbarred uppertail. *See* Appendix for comparison with Saker Falcon. Open dry country and cultivation. AN: nr, GO: nw, KA: nr, KE: nr, MH: nr, TN: nr

4 **Peregrine Falcon** *Falco peregrinus* 38–48 cm

  a **b** ADULT and **c** **d** JUVENILE *F. p. peregrinator*; **e** **f** ADULT and **g** **h** IMMATURE *F. p. babylonicus*; **i** **j** ADULT *F. p. calidus* Heavy-looking falcon with broad-based and pointed wings and short, broad-based tail. Flight strong, with stiff, shallow beats and occasional short glides. *F. p. calidus* has slate-grey upperparts, broad black moustachial stripe, and whitish underparts with narrow blackish barring; juvenile *calidus* (not illustrated) has browner upperparts, heavily streaked underparts, broad moustachial stripe, and barred uppertail. *F. p. peregrinator* has darker upperparts with more extensive black hood, and rufous underparts; juvenile *peregrinator* has darker, browner upperparts than adult, and paler underparts with heavy streaking. *F. p. babylonicus* ('Barbary Falcon') has occurred as a vagrant; has pale blue-grey upperparts, buffish underparts with only sparse markings, rufous on crown and nape, and finer moustachial stripe; juvenile *babylonicus* has darker brown upperparts, heavily streaked underparts, and only a trace of rufous on forehead and supercilium. *See* Appendix for comparison with Saker Falcon. Breeds in open rugged country, also around lakes and large rivers in winter. AN: nr, GO: nr?, KA: nr, KE: nr, LS: nw, MH: nr, MV: v, TN: nr

Little Grebe *Tachybaptus ruficollis*   25–29 cm

   a ADULT BREEDING and **b** **c** ADULT NON-BREEDING   Small size, often with puffed-up rear end. In breeding plumage, has rufous cheeks and neck sides and yellow patch at base of bill. In non-breeding plumage, has brownish-buff cheeks and flanks. Juvenile is similar to non-breeding but has brown stripes across cheeks. *See* Appendix for comparison with Black-necked Grebe. Lakes and pools. AN: cr, GO: nr, KA: cr, KE: nr, MH: cr, TN: cr

Little Cormorant *Phalacrocorax niger*   51 cm

   a **b** ADULT BREEDING, **c** ADULT NON-BREEDING and **d** IMMATURE   Small size with short bill. Adult breeding all black, with a few white plumes on forecrown and sides of head. Non-breeding browner (and lacks white head plumes), with whitish chin. Immature has whitish chin and throat, and foreneck and breast a shade paler than upperparts, with some pale fringes. Lakes, pools and rivers. AN: cr, GO: cr, KA: cr, KE: np, MH: cr, TN: cr

Indian Cormorant *Phalacrocorax fuscicollis*   63 cm

   a **b** ADULT BREEDING, **c** ADULT NON-BREEDING and **d** IMMATURE   Smaller and slimmer than Great, with thinner neck, slimmer oval-shaped head, finer-looking bill and proportionately longer tail. In flight, looks lighter, with thinner neck and quicker wing action. Larger than Little, with longer neck, oval-shaped head and longer bill. Adult breeding glossy black, with tuft of white behind eye and scattering of white filoplumes on neck. Non-breeding lacks white plumes, has whitish throat, and has browner-looking head, neck and underparts. Immature has brown upperparts and whitish underparts. Inland and coastal waters. AN: nr, GO: nr, KA: cr, KE: nr?, MH: nr, TN: nr

Great Cormorant *Phalacrocorax carbo*   80–100 cm

   a **b** ADULT BREEDING, **c** ADULT NON-BREEDING and **d** IMMATURE   Large with thick neck and stout bill. Adult breeding glossy black, with orange facial skin, white cheeks and throat, white head plumes and white thigh-patch. Non-breeding more blackish brown, and lacks white head plumes and thigh-patch. Immature has whitish or pale buff underparts. Lakes and large rivers. AN: nr, GO: v, KA: nr, KE: nr, LS: v, MH: nr, TN: nr

Darter *Anhinga melanogaster*   85–97 cm

   a **b** **c** ADULT MALE BREEDING and **d** IMMATURE   Long, slim head and neck, dagger-like bill, and long tail. Often swims with most of body submerged. In flight, neck is only partly out-stretched with kink at base. As with other cormorants, frequently perches with wings held out-stretched to dry. Adult has white stripe down side of neck, lanceolate white scapular streaks, and white streaking on wing-coverts. Juvenile buffish white below, with buff fringes to coverts forming pale panel on upperwing. Lakes, pools and slow-moving rivers. AN: nr, GO: nr, KA: nr, KE: nr, MH: nr, TN: nr

1 Red-billed Tropicbird *Phaethon aethereus* 48 cm

a **b** ADULT and **c** JUVENILE Adult has red bill, white tail-streamers, black barring on mantle and scapulars, and much black on primaries. Juvenile has yellow bill with black tip, and black band across nape. Pelagic. GO: v, KE: v, LS: np, MH: v, MV: v

2 White-tailed Tropicbird *Phaethon lepturus* 39 cm

a **b** ADULT and **c** JUVENILE Smaller and more graceful than Red-billed. Adult has yellow or orange bill, black diagonal bar across inner upperwing, and white tail-streamers. Juvenile has yellow bill, and lacks black band across nape. Pelagic. AN: v, KA: v, MV: nr, TN: v

3 Masked Booby *Sula dactylatra* 81–92 cm

a ADULT, **b** IMMATURE and **c** JUVENILE Large and robust booby. Adult largely white, with black mask and black flight feathers and tail. Juvenile has brown head, neck and upperparts, with whitish collar and whitish scaling on upperparts; underbody white, and shows much white on underwing-coverts. Head, upper body and upperwing-coverts of immature become increasingly white with age. Pelagic. GO: v, KA: v, KE: v, LS: nr?, MH: v, MV: ns?

4 Brown Booby *Sula leucogaster* 64–74 cm

a ADULT and **b** IMMATURE Dark brown, with sharply demarcated white underbody and underwing-coverts. Juvenile has dusky brown underbody, with pale panel across underwing-coverts, but overall appearance is similar to adult. Pelagic. GO: v, KA: v, KE: v, LS: v, MV: np

5 Red-footed Booby *Sula sula* 66–77 cm

a **b** ADULT WHITE MORPH, **c** INTERMEDIATE MORPH, **d** IMMATURE and **e** JUVENILE Small and graceful booby. Adult has bluish bill, pinkish facial skin and red feet. White, brown and intermediate morphs occur; white morph most likely to be encountered in Indian Ocean. Juvenile has greyish legs and dark bill; underwing uniformly dark. Immature variable; immature white morph has diffuse breast-band. Pelagic. MV: v

Little Egret *Egretta garzetta* 55–65 cm

a ADULT BREEDING and **b** ADULT NON-BREEDING Slim and graceful. Typically, has black bill, black legs with yellow feet, and greyish lores (lores reddish during courtship). Breeding plumage has prominent plumes on nape, breast and mantle. Wetlands. AN: cr, GO: cr, KA: cr, KE: cr, LS: nr?, MH: cr, MV: nw, TN: cr

Western Reef Egret *Egretta gularis* 55–65 cm

a ADULT WHITE MORPH BREEDING, **b** ADULT DARK MORPH NON-BREEDING and **c** INTERMEDIATE MORPH Bill longer and stouter than that of Little and usually appearing very slightly downcurved. Legs also slightly shorter and thicker looking. Bill is usually mainly yellowish or brownish yellow, but may be black when breeding. Typically, has greenish or yellowish lores (although can be greyish as on Little, and Little can, exceptionally, appear to have yellowish tinge to lores). Coastal waters. AN: v, GO: nr, KA: v, KE: nr, LS: nr?, MH: nr, MV: v, TN: v

Great Egret *Casmerodius albus* 65–72 cm

a ADULT BREEDING and **b** ADULT NON-BREEDING Large size, with very long neck and large bill. Black line of gape extends behind eye. In breeding plumage bill is black, lores blue and tibia reddish, and has prominent plumes on breast and mantle. In non-breeding plumage, bill is yellow and lores pale green. Wetlands. AN: cr, GO: nr, KA: nr, KE: nr, MH: nr, MV: v, TN: cr

Intermediate Egret *Mesophoyx intermedia* 65–72 cm

a ADULT BREEDING and **b** ADULT NON-BREEDING Smaller than Great, with shorter bill and neck. Black gape-line does not extend beyond eye. In breeding plumage, bill is black and lores yellow-green, and has breast- and mantle-plumes and prominent crest. Has black-tipped yellow bill and yellow lores outside breeding season. Wetlands. AN: cr, GO: cr, KA: cr, KE: cr, MH: cr, MV: v, TN: cr

Cattle Egret *Bubulcus ibis* 48–53 cm

a ADULT BREEDING and **b** ADULT NON-BREEDING Small stocky egret, with short yellow bill and short legs. In breeding plumage, has orange-buff on head, neck and mantle. Wetlands and grassland; often associated with livestock. AN: cr, GO: cr, KA: cr, KE: cr, LS: nr?, MH: cr, MV: nw, TN: cr

Grey Heron *Ardea cinerea* 90–98 cm
a **b** ADULT and **c** IMMATURE In flight, black flight feathers contrast with grey upperwing- and underwing-coverts. Adult has yellow bill, whitish head and neck with black head plumes, and black patches on belly. Immature has dark cap with variable crest, greyer neck, and lacks or has reduced black on belly. Wetlands. AN: cr, GO: cr, KA: nw, KE: nr?, LS: nr, MH: nw, MV: cr, TN: cw

Purple Heron *Ardea purpurea* 78–90 cm
a **b** ADULT and **c** **d** JUVENILE Rakish, with long, thin neck. In flight, compared with Grey, bulge of recoiled neck is very pronounced and protruding feet are large. Adult has chestnut head and neck with black stripes, grey mantle and upperwing-coverts, and dark chestnut belly and underwing-coverts. Juvenile has buffish neck and underparts, and brownish mantle and upperwing-coverts with rufous-buff fringes. *See* Appendix for comparison with Goliath Heron. Wetlands with tall cover. AN: nr, GO: nr, KA: nw, KE: nr, LS: v, MH: nr, MV: nw, TN: nr

Indian Pond Heron *Ardeola grayii* 42–45 cm
a **b** ADULT BREEDING and **c** ADULT NON-BREEDING Whitish wings contrast with dark saddle. Adult breeding plumage has yellowish-buff head and neck, white nape-plumes and maroon-brown mantle/scapulars. Head, neck and breast streaked in non-breeding plumage. Wetlands. AN: cr, GO: cr, KA: cr, KE: cr, LS: nr, MH: cr, MV: lcr, TN: cr

Little Heron *Butorides striatus* 40–48 cm
a **b** ADULT and **c** JUVENILE Small, stocky and short-legged heron. Adult has black crown and long crest, dark greenish upperparts and greyish underparts. Juvenile has buff streaking on upperparts, and dark-streaked underparts. Wetlands with dense shrub cover. AN: nr, GO: nr, KA: nr, KE: nr, LS: nr, MH: nr, MV: cr, TN: nr

Black-crowned Night Heron *Nycticorax nycticorax* 58–65 cm
a **b** ADULT and **c** JUVENILE Stocky heron, with thick neck. Adult has black crown and mantle contrasting with grey wings and whitish underparts. Breeding plumage has elongated white nape-plumes. Juvenile is boldly streaked and spotted. Immature resembles juvenile but has unstreaked brown mantle/scapulars. Wetlands, often with reedbeds. AN: nr, GO: nr, KA: cr, KE: nr, MH: nr, MV: v, TN: cr

1

Malayan Night Heron *Gorsachius melanolophus* 51 cm
    a b ADULT and **c** IMMATURE Stocky, with stout bill and short neck. Adult has black crown and crest, rufous sides to head and neck, and rufous-brown upperparts. Immature finely vermiculated with white, grey and rufous-buff, and with bold white spotting on crown and crest. Streams and marshes in evergreen forest. GO: v, KA: nr, KE: nr, TN: v

2

Yellow Bittern *Ixobrychus sinensis* 38 cm
    a b ADULT MALE and **c** JUVENILE Small size. Yellowish-buff wing-coverts contrast with dark brown flight feathers. Male has pinkish-brown mantle/scapulars, and face and sides of neck are vinaceous. Female is similar to male, but with rufous streaking on black crown, rufous-orange streaking on foreneck and breast, and diffuse buff edges to rufous-brown mantle/scapulars. Juvenile appears buff with bold dark streaking to upperparts, including wing-coverts; foreneck and breast are heavily streaked. *See* Appendix for comparison with Little Bittern. Reedbeds and marshes. AN: nr, GO: nr?, KA: nw, KE: nr, LS: v, MH: nr, MV: v, TN: nr

3

Cinnamon Bittern *Ixobrychus cinnamomeus* 38 cm
    a b ADULT MALE, **c** ADULT FEMALE and **d** JUVENILE Small size. Uniform-looking cinnamon-rufous flight feathers and tail in all plumages. Male has cinnamon-rufous crown, hindneck and mantle/scapulars. Female has dark brown crown and mantle, and dark brown streaking on foreneck and breast. Juvenile has buff mottling on dark brown upperparts and is heavily streaked with dark brown on underparts. Reedbeds and marshes. AN: nr, GO: nr?, KA: nr, KE: cr, MH: nr, MV: v, TN: nr

4

Black Bittern *Dupetor flavicollis* 58 cm
    a b ADULT and **c** JUVENILE Blackish upperparts, including wings, with orange-buff patch on side of neck. Juvenile has rufous fringes to upperparts. Forest pools, marshes and reed-edged lakes. AN: nr, GO: v, KA: nr, KE: cr, MH: v, MV: v, TN: nr

5

Great Bittern *Botaurus stellaris* 70–80 cm
    a b ADULT Stocky. Cryptically patterned with golden-brown, blackish and buff. Wet reedbeds. AN: v, GO: v, KA: nw, MH: nw, MV: v, TN: nw

Greater Flamingo *Phoenicopterus ruber* 125–145 cm

a **b** ADULT, **c** IMMATURE and **d** JUVENILE Larger than Lesser Flamingo, with longer and thinner neck. Bill is larger and less prominently kinked. Adult has pale pink bill with prominent dark tip, and variable amount of pinkish white on head, neck and body; in flight, crimson-pink upperwing-coverts contrast with whitish body. Immature has greyish-white head and neck, and white body lacking any pink; pink on bill develops with increasing age. Juvenile brownish grey, with white on coverts; bill grey, tipped with black, and legs grey. Shallow brackish lakes, mudflats and saltpans. AN: v, GO: v, KA: xr/nw, KE: v, MH: nw, MV: np, TN: nw

Lesser Flamingo *Phoenicopterus minor* 80–90 cm

a **b** ADULT, **c** IMMATURE and **d** JUVENILE Smaller than Greater Flamingo; neck appears shorter, and bill is smaller and more prominently kinked. Adult has black-tipped dark red bill, dark red iris and facial skin, and deep rose-pink on head, neck and body; blood-red centres to lesser and median upperwing-coverts contrast with paler pink of rest of coverts. Immature has greyish-brown head and neck, pale pink body and mainly pink coverts; bill coloration develops with increasing age. Juvenile mainly grey-brown, with dark-tipped purplish-brown bill and grey legs. Salt and brackish lagoons and saltpans. AN: np, MH: np, TN: np

Glossy Ibis *Plegadis falcinellus* 55–65 cm

a ADULT BREEDING, **b** ADULT NON-BREEDING and **c** JUVENILE Small, dark ibis with rather fine downcurved bill. Adult breeding is deep chestnut, glossed with purple and green, and with metallic green-and-purple wings; has narrow white surround to bare lores. Adult non-breeding is duller, with white streaking on dark brown head and neck. Juvenile similar to adult non-breeding, but is dark brown with white mottling on head and has only faint greenish gloss to upperparts. Inland wetlands. AN: v, GO: nw, KA: xr/nw, KE: v, MH: nw, MV: v, TN: np

Black-headed Ibis *Threskiornis melanocephalus* 75 cm

a ADULT BREEDING and **b** IMMATURE Stocky, mainly white ibis with stout downcurved black bill. Adult breeding has naked black head, white lower-neck plumes, variable yellow wash to mantle and breast, and grey on scapulars and elongated tertials. Adult non-breeding has all-white body and lacks neck plumes. Immature has grey feathering on head and neck, and black-tipped wings. Flooded fields, marshes, rivers and pools. AN: nr, GO: np, KA: nr, KE: xr, MH: nr, TN: nr

Black Ibis *Pseudibis papillosa* 68 cm

ADULT Stocky, dark ibis with relatively stout downcurved bill. Has white shoulder-patch and reddish legs. Adult has naked black head with red patch on rear crown and nape, and is dark brown with green-and-purple gloss. Immature is dark brown, including feathered head. Marshes, lakes and fields, sometimes in dry cultivation. AN: nr, KA: nr, KE: xr?, MH: nr, TN: nr

Eurasian Spoonbill *Platalea leucorodia* 80–90 cm

a ADULT BREEDING and **b** JUVENILE White, with spatulate-tipped bill. Adult has black bill with yellow tip; has crest and yellow breast-patch when breeding. Juvenile has pink bill; in flight, shows black tips to primaries. Marshes, lakes and large rivers. AN: np, GO: np, KA: nr, KE: v, MH: nr, MV: v, TN: nr

Painted Stork *Mycteria leucocephala* 93–100 cm

a **b** ADULT and **c** **d** IMMATURE Adult has downcurved yellow bill, bare orange-yellow or red face and red legs; white barring on mainly black upperwing-coverts, pinkish tertials, and black barring across breast. Juvenile dirty greyish white, with grey-brown (feathered) head and neck, and brown lesser coverts; bill and legs duller than adult's. Marshes and lakes. AN: nr, GO: v, KA: nr, KE: v, MH: nr, TN: nr

Asian Openbill *Anastomus oscitans* 68 cm

a ADULT BREEDING and **b** **c** ADULT NON-BREEDING Stout, dull-coloured 'open bill'. Largely white (breeding) or greyish white (non-breeding), with black flight feathers and tail; legs usually dull pink, brighter in breeding condition. Juvenile has brownish-grey head, neck and breast, and brownish mantle and scapulars slightly paler than the blackish flight feathers. At a distance in flight, best told from White Stork by dull-coloured bill and black tail. Marshes and lakes. AN: nr, GO: nr, KA: nr, KE: nr, MH: nr, TN: nr

Woolly-necked Stork *Ciconia episcopus* 75–92 cm

a **b** ADULT Stocky, largely blackish stork with 'woolly' white neck, black 'skullcap', and white vent and undertail-coverts. In flight, upperwing and underwing entirely dark. Juvenile is similar to adult but with duller brown body and wings, and feathered forehead. Flooded fields, marshes and lakes. AN: nr, GO: nr, KA: nr, KE: nr, MH: nr, TN: nr

White Stork *Ciconia ciconia* 100–125 cm

a **b** ADULT Mainly white stork, with black flight feathers and striking red bill and legs. Generally has cleaner black-and-white appearance than Asian Openbill. Juvenile is similar to adult but with brown greater coverts and duller brownish-red bill and legs. Red bill and white tail help separate it from Asian Openbill at a distance in flight. Wet grassland and fields. AN: nw, GO: v, KA: nw, KE: nw, MH: nw, TN: nw

1

Black Stork *Ciconia nigra* 90–100 cm

a **b** ADULT and **c** IMMATURE Adult mainly glossy black, with white lower breast and belly, and red bill and legs; in flight, white underparts and axillaries contrast strongly with black neck and underwing. Juvenile has brown head, neck and upperparts flecked with white; bill and legs greyish green. Marshes and rivers. AN: v, GO: v, KA: nw, KE: nw, MH: nw, TN: v

2

Black-necked Stork *Ephippiorhynchus asiaticus* 129–150 cm

a **b** ADULT and **c** **d** IMMATURE Large black-and-white stork with long red legs and huge black bill. In flight, wings white except for broad black band across coverts, and tail black. Male has brown iris; yellow in female. Juvenile has fawn-brown head, neck and mantle, mainly brown wing-coverts, and mainly blackish-brown flight feathers; legs dark. Marshes and large rivers. AN: nr, GO: v, KA: nr, MH: nr, TN: nr

3

Lesser Adjutant *Leptoptilos javanicus* 110–120 cm

a ADULT BREEDING and **b** **c** ADULT NON-BREEDING Flies with neck retracted, as Greater Adjutant. Smaller than Greater, with slimmer bill that has straighter ridge to culmen. Compared with Greater, adult shows pale frontal plate on head, and denser feathering on head and hind-neck, which forms small crest. Adult has glossy black mantle and wings, largely black underwing (with white axillaries), white undertail-coverts, and largely black neck ruff (appearing as black patch on breast sides in flight); in breeding plumage, has narrow white fringes to scapulars and inner greater coverts, and copper spots on median coverts. Juvenile similar to adult, but upperparts are dull black and head and neck more densely feathered. Marshes, pools and wet fields. Globally threatened. AN: np, GO: nr?, KA: nr?, KE: nr?, MH: np, TN: v

4

Greater Adjutant *Leptoptilos dubius* 120–150 cm

a **b** **c** ADULT BREEDING and **d** IMMATURE Larger than Lesser Adjutant, with stouter, conical bill with convex ridge to culmen. Adult breeding has bluish-grey mantle, silvery-grey panel across greater coverts, greyish or brownish underwing-coverts, grey undertail-coverts, and more extensive white neck ruff. Further, has blackish face and forehead (with appearance of dried blood) and has neck pouch (visible only when inflated). Adult non-breeding and immature have darker grey mantle and inner wing-coverts, and brown greater coverts (which barely contrast with rest of wing); immature with brownish (rather than pale) iris. Marshes. Globally threatened. KA: v, MH: np, TN: np

Great White Pelican *Pelecanus onocrotalus* 140–175 cm
a ADULT BREEDING, **b** **c** ADULT NON-BREEDING, **d** IMMATURE and **e** JUVENILE Adult and immature have black underside to primaries and secondaries that contrast strongly with white (or largely white) underwing-coverts. Adult breeding has white body and wing-coverts tinged with pink, bright yellow pouch and pinkish skin around eye. Adult non-breeding has duller bare parts, and lacks pink tinge and white crest. Immature has variable amounts of brown on wing-coverts and scapulars. Juvenile has largely brown head, neck and upperparts, including upperwing-coverts, and brown flight feathers; upperwing appears more uniform brown, and underwing shows pale central panel contrasting with dark inner coverts and flight feathers; greyish pouch becomes yellower with age. *See* Appendix for comparison with Dalmatian Pelican. Large lakes and lagoons. AN: nw, KA: v, KE: v, MV: v

Spot-billed Pelican *Pelecanus philippensis* 140 cm
a **b** ADULT BREEDING, **c** ADULT NON-BREEDING, **d** IMMATURE and **e** JUVENILE Much smaller than Great White, with dingier appearance, rather uniform pinkish bill and pouch (except in breeding condition), and black spotting on upper mandible (except juveniles). Tufted crest/hind-neck usually apparent even on young birds. Underwing pattern quite different from Great White, showing little contrast between wing-coverts and flight feathers, and with paler greater coverts producing distinct central panel. Adult breeding has cinnamon-pink rump, underwing-coverts and undertail-coverts; head and neck appear greyish; has purplish skin in front of eye, and pouch is pink to dull purple and blotched with black. Adult non-breeding is dirtier greyish white, with pinkish pouch. Immature has variable grey-brown markings on upperparts. Juvenile has brownish head and neck, brown mantle and upperwing-coverts (fringed with pale buff) and brown flight feathers; spotting on bill initially lacking (and still indistinct at 12 months). *See* Appendix for comparison with Dalmatian Pelican. Large inland and coastal waters. AN: nr, KA: nr, KE: np, MH: np, TN: nr

Great Frigatebird *Fregata minor* 85–105 cm
a ADULT MALE, **b** ADULT FEMALE, **c** JUVENILE and **d** IMMATURE Adult male is only frigatebird with all-black underparts. Adult female has black cap and pink eye-ring; also has grey throat and black neck sides, and lacks spur of white on underwing. Juvenile and immature have rufous or white head, blackish breast-band and largely white underparts, which are gradually replaced by adult plumage; they lack white spur on underwing (shown by all Lesser). Pelagic. AN: v, KA: v, KE: v, LS: v, MH: v, MV: np

Lesser Frigatebird *Fregata ariel* 70–80 cm
a ADULT MALE, **b** ADULT FEMALE, **c** IMMATURE MALE and **d** JUVENILE Smaller and more finely built than Great Frigatebird. Adult male is entirely black except for white spur extending from breast sides onto inner underwing. Adult female has black head and red eye-ring; also black throat, white neck sides, white spur extending from white breast onto inner underwing, and black belly and vent. Juvenile and immature have rufous or white head, blackish breast-band and much white on underparts, which are gradually replaced by adult plumage; they always show white spur on underwing (lacking on Great). Pelagic. KA: v, KE: v, MH: v, MV: nr, TN: v

1 Wedge-tailed Shearwater *Puffinus pacificus* 41–46 cm

a PALE MORPH and **b** **c** DARK MORPH Large size, with long, pointed or wedge-shaped tail, fine greyish bill with dark tip, and pale legs and feet. Comparatively broad rounded wing-tips. In calm conditions, flight comprises lazy flapping and short glides with wings held forward and bowed; in strong winds, soars in low arcs between short bursts of flapping. Two colour morphs; dark morph has all-dark underwing. *See* Appendix for comparison with Jouanin's Petrel. Pelagic. GO: v, KA: v, LS: v, MV: np

2 Flesh-footed Shearwater *Puffinus carneipes* 41–45 cm

a **b** ADULT Large, dark, broad-winged shearwater. Pink legs and feet. Greyish patch on underside of primaries. Stout pinkish bill with dark tip. Flight typically relaxed, with strong flapping interspersed with stiff-winged glides; banks and glides with less flapping in stronger winds. Offshore. KE: v, LS: v, MV: np, TN: v

3 Audubon's Shearwater *Puffinus lherminieri* 30 cm

a **b** ADULT Small size. Dark brown upperparts, white underparts with dark on breast sides; white wing-linings, axillaries and flanks, with broad, dark margins to underwing. Flies with fairly fast wing-beats interspersed with short glides. *See* Appendix for comparison with Persian Shearwater. Offshore and pelagic waters. KE: v, LS: nr?, MV: nr

4 Wilson's Storm-petrel *Oceanites oceanicus* 15–19 cm

a **b** ADULT Dark underparts and underwing. White rump-band. Feet project noticeably beyond tail. When fluttering over water, dangling feet show yellow webbing. Pelagic. GO: cp, KA: v, KE: nw, LS: np, MH: np, MV: cp, TN: np

5 Swinhoe's Storm-petrel *Oceanodroma monorhis* 20 cm

a **b** ADULT All-dark storm-petrel, lacking white rump-band. Tail slightly forked, and feet do not project beyond tail. Pelagic and coastal waters. *See* Appendix for comparison with Leach's Storm-petrel. LS: np, MV: v, TN: v

Indian Pitta *Pitta brachyura* 19 cm
ADULT Black stripe through eye; white throat, buff lateral crown-stripes, and buff breast and flanks. Song is a sharp two-noted whistle, second note descending, *pree-treer*. Broadleaved forest with dense undergrowth. AN: np, GO: nw, KA: nr, KE: cw, LS: v, MH: nr, TN: nw

Asian Fairy Bluebird *Irena puella* 25 cm
a MALE and **b** FEMALE Male has glistening violet-blue upperparts and black underparts. Female and first-year male entirely dull blue-green. Calls include a loud, liquid *tu-lip*. Moist broadleaved forest. AN: nr, GO: nr, KA: nr, KE: nr, MH: nr, TN: lcr

Blue-winged Leafbird *Chloropsis cochinchinensis* 20 cm
a MALE, **b** FEMALE and **c** JUVENILE Male has smaller black throat-patch than Golden-fronted, with yellowish forehead. Female and juvenile have turquoise throat with yellowish border. Race in southern India lacks the blue in wing and tail of the nominate race of NE subcontinent. Open forest and well-wooded areas. AN: nr, GO: nr, KA: nr, KE: nr, MH: nr, TN: nr

Golden-fronted Leafbird *Chloropsis aurifrons* 19 cm
a ADULT and **b** JUVENILE Adult has golden-orange forehead, and more extensive black throat than Blue-winged. Juvenile has green head, with hint of turquoise moustachial stripe. Broadleaved forest and secondary growth. AN: nr, GO: nr, KA: nr, KE: nr, MH: nr, TN: lcr

Rufous-tailed Shrike *Lanius isabellinus* 18–19 cm
a MALE and **b** FEMALE Typically, has paler sandy-brown/grey-brown mantle and warmer rufous rump and tail than Brown. Male has small white patch at base of primaries, which is lacking in Brown. Female is similar to male, but lacks white patch in wing, has grey-brown (rather than blackish) ear-coverts, and usually has some scaling on underparts. First-winter birds are similar to female, but with pale fringes and dark subterminal lines to scapulars, wing-coverts and tertials. Open dry scrub country. AN: v, GO: nw, MH: nw, MV: v

Brown Shrike *Lanius cristatus* 18–19 cm
a MALE and **b** 1ST-WINTER Compared with Rufous-tailed, typically has darker rufous-brown upperparts and tail; also thicker bill and more graduated tail. Female has a darker mask than female Rufous-tailed, and a more prominent white supercilium. Forest edges, scrub, open forest and bushy hillsides. AN: cw, GO: nw, KA: cw, KE: cw, LS: nw, MH: nw, MV: v, TN: lcw

Bay-backed Shrike *Lanius vittatus* 17 cm
a ADULT and **b** JUVENILE Adult has black forehead and mask contrasting with pale grey crown and nape, deep maroon mantle, whitish rump, and white patch at base of primaries. Juvenile told from juvenile Long-tailed by smaller size and shorter tail, more uniform greyish/buffish base colour to upperparts, pale rump, more intricately patterned wing-coverts and tertials (with buff fringes and dark subterminal crescents and central marks), and primary coverts that are prominently tipped with buff. First-year like washed-out version of adult; lacks black forehead. Open dry scrub, and bushes in cultivation. AN: nr, GO: nr, KA: nr, KE: nr, MH: nr, TN: cr

Long-tailed Shrike *Lanius schach* 25 cm
a ADULT and **b** JUVENILE *L. s. erythronotus*; **c** ADULT *L. s. caniceps*; **d** ADULT *L. s. tricolor* Adult *L. s. erythronotus* has grey mantle, rufous scapulars and upper back, narrow black forehead, rufous sides to black tail, and small white patch on primaries. Juvenile has (dark-barred) rufous-brown scapulars, back and rump; dark greater coverts and tertials fringed rufous. Birds in the southern peninsula *L. s. caniceps* lack rufous to scapulars and back. The black-hooded race, *tricolor*, winters south to N Andhra Pradesh and NE Maharashtra. *See* Appendix for comparison with Grey-backed Shrike. Bushes in cultivation and in open country, lightly wooded areas and gardens. AN: nr, GO: cr?, KA: nr, KE: nr, MH: cr, MV: v, TN: lcr

Southern Grey Shrike *Lanius meridionalis* 24 cm
a ADULT and **b** JUVENILE Narrow black forehead and broad black mask, grey mantle with white scapulars, broad white tips to secondaries, white sides and tip to tail, and white underparts. Juvenile has sandy cast to grey upperparts, buff tips to tertials and coverts, and grey mask. Open dry scrub country. AN: nr, GO: nr, KA: lcr, KE: v, MH: nr, TN: nr

Rufous Treepie *Dendrocitta vagabunda* 46–50 cm

ADULT Slate-grey hood, rufous-brown mantle, pale grey wing-panel, buffish underparts and rump, and whitish subterminal tail-band. Juvenile has brown hood. Open wooded country, groves and trees at edges of cultivation. AN: nr, GO: nr, KA: lcr, KE: cr, MH: nr, TN: cr

Grey Treepie *Dendrocitta formosae* 36–40 cm

ADULT Dark grey face, grey underparts and rump, and black wings with white patch at base of primaries. Juvenile duller version of adult. Broadleaved forest and secondary growth. AN: nr

White-bellied Treepie *Dendrocitta leucogastra* 48 cm

ADULT Black face, white nape and underparts, white rump, black wings with white patch, and extensive black tip to tail. Evergreen hill forest and secondary growth. AN: nr, GO: nr, KA: lcr, KE: nr, TN: lcr

House Crow *Corvus splendens* 40 cm

ADULT Two-toned appearance, with paler nape, neck and breast. Around human habitation and cultivation. AN: cr, GO: cr, KA: cr, KE: cr, LS: nr, MH: cr, TN: cr

Large-billed Crow *Corvus macrorhynchos* 46–59 cm

ADULT All black, lacking paler collar of House Crow. Domed head, and large bill with arched culmen. *See* Appendix for comparison with Common Raven. Forest, cultivation and open country above the treeline; usually associated with towns and villages. AN: cr, GO: nr, KA: cr, KE: cr, MH: cr, TN: cr

Eurasian Golden Oriole *Oriolus oriolus* 25 cm

a MALE, **b** FEMALE and **c** IMMATURE Male golden-yellow, with black mask and mainly black wings. Female and immature variable, usually with streaking on underparts and yellowish-green upperparts. Song is a loud, fluty *weela-wheo-oh*. Open woodland, and trees in cultivation. AN: cr, GO: cw, KA: nr, KE: nr, MH: cr, MV: v, TN: nw

Black-naped Oriole *Oriolus chinensis* 27 cm

a MALE, **b** FEMALE and **c** IMMATURE Large, stout bill; nasal call. Black eye-stripe and nape-band poorly defined in immature. Male has yellow mantle and wing-coverts concolorous with underparts (upperparts greener in female). Broadleaved forest and well-wooded areas. AN: v, GO: nw, KA: np, KE: nw, MH: nw, TN: v

Black-hooded Oriole *Oriolus xanthornus* 25 cm

a MALE, **b** FEMALE and **c** IMMATURE Adult has black head and breast; female's upperparts duller than male's. Immature has yellow forehead and black-streaked white throat. Song is a mixture of mellow, fluty notes, *wye-you* or *wye-you-you*. Open broadleaved forest and well-wooded areas. AN: nr, GO: lcr, KA: nr, KE: cr, MH: cr, TN: cr

Ashy Woodswallow *Artamus fuscus* 19 cm

a **b** ADULT Slate-grey head, pinkish-grey underparts, and narrow whitish horseshoe-shaped band across uppertail-coverts. Spends much time hawking insect prey on the wing, with plenty of gliding interspersed with short bouts of rapid wing-flapping. Open wooded country. AN: nr, GO: nr, KA: nr, KE: cr, MH: nr, TN: lcr

Large Cuckooshrike *Coracina macei* 30 cm

a MALE and **b** FEMALE Large and mainly pale grey in coloration. Female has grey barring on underparts. Song is a rich, fluty *pi-io-io*. Open woodland, and trees in cultivation. AN: nr, GO: nr, KA: nr, KE: nr, MH: nr, TN: nr

Black-winged Cuckooshrike *Coracina melaschistos* 24 cm

a MALE and **b** FEMALE Male slate-grey, with black wings and bold white tips to tail feathers. Female paler grey, with faint barring on underparts. Open forest and groves. AN: nw, GO: nw, KA: nw, MH: nr, TN: v

Black-headed Cuckooshrike *Coracina melanoptera* 18 cm

a MALE and **b** FEMALE Male has slate-grey head and breast, and pale grey mantle. Female has whitish supercilium, barred underparts, pale grey back and rump contrasting with blackish tail, and broad white fringes to coverts and tertials. Open broadleaved forest and secondary growth. AN: nr, GO: nr?, KA: lcr, KE: nr, MH: cr, TN: nr

Rosy Minivet *Pericrocotus roseus* 20 cm

a MALE and **b** FEMALE Male has grey-brown upperparts, white throat, and pinkish underparts and rump. Female has greyish forehead, white throat, pale yellow underparts and dull olive-yellow rump. Broadleaved forest. AN: nw, GO: v, KA: v, MH: nw

Ashy Minivet *Pericrocotus divaricatus* 20 cm

a MALE and **b** FEMALE Grey and white, lacking any yellow or red in plumage. Male has black 'hood'. Light forest. AN: v, GO: v, KA: v, KE: v, MH: v, TN: np

Small Minivet *Pericrocotus cinnamomeus* 16 cm

a MALE and **b** FEMALE *P. c. cinnamomeus*; **c** MALE and **d** FEMALE *P. c. malabaricus* Small size. Male has grey upperparts, dark grey throat and orange underparts. Female has pale throat and orange wash on underparts. The richly coloured *P. c. malabaricus* occurs in the Western Ghats. Open wooded areas. AN: cr, GO: cr, KA: nr, KE: cr, MH: cr, TN: cr

White-bellied Minivet *Pericrocotus erythropygius* 15 cm

a MALE and **b** FEMALE White wing-patch and orange rump. Male has black head and upperparts, and white underparts with orange breast. Female has brown upperparts and white underparts. Dry open scrub and forest. AN: nr, KA: v, MH: nr, TN: v

Scarlet Minivet *Pericrocotus flammeus* 20–22 cm

a MALE and **b** FEMALE Much larger than Small Minivet, with isolated patch of colour on secondaries (red in male and yellow in female). Male has glossy black upperparts and throat, and entire underparts are orange-red. Female has yellow forehead and underparts. *See* Appendix for comparison with Long-tailed Minivet. Broadleaved and coniferous forests. AN: nr, GO: lcr, KA: nr, KE: cr, MH: nr, TN: lcr

Bar-winged Flycatcher-shrike *Hemipus picatus* 15 cm

a MALE and **b** FEMALE Dark cap and upperparts of male contrasts with greyish-white underparts; has white wing-patch and white rump. Female has browner upperparts than male. Broadleaved forest and forest edges. AN: nr, GO: nr, KA: nr, KE: nr, MH: nr, TN: lcr

Black Drongo *Dicrurus macrocercus* 28 cm
a IMMATURE and **b** ADULT Adult has glossy blue-black underparts and white rictal spot. Tail-fork may be lost during moult. Immature has black underparts with bold whitish fringes. Around habitation and cultivation. AN: cr, GO: cr, KA: cr, KE: cr, MH: cr, TN: cr

Ashy Drongo *Dicrurus leucophaeus* 29 cm
a IMMATURE and **b** ADULT Adult has dark grey underparts and slate-grey upperparts with blue-grey gloss; iris bright red. Immature has brownish-grey underparts with indistinct pale fringes. Broadleaved and coniferous forests. AN: nw, GO: nw, KA: cw, KE: nw, MH: cw, TN: nw

White-bellied Drongo *Dicrurus caerulescens* 24 cm
ADULT Similar to Ashy Drongo, but with white belly and shorter tail that has a shallower tail-fork. Immature is similar to adult, but throat and breast are browner and border with white belly is less clearly defined. Open forest and well-wooded areas. AN: nr, GO: nr, KA: lcr, KE: nr, MH: nr, TN: nr

Bronzed Drongo *Dicrurus aeneus* 24 cm
ADULT Small size, with shallow tail-fork. Heavily spangled. Clearings and edges of moist broadleaved forest. AN: nr, GO: nr, KA: lcr, KE: cr, MH: nr, TN: lcr

Spangled Drongo *Dicrurus hottentottus* 32 cm
ADULT Broad tail with upward-twisted corners, and long downcurved bill. Adult has extensive spangling, and hair-like crest. Moist broadleaved forest; associated with flowering trees, especially silk cotton. AN: nr, GO: nr, KA: nr, KE: nr, MH: nr, TN: nr

Greater Racket-tailed Drongo *Dicrurus paradiseus* 32 cm
a IMMATURE and **b** ADULT Large size with long tail streamers that have 'rackets' at the end (tail-streamers and rackets may be broken off). Has prominent crest and forked tail; crest much reduced in immature. Open broadleaved forest. AN: nr, GO: cr, KA: nr, KE: nr, MH: nr, TN: lcr

White-throated Fantail *Rhipidura albicollis* 19 cm
ADULT Narrow white supercilium and white throat; lacks spotting on wing-coverts. Grey breast is spotted with white. Broadleaved forest and secondary growth. AN: nr, GO: nr, KA: nr, MH: cr, TN: lcr

White-browed Fantail *Rhipidura aureola* 18 cm
ADULT Broad white supercilia that meet over forehead, blackish throat, white breast and belly, and white spotting on wing-coverts. Forest undergrowth. AN: nr, GO: nr, KA: nr, KE: nr, MH: nr, TN: nr

Black-naped Monarch *Hypothymis azurea* 16 cm
a MALE and **b** FEMALE Male mainly blue, with black nape and gorget. Female lacks these features and is duller, with grey-brown mantle and wings. Middle storey of broadleaved forest. AN: nr, GO: nr, KA: nr, KE: cr, MH: nr, TN: nr

Asian Paradise-flycatcher *Terpsiphone paradisi* 20 cm
a WHITE MALE, **b** RUFOUS MALE and **c** FEMALE Male has black head and crest, with white or rufous upperparts and long tail-streamers. Female and immatures have reduced crest and lack streamers. Open forest, groves and gardens. AN: nr, GO: nr?, KA: nr, KE: nr?, MH: nr, MV: v, TN: cr

Common Iora *Aegithina tiphia* 14 cm
a MALE BREEDING, **b** MALE NON-BREEDING and **c** FEMALE *A. t. humei*; **d** MALE BREEDING *A. t. multicolor* Yellow underparts and prominent white wing-bars. Male has black tail (green in female). Crown and nape are black in breeding plumage (with variable amounts of black feathering in mantle). Entire upperparts are black in breeding male *A. t. multicolor* in southern peninsula. *See* Appendix for comparison with Marshall's Iora. Open broadleaved forest and well-wooded areas. AN: cr, GO: cr, KA: cr, KE: cr, MH: cr, TN: cr

Large Woodshrike *Tephrodornis gularis* 23 cm
a MALE and **b** FEMALE Male has black mask and grey crown and nape; mask, crown and nape browner in female. Larger than Common Woodshrike; lacks white supercilium and white on tail. Broadleaved forest and well-wooded areas. AN: nr, GO: nr, KA: nr, KE: nr, TN: nr

Common Woodshrike *Tephrodornis pondicerianus* 18 cm
ADULT Smaller than Large Woodshrike, with broad white supercilium and white tail sides. Open broadleaved forest, secondary growth and well-wooded areas. AN: nr, GO: nr, KA: nr, KE: cr, MH: cr, TN: cr

Blue-capped Rock Thrush *Monticola cinclorhynchus* 17 cm
a MALE BREEDING, **b** FEMALE and **c** 1ST-WINTER MALE Male has white wing-patch, blue crown and throat, and orange rump and underparts; bright coloration obscured by pale fringes in non-breeding and first-winter plumages. Female has uniform olive-brown upperparts. Open dry forest and rocky slopes with scattered trees. AN: v, GO: nw, KA: nw, KE: nw, MH: nw, TN: lcw

Blue Rock Thrush *Monticola solitarius* 20 cm
a MALE BREEDING, **b** FEMALE and **c** 1ST-WINTER MALE Male indigo-blue, with bright coloration obscured by pale fringes in non-breeding and first-winter plumages. Female has bluish cast to slaty-brown upperparts, and buff scaling on underparts. Winters along streams, rivers and amongst old buildings. AN: nw, GO: nw, KA: nw, KE: nw, MH: nw, TN: lcw

Malabar Whistling Thrush *Myophonus horsfieldii* 25 cm
ADULT Adult blackish, with blue forehead and shoulders. Juvenile more sooty-brown, and lacks blue forehead. Rocky hill streams in forest and well-wooded areas. AN: nr, GO: nr, KA: nr, KE: cr, MH: cr, TN: lcr

Pied Thrush *Zoothera wardii* 22 cm
a MALE and **b** FEMALE Male black and white, with white supercilium and wing-bars, and yellow bill. Female has buff supercilium, buff wing-bars and tips to tertials, and scaled underparts. *See* Appendix for comparison with Siberian Thrush. Open broadleaved forest and secondary growth. AN: np, GO: v, KA: np, KE: np, TN: nwp

Orange-headed Thrush *Zoothera citrina* 21 cm
a MALE and **b** FEMALE *Z. c. cyanotus*; **c** MALE and **d** FEMALE *Z. c. citrina* Adult has orange crown and underparts, and black-and-white face pattern; male has blue-grey mantle, female has olive-brown wash to mantle. Head is entirely orange in *Z. c. citrina*, which occurs as a winter visitor to southern India. Damp, shady places in forest, often in wet ravines. AN: nr, GO: nr, KA: nr, KE: nr, MH: nr, TN: lcr

Scaly Thrush *Zoothera dauma* 26–27 cm
a ADULT *Z. d. neilgherriensis*; **b** ADULT *Z. d. dauma* Boldly scaled upperparts and underparts. *Z. d. neilgherriensis*, resident in the Western Ghats, differs from the migrant nominate race in having darker, browner and more uniform upperparts, plainer face (lacking prominent dark patches) and longer bill. Thick forest with dense undergrowth, often near streams. AN: v, KA: nr, KE: nr, MH: nr, TN: nr

Tickell's Thrush *Turdus unicolor* 21 cm

a MALE, **b** FEMALE and **c** 1ST-WINTER MALE Small thrush. Male is pale bluish grey, with whitish belly and vent. Female and first-winter male have pale throat and submoustachial stripe, dark malar stripe, and often have spotting on breast. Open broadleaved forest. AN: nw, GO: nw, KA: nw, MH: v

Eurasian Blackbird *Turdus merula* 25–28 cm

a MALE and **b** FEMALE *T. m. nigropileus*; **c** MALE and **d** FEMALE *T. m. simillimus*; **e** MALE and **f** FEMALE *T. m. bourdilloni* The southern Indian races of Eurasian Blackbird are distinct from those races occurring in the Himalayas, and deserve full taxonomic examination since separate species are likely to be involved. Male *nigropileus* (Satpuras and N Western Ghats) has blackish crown and ear-coverts that contrast with fawn-brown throat and neck, resulting in pronounced dark cap and pale collar; mantle is brownish grey, with slate-grey wings, and underparts are pale brown with greyer flanks and vent. Female *nigropileus* has browner crown and ear-coverts, and capped appearance is less marked. Male *spencei* (Eastern Ghats) is similar to male *nigropileus* but with browner crown and ear-coverts, resulting in less marked cap and collar; underparts similar but with whiter center of belly and vent. Female *spencei* is rather uniform brown above, lacking capped appearance; underparts paler brown with whiter centre of belly and vent. Male *simillimus* (Western Ghats south of *nigropileus*, e.g. Palnis) is similar to *nigropileus* but with less distinct capped appearance owing to browner crown and richer dark brown upperparts, and has more uniform darker brown underparts, including belly and vent. Female *simillimus* is fairly uniform dark brown, including on belly and vent. Male *bourdilloni* (Kerala hills south of *simillimus*) is fairly uniform brownish slate-grey, slightly paler and browner on underparts (with a slight suggestion of a darker cap in some); closest to *simillimus* in appearance but more uniform in coloration. Female *bourdilloni* is browner than male and much as female *simillimus*. AN: nr, GO: nr?, KA: lcr, KE: nr, MH: nr, TN: lcr

Asian Brown Flycatcher *Muscicapa dauurica* 13 cm
ADULT Large bill with prominent pale base to lower mandible. Pale underparts, with light brownish wash to breast and flanks. Open broadleaved forest. AN: nw, GO: nw, KA: lcw, KE: nw, MH: nr, TN: nw

Rusty-tailed Flycatcher *Muscicapa ruficauda* 14 cm
ADULT Rufous uppertail-coverts and tail, rather plain face, and pale orange lower mandible. Forests. AN: np, GO: nw, KA: np, KE: nw, MH: nw, TN: v

Brown-breasted Flycatcher *Muscicapa muttui* 14 cm
ADULT Compared with Asian Brown, has larger bill with entirely pale lower mandible, pale legs and feet, rufous-buff edges to greater coverts and tertials, and slightly rufescent tone to rump and tail. Crown and nape are darker and greyer than olive-brown mantle. Dense thickets in evergreen forest. AN: np, GO: nw, KA: np, KE: nw, MH: v, TN: v

Red-throated Flycatcher *Ficedula parva* 11.5–12.5 cm
a MALE and **b** FEMALE *F. p. parva*; **c** MALE *F. p. albicilla* White sides to tail. Male has reddish-orange throat. Female and many males have whitish underparts with greyish breast-band. Frequently calls with a distinctive sharp *chack* and rattling *purrr*. Open forest, bushes and wooded areas. AN: cw, GO: nw, KA: lcw, KE: nw, MH: nw, TN: nw

Kashmir Flycatcher *Ficedula subrubra* 13 cm
a MALE and **b** FEMALE Male has more extensive and deeper red on underparts than Red-throated, with diffuse black border to throat and breast. Female and first-winter male can rather resemble some male Red-throated, but coloration of throat is more rufous, and this coloration is often more pronounced on breast than throat and often continues as wash onto belly and/or flanks. Open broadleaved forest. Globally threatened. AN: v, MH: v, TN: nw

Ultramarine Flycatcher *Ficedula superciliaris* 12 cm
a MALE, **b** FEMALE and **c** 1ST-YEAR MALE Male has deep blue upperparts and sides of neck/breast, and white underparts. Female has greyish-brown breast-side patches and lacks rufous on rump/uppertail-coverts. First-winter/first-summer male resembles female but with blue cast to upperparts. Winters in open woodland and wooded areas. AN: nw, GO: v, KA: nw, MH: nw

Black-and-orange Flycatcher *Ficedula nigrorufa* 11 cm
a MALE and **b** FEMALE Male rufous-orange and black; female duller. Evergreen sholas and moist thickets in ravines. GO: nr?, KA: nr, KE: nr, TN: lcr

Verditer Flycatcher *Eumyias thalassina* 15 cm

a MALE and **b** FEMALE Partial migrant; common and widespread in summer, 1200–2625 m, uncommon up to 3200 m and down to 1000 m; occasionally recorded in winter, mainly 75–350 m. Male greenish blue, with black lores. Female duller and greyer, with dusky lores. Open forest and wooded areas, especially of broadleaved species. AN: nw, GO: nw, KA: nw, KE: nw, MH: nw, TN: nw

Nilgiri Flycatcher *Eumyias albicaudata* 15 cm

a MALE and **b** FEMALE White on tail-base and diffuse whitish fringes to blue-grey undertail-coverts. Male indigo-blue, with blue-grey belly, black lores, and bright blue forehead and supercilium. Female blue-grey, paler on underparts. Evergreen biotope in hills. GO: nr?, KA: nr, KE: cr, TN: lcr

White-bellied Blue Flycatcher *Cyornis pallipes* 15 cm

a MALE and **b** FEMALE Large bill, and lacks white at base of tail. Male indigo-blue, with white belly and unmarked undertail-coverts (compare with Nilgiri Flycatcher). Female has orange-red throat and breast, and greyish head; these features more striking than in female Blue-throated; also has more extensive cream lores, brighter chestnut tail, and has longer bill than that species. Undergrowth in dense evergreen forest. GO: nr, KA: nr, KE: nr, MH: nr, TN: nr

Pale-chinned Flycatcher *Cyornis poliogenys* 18 cm

a MALE and **b** FEMALE Male has variable bluish-slate coloration to upperparts (some with bluish coloration restricted to head); bluest birds resemble female Tickell's Blue Flycatcher, and are best told by more uniform creamy-orange underparts (especially throat, lower breast and flanks, which are whiter on Tickell's), narrow whitish eye-ring and paler pinkish legs; tail can be either bluish slate or rufescent brown (younger males?). Female is more olive-brown on mantle, and orange on underparts is paler and less extensive; tail and uppertail-coverts are rufescent brown. Bushes and undergrowth in broadleaved forest. AN: nr

Blue-throated Flycatcher *Cyornis rubeculoides* 14 cm

a MALE and **b** FEMALE Male has blue throat (some with orange wedge) and well-defined white belly and flanks. Female has poorly defined creamy-orange throat, orange breast well demarcated from white belly, and creamy lores (compare with female Pale-chinned). Olive-brown head and upperparts and rufescent tail are best features separating it from female Tickell's. Open forest and wooded areas. AN: nw, GO: nw, KA: nw, KE: nw, MH: v, TN: nw

Tickell's Blue Flycatcher *Cyornis tickelliae* 14 cm

a MALE and **b** FEMALE Male has orange throat and breast, with clear horizontal division from white flanks and belly. Female has greyish-blue upperparts (especially rump and tail). Open dry broadleaved forest. AN: cr, GO: cr, KA: nr, KE: nr, MH: nr, TN: nr

Grey-headed Canary Flycatcher *Culicicapa ceylonensis* 13 cm

ADULT Grey head and breast, rest of underparts yellow, and greenish upperparts. Forest and wooded areas. AN: nw, GO: nw, KA: nw, KE: lcr, MH: nw, TN: lcr

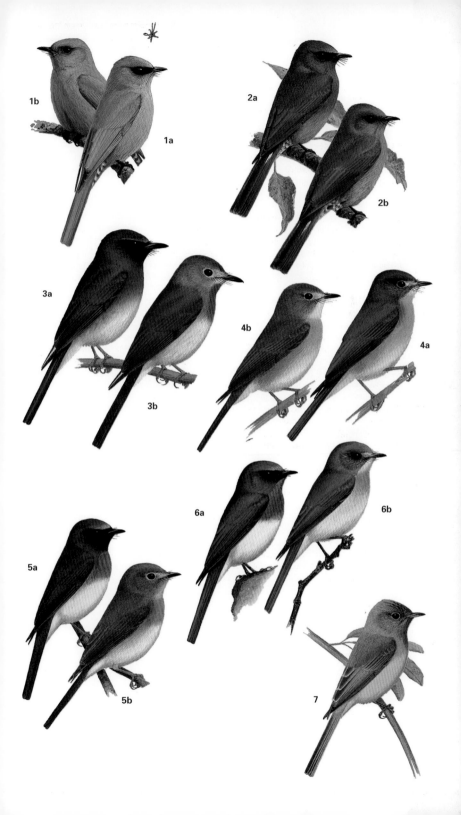

1

White-bellied Shortwing *Brachypteryx major* 15 cm
a ADULT *B. m. major*; **b** ADULT *B. m. albiventris* Slaty-blue upperparts and breast, and white belly. Flanks rufous in nominate *major* from S Karnataka and N Tamil Nadu, and grey in *albiventris* from Kerala and W Tamil Nadu. Dense undergrowth in ravines and evergreen forest. KA: nr, KE: nr, TN: lcr

2

Siberian Rubythroat *Luscinia calliope* 14 cm
a MALE and **b** FEMALE Olive-brown upperparts and tail, and white supercilium and moustachial stripe. Adult male and first-winter male have ruby-red throat and grey breast. Female has olive-buff wash to breast. *See* Appendix for differences from White-tailed Rubythroat. Bushes and thick undergrowth, often near water. AN: nw, MH: v

3

Bluethroat *Luscinia svecica* 15 cm
a MALE NON-BREEDING, **b** 1ST-WINTER FEMALE and **c** MALE BREEDING White supercilium and rufous tail sides. Male has variable blue, black and rufous patterning to throat and breast (patterning obscured by whitish fringes in fresh plumage). Female is less brightly coloured but usually with blue and rufous breast-bands. First-winter female may have just black submoustachial stripe and band of black spotting across breast. Winters in scrub and tall grass. AN: nw, GO: nw, KA: lcw, KE: nw, MH: cw

4

Indian Blue Robin *Luscinia brunnea* 15 cm
a MALE and **b** FEMALE Male has blue upperparts and orange underparts, with white supercilium and black ear-coverts. Female has olive-brown upperparts and buffish underparts with white throat and belly. Forest, secondary scrub and plantations. AN: np, GO: np, KA: nwp, KE: nw, MH: nw, TN: nw

5

Oriental Magpie Robin *Copsychus saularis* 23 cm
a MALE and **b** FEMALE Black/slate-grey and white, with white on wing and at sides of tail. Gardens, groves, open broadleaved forest and secondary growth. AN: cr, GO: cr, KA: cr, KE: cr, MH: cr, TN: cr

6

White-rumped Shama *Copsychus malabaricus* 22 cm
a MALE and **b** FEMALE Long, graduated tail and white rump. Male has glossy blue-black upperparts and breast, and rufous-orange underparts. Female duller, with brownish-grey upperparts. Undergrowth in broadleaved forest. AN: nr, GO: nr, KA: nr, KE: nr, MH: nr, TN: nr

7

Brown Rock-chat *Cercomela fusca* 17 cm
ADULT Both sexes uniform brown, with more rufescent underparts. Buildings in open country. MH: nr

1

Indian Robin *Saxicoloides fulicata* 19 cm
a MALE and **b** FEMALE Reddish vent and black tail in all plumages. Male has white shoulders and black underparts. Female has greyish underparts. Dry stony areas with scrub, and cultivation edges. AN: cr, GO: nr, KA: cr, KE: cr, MH: cr, MV: v, TN: cr

2

Black Redstart *Phoenicurus ochruros* 15 cm
a MALE and **b** FEMALE Male has blackish upperparts and breast, and rufous underparts. Female is dusky-brown with orange-buff wash to flanks and vent. Cultivation, stony areas and thin scrub. AN: cw, GO: nw, KA: nw, KE: v, MH: nw, TN: nw

3

Common Stonechat *Saxicola torquata* 17 cm
a MALE BREEDING, **b** MALE NON-BREEDING and **c** FEMALE Male has black head, white patch on neck, orange breast and whitish rump (features obscured in fresh plumage). Female has streaked upperparts and orange on breast and rump. Winters in scrub, reedbeds and cultivation. AN: nw, GO: nw, KA: nw, KE: nw, MH: nw, TN: nw

4

Pied Bushchat *Saxicola caprata* 13.5 cm
a MALE BREEDING, **b** FEMALE and **c** 1ST-WINTER MALE Male black, with white rump and wing-patch; rufous fringes to body in non-breeding and first-winter plumages. Female has dark brown upperparts and rufous-brown underparts, with rufous-orange rump. Mainly cultivation and open country with scattered bushes or tall grass. AN: cr, GO: nr, KA: lcr, KE: nr, MH: nr, TN: lcr

5

Desert Wheatear *Oenanthe deserti* 14–15 cm
a MALE BREEDING, **b** MALE NON-BREEDING and **c** FEMALE NON-BREEDING Sandy-brown upperparts, with largely black tail and contrasting white rump. Male has black throat (partly obscured by pale fringes in fresh plumage). Female has blackish centres to wing-coverts and tertials in fresh plumage and largely black wings when worn (useful distinction from Isabelline). Arid, semi-desert and open fields. AN: v, GO: v, KE: v, MH: nw, TN: v

6

Isabelline Wheatear *Oenanthe isabellina* 16.5 cm
ADULT Rather plain sandy-brown and buff. Tail shorter than in Desert, with more white at base and sides. Has paler, sandy-brown wings with contrasting dark alula (lacking black centres to coverts and tertials/secondaries). *See* Appendix for comparison with Northern and Rufous-tailed wheatears. Dry cultivation. GO: v, MH: nw, MV: np

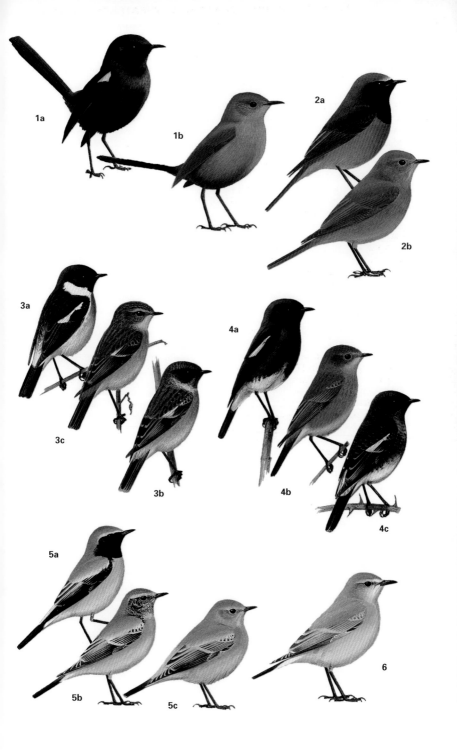

Chestnut-tailed Starling *Sturnus malabaricus* 20 cm
a ADULT and **b** JUVENILE *S. m. malabaricus*; **c** MALE *S. m. blythii* Adult *malabaricus* has grey upperparts, rufous underparts and chestnut tail. Juvenile is rather uniform, with rufous sides and tips to outer tail feathers. Male *S. m. blythii*, of the southwest peninsula, has whitish head and breast (with white confined to forehead and forecrown in female). Open wooded areas and groves. AN: np, GO: nr?, KA: nr, KE: nr, MH: nr, TN: cw

Brahminy Starling *Sturnus pagodarum* 21 cm
a ADULT and **b** JUVENILE Adult has black crest and rufous-orange sides of head and underparts. Juvenile lacks crest; has grey-brown cap and paler orange-buff underparts. Dry, well-wooded areas and thorn scrub. AN: cr, GO: nr?, KA: nr, KE: cr, MH: nr, TN: lcr

Rosy Starling *Sturnus roseus* 21 cm
a ADULT and **b** JUVENILE Adult has blackish head with shaggy crest, pinkish mantle and underparts, and blue-green gloss to wings. In non-breeding and first-winter plumage, much duller than shown; pink of plumage partly obscured by buff fringes, black obscured by greyish fringes. Juvenile mainly sandy-brown, with stout yellowish bill and broad pale fringes to wing feathers. Cultivation and damp grassland. AN: cw, GO: nw, KA: cw, KE: nw, MH: cw, TN: nw

Common Starling *Sturnus vulgaris* 21 cm
a ADULT BREEDING, **b** ADULT NON-BREEDING and **c** JUVENILE Adult is metallic green and purple; heavily marked with buff and white in winter. Juvenile is dusky brown with whiter throat. Cultivation and damp grassland. AN: v, GO: v, KA: nw, KE: v, MH: nw, MV: v, TN: v

Asian Pied Starling *Sturnus contra* 23 cm
a ADULT and **b** JUVENILE Adult is black and white, with orange orbital skin and large, pointed yellowish bill. Juvenile has brown plumage in place of black. Cultivation, damp grassland and habitation. AN: nr, MH: nr, TN: nr

Common Myna *Acridotheres tristis* 25 cm
a **b** ADULT Brownish myna with yellow orbital skin, white wing-patch and white tail-tip. Juvenile duller. Habitation and cultivation. AN: cr, GO: nr, KA: cr, KE: cr, MH: cr, MV: irx/v, TN: cr

Bank Myna *Acridotheres ginginianus* 23 cm
a **b** ADULT and **c** JUVENILE Orange-red orbital patch, orange-yellow bill, and tufted forehead. Wing-patch, underwing-coverts and tail-tip orange-buff. Adult is bluish grey with blackish cap. Juvenile duller and browner than adult. Cultivation, damp grassland near villages, often associated with grazing animals. AN: nr, GO: nr, KA: nr, MH: nr, TN: v

Jungle Myna *Acridotheres fuscus* 23 cm
ADULT Tufted forehead, and white wing-patch and tail-tip; lacks bare orbital skin. Juvenile browner, with reduced forehead tuft. Cultivation near well-wooded areas, and edges of habitation. AN: nr, GO: cr, KA: cr, KE: nr, MH: nr, TN: lcr

Hill Myna *Gracula religiosa* 25–29 cm
ADULT Large myna with yellow wattles, large orange-yellow bill and white wing-patches. Juvenile has duller bill, paler yellow wattles and less gloss to plumage. Moist broadleaved forest. AN: nr, GO: nr, KA: nr, KE: cr, MH: nr, TN: lcr

Chestnut-bellied Nuthatch *Sitta castanea* 12 cm
a MALE and **b** FEMALE Male has deep chestnut underparts and white cheeks. Female has paler cinnamon-brown on underparts. Broadleaved forest and groves. AN: nr, GO: v, KA: nr, KE: nr, MH: nr, TN: nr

Velvet-fronted Nuthatch *Sitta frontalis* 10 cm
MALE Violet-blue upperparts, black forehead, black-tipped red bill and lilac underparts. Female is as male but lacks black eye-stripe. Open broadleaved forest and well-wooded areas. AN: nr, GO: nr, KA: nr, KE: cr, MH: nr, TN: lcr

Spotted Creeper *Salpornis spilonotus* 13 cm
ADULT Long, downcurved bill, and shortish tail. Plumage spotted with white. Open deciduous forest and groves. AN: nr, MH: nr

Great Tit *Parus major* 14 cm
ADULT Black breast centre and line down belly, greyish mantle, greyish-white breast sides and flanks, and white wing-bar. Juvenile has yellowish-white cheeks and underparts, and yellowish-olive wash to mantle. Open forest and well-wooded country, favours broadleaves. AN: nr, GO: nr?, KA: lcr, KE: nr, MH: nr, TN: lcr

White-naped Tit *Parus nuchalis* 12 cm
ADULT Black mantle and wing-coverts (grey on Great Tit); much white on tertials and at bases of secondaries and primaries. Thorn-scrub forest. AN: nr, KA: nr

Black-lored Tit *Parus xanthogenys* 13 cm
a MALE and **b** FEMALE *P. x. aplonotus*; **c** FEMALE *P. x. travancoreensis* Male *P. x. aplonotus*, of northern and eastern peninsula, has black crest, yellow cheeks, black centre to yellow throat and breast, and greenish upperparts. Female *aplonotus* is duller than male, with greyish-olive throat and centre to breast, and paler yellow cheeks and underparts. Male *P. x. travancoreensis*, of southern peninsula, is similar to male *aplonotus* but duller; female *travancoreensis* is similar to female *aplonotus* but has greyish-olive crest. Open forest, forest edges and groves. AN: nr, GO: nr, KA: lcr, KE: lcr, MH: nr, TN: nr

Sand Martin *Riparia riparia* 13 cm
a **b** **c** ADULT White throat and half-collar, and brown breast-band. Very similar to Pale Martin; upperparts darker brown, breast-band clearly defined and tail-fork deeper. Rivers and lakes. GO: v, KA: v, LS: v, MH: nw, MV: np, TN: v

Pale Martin *Riparia diluta* 13 cm
a **b** **c** ADULT Upperparts paler and greyer than on Sand and Plain martins; throat greyish white; breast-band not clearly defined; tail-fork very shallow. Rivers and lakes. GO: v, MH: nw

Plain Martin *Riparia paludicola* 12 cm
a **b** **c** ADULT Pale brownish-grey throat and breast, merging into dingy-white rest of underparts; some have suggestion of breast-band. Underwing darker than on Sand and Pale, flight weaker and more fluttering, and has shallower indent to tail. Upperparts darker than on Pale. Rivers and lakes. AN: v, GO: v, KA: v, KE: v, MH: nr, MV: v

Eurasian Crag Martin *Hirundo rupestris* 15 cm

 a **b** **c** ADULT Larger and stockier than the *Riparia* martins. Dark underwing-coverts, dusky throat, and brown flanks and undertail-coverts (the latter with pale fringes). Lacks breast-band. Shows white spots in tail when spread. Rocky cliffs and gorges. GO: nw, KA: nw, MH: nw, TN: nw

Dusky Crag Martin *Hirundo concolor* 13 cm

 a **b** **c** ADULT Upperparts and underparts dark brown and rather uniform. Cliffs, gorges and old buildings. AN: cr, GO: nr, KA: nr, KE: nr, MH: cr, TN: nr

Barn Swallow *Hirundo rustica* 18 cm

 a **b** **c** ADULT and **d** JUVENILE Reddish throat, long tail-streamers, and blue-black breast-band. Juvenile duller; lacks tail-streamers. Cultivation, habitation, lakes and rivers. AN: cw, GO: nw, KA: cw, KE: cw, LS: np, MH: cw, MV: nw, TN: lcw

Pacific Swallow *Hirundo tahitica* 13 cm

 a **b** ADULT Told from Barn by more extensive rufous on throat, lack of breast-band, dingy underparts and underwing-coverts, and blackish undertail-coverts with whitish fringes; lacks tail-streamers. Grassy hills, rivers and habitation. GO: v, KA: nr, KE: nr, TN: lcr

Wire-tailed Swallow *Hirundo smithii* 14 cm

 a **b** **c** ADULT and **d** JUVENILE Chestnut crown, white underparts, and fine tail projections. Juvenile has brownish cast to blue upperparts, and dull brownish crown. Open country and cultivation near fresh waters. AN: cr, GO: cr, KA: lcr, KE: nr, MH: nr, TN: nw

Red-rumped Swallow *Hirundo daurica* 16–17 cm

 a **b** **c** ADULT and **d** JUVENILE Rufous-orange neck-sides and rump, finely streaked buffish-white underparts, and black undertail-coverts. Cultivation and upland pastures. AN: cr, GO: cr, KA: cr, KE: nr, LS: np, MH: nr, MV: v, TN: lcr

Streak-throated Swallow *Hirundo fluvicola* 11 cm

 a **b** **c** ADULT and **d** JUVENILE Small, with slight fork to long, broad tail. Chestnut crown, streaked throat and breast, white mantle streaks and brownish rump. Juvenile is duller, with browner crown. Rivers and lakes. AN: nr, GO: nr?, KA: nr, KE: v, MH: nr, MV: v, TN: v

Northern House Martin *Delichon urbica* 12 cm

a **b** **c** ADULT Striking contrast between blue-black upperparts and white underparts, and with prominent white rump. Tail is deeply forked. *See* Appendix for differences from Asian House Martin. AN: v, GO: nw, KA: nw, KE: nw, LS: np, MH: nw, MV: nw, TN: nw

Grey-headed Bulbul *Pycnonotus priocephalus* 19 cm
ADULT Crestless grey-and-green bulbul. Greyish head, greenish-yellow forehead, and yellowish bill and iris. Tail appears grey at rest, but in flight shows blackish outer feathers with grey tips. Some birds have olive-green head and greener coloration to rump and tail. Evergreen forest and dense thickets. GO: nr, KA: nr, KE: nr, MH: nr, TN: nr

Black-crested Bulbul *Pycnonotus melanicterus* 19 cm
a ADULT *P. m. gularis*; **b** ADULT *P. m. flaviventris* Black head, yellow underparts and uniform greenish upperparts. *P. m. gularis*, of the Western Ghats, lacks crest and has a ruby-red throat. *P. m. flaviventris*, which occurs in the northeastern peninsula, has a prominent crest and black throat. Moist broadleaved forest and thick secondary growth. AN: nr, GO: nr, KA: nr, KE: nr, MH: nr, TN: nr

Red-whiskered Bulbul *Pycnonotus jocosus* 20 cm
a ADULT and **b** JUVENILE Black crest, red 'whiskers', white underparts with complete or broken breast-band, and red vent. Juvenile duller and lacks 'whiskers'. Open forest and secondary growth. AN: cr, GO: cr, KA: cr, KE: cr, MH: cr, TN: cr

Red-vented Bulbul *Pycnonotus cafer* 20 cm
ADULT Blackish head with slight crest, scaled appearance to upperparts and breast, red vent and white rump. Open deciduous forest, secondary growth and trees around habitation. AN: cr, GO: cr, KA: cr, KE: cr, MH: cr, TN: cr

Yellow-throated Bulbul *Pycnonotus xantholaemus* 20 cm
ADULT Plain yellow-green head, bright yellow throat, grey breast-band, and yellow undertail-coverts and tail-tip. Thorn jungle and moist deciduous habitats in stony hills. AN: nr, KA: nr, KE: xr, TN: nr

White-browed Bulbul *Pycnonotus luteolus* 20 cm
ADULT White supercilium and crescent below eye, and dark eye-stripe and moustachial stripe. Otherwise nondescript. Dry scrub and forest edges. AN: nr, GO: cr, KA: lcr, KE: nr, MH: nr, TN: cr

Yellow-browed Bulbul *Iole indica* 20 cm
ADULT Yellow supercilium, eye-ring and underparts. Striking black bill and dark eye. Moist forest and secondary growth. AN: nr, GO: nr, KA: nr, KE: cr, MH: nr, TN: nr

Black Bulbul *Hypsipetes leucocephalus* 25 cm
ADULT Slate-grey bulbul with black crest. Has shallow fork to tail, and red bill, legs and feet. Mainly broadleaved forest. GO: nr?, KA: nr, KE: nr, MH: nr, TN: lcr

In the gooseberry tree.

Zitting Cisticola *Cisticola juncidis* 10 cm
a ADULT BREEDING and **b** ADULT NON-BREEDING Small, with short tail that has prominent white tip. Bold streaking on buff upperparts, including nape, and thin whitish supercilium. Tail is longer in non-breeding plumage. Song, uttered in display flight, is a repetitive *pip pip pip...*; call is a single *plit*. Fields and grassland. AN: cr, GO: nr, KA: cr, KE: cr, MH: ns, TN: nr

Bright-headed Cisticola *Cisticola exilis* 10 cm
a MALE BREEDING and **b** NON-BREEDING Breeding males have unstreaked rufous head and underparts. Female and non-breeding male have streaked crown and more closely resemble Zitting; best told from the latter by unstreaked rufous nape, rufous supercilium and neck sides, blacker crown and mantle with less distinct streaking, and longer and more uniformly dark tail with narrow buff tips. Tail is longer in non-breeding plumage. Song is a *cheeezz...joo-ee, di-do*, given in display flight or from perch; the *cheeezz* often given alone. Tall grassland; scrubby hillsides in S India. AN: nr, KA: nr, KE: nr, MH: nr, TN: nr

Rufous-fronted Prinia *Prinia buchanani* 12 cm
ADULT Rufous-brown crown and broad white tip to tail (very prominent in flight). Call is a distinctive rippling trill. Rufous to crown may be difficult to see when worn. Upperparts uniform pale rufous-brown on juvenile. Scrub in semi-desert. AN: nr, MH: nr

Rufescent Prinia *Prinia rufescens* 11 cm
a ADULT BREEDING and **b** ADULT NON-BREEDING Grey cast to crown, nape and ear-coverts in summer. In non-breeding plumage has more rufescent mantle and edgings to tertials, and has stronger buffish wash to throat and breast, compared with Grey-breasted. Buzzing call and large bill are also helpful features. Tall grassland, grass under forest and secondary growth. AN: nr

Grey-breasted Prinia *Prinia hodgsonii* 11 cm
a ADULT BREEDING and **b** ADULT NON-BREEDING Small size. Diffuse grey breast-band in summer. In non-breeding plumage has fine dark bill, fine whitish supercilium, grey-brown upperparts with rufescent cast to wings, and whitish underparts. Where range overlaps with Rufescent, non-breeding is best distinguished by finer bill, grey-brown tail, greyish wash to sides of neck and breast, and laughing, high-pitched call. Bushes at forest edges, scrub and secondary growth. AN: cr, GO: nr, KA: nr, KE: cr, MH: cr, TN: nr

Jungle Prinia *Prinia sylvatica* 13 cm
a ADULT BREEDING and **b** ADULT NON-BREEDING Larger than Plain, with stouter bill and uniform wing. In breeding plumage has greyer upperparts, dark lores and bill, and shorter tail with prominent white outertail feathers. More rufescent in non-breeding plumage, with prominent supercilium, and longer tail. Song is a loud, pulsing *zong zee chu*, repeated monotonously; calls include a dry rattle and a loud *tiu*. Scrub and tall grass in open dry areas. AN: nr, GO: ?, KA: lcr, KE: nr, MH: nr, TN: lcr

Ashy Prinia *Prinia socialis* 13 cm
ADULT BREEDING Slate-grey crown and ear-coverts, red eyes, slate-grey or rufous-brown upperparts, and orange-buff wash to underparts. Tall grass and scrub, open secondary growth, reedbeds and forest edges. AN: cr, GO: nr, KA: lcr, KE: lcr, MH: cr, TN: cr

Plain Prinia *Prinia inornata* 13 cm
a ADULT BREEDING and **b** ADULT NON-BREEDING *P. i. inornata*; **c** ADULT BREEDING *P. i. franklinii* Smaller than Jungle, with finer bill and pale or rufous fringes to tertials. Song is a rapid wheezy trill, *tlick-tlick-tlick...*; calls include a plaintive *tee-tee*-Reeds, grassland, edges of cultivation, scrub and forest edges. AN: nr, GO: nr, KA: lcr, KE: lcr, MH: cr, TN: cr

Oriental White-eye *Zosterops palpebrosus* 10 cm
ADULT Black lores and white eye-ring, bright yellow throat and breast, and whitish belly. Open broadleaved forest and wooded areas. AN: nr, GO: nr, KA: cr, KE: nr, LS: cr, MH: cr, TN: cr

1   Pale-footed Bush Warbler *Cettia pallidipes*   11 cm
ADULT Pale pinkish legs and feet. Upperparts rufescent brown, with white underparts and supercilium. Song is a loud, explosive *zip...zip-tschuck-o-tschuck*. Tall grass and bushes at forest edges. AN: nr

2   Grasshopper Warbler *Locustella naevia*   13 cm
a b ADULT Streaked olive-brown upperparts, indistinct supercilium, and (usually) unmarked or only lightly streaked throat and breast. *See* Appendix for comparison with Rusty-rumped Warbler. Tall grassland, reedbeds and paddy-fields. AN: nw, GO: v, KA: nw, KE: nw, MH: nw, TN: v

3   Paddyfield Warbler *Acrocephalus agricola*   13 cm
a ADULT FRESH and **b** ADULT WORN Prominent white supercilium behind eye, and stout bill with dark tip. Often shows dark edge to supercilium. Rufous cast to upperparts in fresh plumage. Typically shows dark centres and pale edges to tertials (wings usually uniform in Blyth's Reed). (*See also* Table 6 on p.233.) Reedbeds and damp grassland. AN: nw, GO: nw, KA: nw, KE: nw, MH: nw, TN: nw

4   Blyth's Reed Warbler *Acrocephalus dumetorum*   14 cm
a ADULT FRESH and **b** ADULT WORN Long bill, olive-brown to olive-grey upperparts, and uniform wings. Supercilium indistinct compared with Paddyfield, barely apparent behind eye. (*See also* Table 6 on p.233.) Bushes and trees at edges of forest and cultivation. AN: cw, GO: cw, KA: cw, KE: cw, LS: v, MH: cw, MV: v, TN: lcw

5   Clamorous Reed Warbler *Acrocephalus stentoreus*   19 cm
ADULT Large size, long bill, short primary projection, and whitish supercilium. Reedbeds and bushes around wetlands. AN: nw, GO: nr?, KA: nr, KE: nr, MH: nr?, TN: nw

6   Thick-billed Warbler *Acrocephalus aedon*   19 cm
ADULT Large size. Short, stout bill and rounded head. 'Plain-faced' appearance, lacking prominent supercilium or eye-stripe. Tall grass, scrub, reeds and bushes at edges of forest and cultivation. AN: nw, GO: nw, KA: nw, KE: nw, MH: nw, TN: nw

7   Booted Warbler *Hippolais caligata*   12 cm
a ADULT *H. c. caligata*; **b** ADULT *H. c. rama* Small size and *Phylloscopus*-like behaviour (especially *caligata*). Tail looks long and square-ended, and undertail-coverts look short. Often shows faint whitish edges and tip to tail and fringes to tertials. Supercilium usually fairly distinct, and often shows dark upper edge in *caligata*. (*See also* Table 6 on p.233.) Scrub and bushes at cultivation edges in dry habitats. AN: cw, GO: nw, KA: nw, KE: nw, MH: cw, TN: lcw

8   Common Tailorbird *Orthotomus sutorius*   13 cm
a MALE and **b** FEMALE Rufous forehead, greenish upperparts, and whitish underparts, including undertail-coverts. Bushes in gardens, cultivation edges and forest edges. AN: cr, GO: cr, KA: cr, KE: cr, MH: cr, TN: cr

1

Common Chiffchaff *Phylloscopus collybita*   11 cm
ADULT Brownish to greyish upperparts; olive-green edges to wing-coverts, remiges and rectrices. Black bill and legs. No wing-bar. (*See also* Table 2 on p.231.) Forest, bushes and secondary growth. GO: nw, KA: nw, MH: nw, TN: v

2

Dusky Warbler *Phylloscopus fuscatus*   11 cm
ADULT Brown upperparts and whitish underparts, with buff flanks. Prominent supercilium, and hard *chack* call. (*See also* Table 2 on p.231.) Bushes and long grass, especially near water. MH: nw

3

Tickell's Leaf Warbler *Phylloscopus affinis*   11 cm
ADULT FRESH Dark greenish to greenish-brown upperparts, and bright yellow supercilium and underparts. (*See also* Table 2 on p.231.) *Chit* call. Breeds in open country with bushes; winters in bushes at edges of forest and cultivation. AN: nw, GO: nw, KA: nw, KE: nw, MH: nw, TN: lcw

4

Sulphur-bellied Warbler *Phylloscopus griseolus*   11 cm
ADULT FRESH Dark greyish upperparts, bright yellow supercilium, and dusky yellow underparts strongly washed with buff. (*See also* Table 2 on p.231.) Soft *quip* call. Has distinctive habit of climbing about rocks and nuthatch-like on tree trunks and branches. Rocky areas and around old buildings. AN: nw, GO: nw, KA: nw, MH: nw, TN: v

5

Hume's Warbler *Phylloscopus humei*   10–11 cm
a ADULT FRESH and **b** ADULT WORN Has buffish or whitish wing-bars and supercilium. Bill appears all-dark, and legs are normally blackish brown. (*See also* Table 4 on p.232.) Call is a rolling *whit-hoo*. *See* Appendix for comparison with Yellow-browed Warbler. Winters in forest and secondary growth. AN: nw, GO: nw, KA: nw, KE: nw, MH: nw, TN: v

6

Greenish Warbler *Phylloscopus trochiloides*   10–11 cm
a ADULT FRESH and **b** ADULT WORN *P. t. viridanus*; **c** ADULT FRESH *P. t. nitidus* Slurred, loud *chli-wee* call. No crown-stripe; fine wing-bar (sometimes two). (*See also* Table 3 on p.231.) Well-wooded areas. AN: nw, GO: cw, KA: cw, KE: cw, MH: nw, TN: cw

7

Large-billed Leaf Warbler *Phylloscopus magnirostris*   13 cm
ADULT FRESH Clear, loud *der-tee* call is best feature separating it from Greenish. Large, with large dark bill. Very bold yellow-white supercilium and broad dark eye-stripe. (*See also* Table 3 on p.231.) Forest. AN: nw, GO: nw, KA: nw, KE: cw, MH: nw, TN: nw

8

Tytler's Leaf Warbler *Phylloscopus tytleri*   11 cm
ADULT FRESH Slender, mainly dark bill, long fine supercilium, no wing-bars, shortish tail. (*See also* Table 2 on p.231.) Forest. KA: nw, KE: v, MH: nw, TN: v

1 Western Crowned Warbler *Phylloscopus occipitalis* 11 cm

ADULT FRESH Pale crown-stripe, large size, greyish-green upperparts, and greyish-white underparts. *See* Appendix for comparison with Blyth's Leaf Warbler. (*See also* Table 5 on p.232.) Winters in moist deciduous and evergreen forests. AN: nw, GO: nw, KA: nw, KE: cw, MH: nw, TN: nw

2 Golden-spectacled Warbler *Seicercus burkii* 10 cm

ADULT Yellow eye-ring, dark sides to crown, and yellow underparts. *See* Appendix for comparison with Whistler's Warbler. Forest understorey and secondary growth. AN: nw, MH: v

3 Striated Grassbird *Megalurus palustris* 25 cm

ADULT Streaked upperparts, finely streaked breast and long, graduated tail. Has longer and finer bill and more prominent supercilium than Bristled. Tall damp grassland and reedbeds. MH: nr

4 Bristled Grassbird *Chaetornis striatus* 20 cm

ADULT Streaked upperparts and fine streaking on lower throat. Has shorter, stouter bill and less prominent supercilium than Striated; also shorter and broader tail with buffish-white tips. Short grassland with scattered bushes and some tall vegetation. Globally threatened. AN: nr, MH: nr, TN: nr

5 Broad-tailed Grassbird *Schoenicola platyura* 18 cm

a ADULT FRESH and **b** ADULT WORN Stout bill, long and broad tail, unstreaked rufous-brown to greyish-brown upperparts, and whitish underparts. Tail diffusely barred. Tall grass and reeds on open hillsides. AN: nr, KA: nr, KE: nr, TN: nr

6 Lesser Whitethroat *Sylvia curruca* 13 cm

a ADULT *S. c. blythi*; **b** ADULT *S. c. althaea* Brownish-grey upperparts, grey crown with darker ear-coverts, blackish bill, and dark grey legs and feet. *S. c. althaea* is larger with darker head than *S. c. blythi*. Scrub. AN: nw, GO: nwp, KA: nw, KE: v, MH: nw, TN: nw

7 Orphean Warbler *Sylvia hortensis* 15 cm

a ADULT MALE, **b** ADULT FEMALE and **c** 1ST-WINTER Larger and bigger-billed than Lesser Whitethroat; more ponderous movements, and heavier appearance in flight. Adult has blackish crown, pale grey mantle, blackish tail and pale iris. First-year has crown concolorous with mantle, with darker grey ear-coverts; very similar to many Lesser Whitethroats (that species has dark iris). Orphean often shows darker-looking uppertail, eye-ring is absent or indistinct, and has greyish centres and pale fringes to undertail-coverts; these features variable and difficult to observe in the field. Scrub and groves. AN: v, GO: v, KA: nw, KE: v, MH: nw, TN: nw

1

Wynaad Laughingthrush *Garrulax delesserti* 23 cm
ADULT Slate-grey crown with blackish ear-coverts, and white throat contrasting with grey breast. Has striking yellowish or pink lower mandible. Mainly moist evergreen forest. GO: nw, KA: nr, KE: nr, TN: nr

2

Nilgiri Laughingthrush *Garrulax cachinnans* 20 cm
ADULT Prominent white supercilium, grey crown and black chin, rufous throat and breast, and rufous ear-coverts. Forest undergrowth and scrub. KE: nr, TN: lcr

3

Grey-breasted Laughingthrush *Garrulax jerdoni* 20 cm
a ADULT *G. j. fairbanki*; b ADULT *G. j. jerdoni*; c ADULT *G. j. meridionale* The race *G. j. fairbanki* occurs in N Kerala and W Tamil Nadu; *G. j. jerdoni* occurs in SW Karnataka; and *G. j. meridionale* occurs in S Kerala. White supercilium. Grey or grey-streaked white throat and breast, greyish ear-coverts. Only *jerdoni* has black chin. Thickets with wild raspberry. GO: nr, KA: nr, KE: nr, TN: lcr

4

Abbott's Babbler *Malacocincla abbotti* 17 cm
ADULT Top heavy, with large bill and rather short tail. White throat and breast, grey lores and supercilium, rufous uppertail-coverts and tail, and rufous-buff flanks and vent. Gives three to four whistled notes, *three cheers for me*, with the last note highest. Thickets in moist forest. AN: nr

5

Puff-throated Babbler *Pellorneum ruficeps* 15 cm
ADULT Rufous crown, prominent buff supercilium, white throat (often puffed out), and bold brown spotting/streaking on breast and sides of neck. Song is a halting, impulsive *swee ti-ti-hwee hwee hwee ti swee-u*, rambling up and down the scale. Undergrowth in broadleaved forest and secondary growth. AN: nr, GO: nr, KA: nr, KE: nr, MH: cr, TN: lcr

6

Indian Scimitar Babbler *Pomatorhinus horsfieldii* 22 cm
ADULT Yellow bill, white supercilium, and grey to blackish breast sides and flanks. Forest and secondary growth. AN: nr, GO: nr, KA: nr, KE: cr, MH: nr, TN: lcr

7

Rufous-fronted Babbler *Stachyris rufifrons* 12 cm
ADULT Small size, with rufous cap, olive upperparts, white throat and buff underparts. Thick undergrowth in open forest and ravines. AN: nr

8

Tawny-bellied Babbler *Dumetia hyperythra* 13 cm
a ADULT *D. h. hyperythra*; b ADULT *D. h. albogularis* Rufous-brown forehead and forecrown, and orange-buff underparts. *D. h. albogularis* of the eastern peninsula has throat concolorous with underparts; other races in region have white throat. Thorny scrub and tall grass. AN: nr, GO: nr, KA: nr, KE: nr, MH: nr, TN: nr

9

Dark-fronted Babbler *Rhopocichla atriceps* 13 cm
ADULT Stocky babbler with stout pinkish bill, blackish hood, and strikingly white underparts. Dense undergrowth in evergreen biotope. GO: nr, KA: nr, KE: cr, MH: nr, TN: lcr

1

Striped Tit Babbler *Macronous gularis* 11 cm
ADULT Rufous-brown cap, pale yellow supercilium, and finely streaked pale yellow throat and breast. Undergrowth in broadleaved forest. AN: nr, KA: nr

2

Yellow-eyed Babbler *Chrysomma sinense* 18 cm
ADULT Yellow iris and orange eye-ring, white lores and supercilium, and striking white throat and breast. Tall grass, bushes and reeds. AN: nr, GO: nr, KA: nr, KE: nr, MH: cr, TN: nr

3

Common Babbler *Turdoides caudatus* 23 cm
ADULT Streaked brownish-buff upperparts, and long tail. Unstreaked whitish throat and breast centre. Dry cultivation and scrub. AN: nr, GO: nr, KA: lcr, MH: nr, TN: cr

4

Large Grey Babbler *Turdoides malcolmi* 28 cm
ADULT Large size. Dull white sides to long, graduated tail; unmottled pinkish-grey throat and breast, pale grey forehead and dark grey lores. Open dry scrub and cultivation. AN: cr, GO: nr, KA: lcr, MH: nr, TN: nr

5

Rufous Babbler *Turdoides subrufus* 25 cm
ADULT Grey forehead and forecrown, black-and-yellow bill, blackish lores and unstreaked rufous underparts. Tall grass and bamboo at forest edges. GO: nr, KA: lcr, KE: nr, MH: nr, TN: nr

6

Jungle Babbler *Turdoides striatus* 25 cm
a ADULT *T. s. orientalis*; **b** ADULT *T. s. somervillei* Uniform tail; variable dark mottling and streaking on throat and breast. *T. s. somervillei*, of Maharashtra, is a distinctive race with orange-brown tail and dark primaries. Cultivation and secondary scrub. AN: nr, GO: cr, KA: lcr, KE: lcr, MH: cr, TN: cr

7

Yellow-billed Babbler *Turdoides affinis* 23 cm
ADULT Creamy-white crown, dark mottling on throat and breast, and pale rump and tail-base (although juvenile more similar to Jungle). Scrub. AN: cr, KA: cr, KE: cr, MH: nr, TN: cr

8

Brown-cheeked Fulvetta *Alcippe poioicephala* 15 cm
ADULT Nondescript, lacking any patterning to head or wings. Undergrowth in moist forest and secondary growth. AN: nr, GO: nr, KA: nr, KE: cr, MH: nr, TN: lcr

1 Singing Bushlark *Mirafra cantillans* 14 cm

ADULT Stout bill, and rufous on wing; white outer tail feathers, weak and rather restricted spotting on upper breast, and whitish throat with brownish to rufous-buff breast-band. Song, delivered in flight, is sweet and full, with much mimicry. Grassland. AN: nr, KA: lcr, KE: nr, MH: nr, TN: v

2 Indian Bushlark *Mirafra erythroptera* 14 cm

ADULT Stout bill, and rufous on wing; rufous-buff on outer tail feathers, pronounced dark spotting on breast, dark spotting on ear-coverts and malar region, and more uniform whitish underparts. Shows more rufous on wing than other bushlarks. Song is a *tit-tit-tit*, followed by a long, drawn-out *tsweeeih-tsweeeih-tsweeeih*. Stony scrub and fallow cultivation. AN: nr, GO: nr, KA: nr, MH: nr, TN: nr

3 Jerdon's Bushlark *Mirafra affinis* 15 cm

ADULT Stout bill, short tail, and rufous on wing; rufous-buff on outer tail feathers, pronounced dark spotting on breast, dark spotting on ear-coverts and malar region, and pale rufous-buff wash to underparts. Song is a dry metallic rattle delivered from a perch or during short song flight. AN: nr, KA: nr, KE: nr, TN: cr

4 Ashy-crowned Sparrow Lark *Eremopterix grisea* 12 cm

a MALE and **b** **c** FEMALE Male has grey crown and nape, and brownish-black underparts. Female has stout greyish bill, rather uniform head and upperparts, and dark grey underwing-coverts. Open dry scrub, dry cultivation. AN: cr, GO: nw, KA: nr, KE: cr, MH: cr, TN: cr

5 Rufous-tailed Lark *Ammomanes phoenicurus* 16 cm

ADULT Dusky grey-brown upperparts, rufous-orange underparts, prominent dark streaking on throat and breast, and rufous-orange uppertail-coverts and tail, with dark terminal bar. Open dry scrub, cultivation. AN: nr, GO: nr?, KA: nr, KE: v, MH: cr, TN: nw

6 Greater Short-toed Lark *Calandrella brachydactyla* 14 cm

a ADULT *C. b. dukhunensis*; **b** ADULT *C. b. longipennis* Lacks crest and rufous panel in wing; has prominent white outertail feathers and prominent supercilium. Bill is short and stout. Underparts comparatively unmarked, either with dark patches on sides of breast or a narrow gorget of dark streaking. Compared with *C. b. longipennis*, *C. b. dukhunensis* has warmer rufous-buff upperparts and rufous-buff wash across breast. Open stony and short grass areas, fallow cultivation. AN: v, GO: nw, KA: nw, KE: nw, MH: cw, TN: nw

7 Crested Lark *Galerida cristata* 18 cm

ADULT Large size and very prominent crest. Sandy upperparts and well-streaked breast; broad, rounded wings, rufous-buff underwing-coverts and outer tail feathers. Dry cultivation. MH: nr

8 Malabar Lark *Galerida malabarica* 16 cm

ADULT Prominent crest, heavily streaked rufous upperparts, rufous-buff breast with heavy black spotting, and pale rufous outer tail feathers and underwing-coverts. Bill longer than Sykes's, and has buffish-white belly and flanks. Cultivation, grass-covered hills and open scrub. GO: nr, KA: nr, KE: nr, MH: cr, TN: nr

9 Sykes's Lark *Galerida deva* 14 cm

ADULT Prominent crest and pale rufous outer tail feathers. Smaller than Malabar, with pale rufous underparts and finer and less extensive breast streaking. Stony, scrubby areas and dry cultivation. AN: nr, GO: v, KA: nr, MH: lcr, TN: nr

10 Oriental Skylark *Alauda gulgula* 16 cm

a ADULT *A. g. gulgula*; **b** ADULT *A. g. australis* Fine bill, buffish-white outer tail feathers, and indistinct rufous wing-panel. Race of western peninsula, *A. g. australis*, is warmer buff compared with other races; note smaller bill and shorter crest, which are useful differences from Malabar Lark. Grassland and cultivation. AN: nr, GO: nr, KA: cr, KE: cr, MH: nr, TN: nr

Thick-billed Flowerpecker *Dicaeum agile* 10 cm
ADULT Thick bill; diffuse malar stripe, streaking on breast, and indistinct white tip to tail. Broadleaved forest and well-wooded country. AN: nr, GO: nr, KA: lcr, KE: nr, MH: nr, TN: nr

Pale-billed Flowerpecker *Dicaeum erythrorynchos* 8 cm
ADULT Pale bill. Greyish-olive upperparts and pale grey underparts. Open broadleaved forest and well-wooded areas. AN: cr, GO: cr, KA: cr, KE: cr, MH: cr, TN: lcr

Plain Flowerpecker *Dicaeum concolor* 9 cm
ADULT Dark bill. Darker olive-brown upperparts and paler greyish-white underparts compared with Pale-billed. Edges of broadleaved forest and well-wooded areas. GO: cr, KA: nr, KE: cr, MH: nr, TN: lcr

Ruby-cheeked Sunbird *Anthreptes singalensis* 11 cm
a MALE, **b** FEMALE and **c** JUVENILE Rufous-orange throat and yellow underparts. Male has metallic green upperparts and 'ruby' cheeks. Juvenile is uniform yellow below. Open broadleaved forest and forest edges; favours evergreens. AN: nr

Purple-rumped Sunbird *Nectarinia zeylonica* 10 cm
a MALE, **b** FEMALE and **c** JUVENILE Male has narrow maroon breast-band, maroon head sides and mantle, and greyish-white flanks. Female has greyish-white throat, yellow breast, whitish flanks and rufous-brown on wing. Juvenile is uniform yellow below, with rufous-brown on wing. Calls include a high-pitched *ptsee-ptsee* and a metallic *chit*. Cultivation and secondary growth. AN: cr, GO: cr, KA: cr, KE: cr, MH: cr, TN: cr

Crimson-backed Sunbird *Nectarinia minima* 8 cm
a MALE, **b** FEMALE and **c** ECLIPSE MALE Smaller and finer-billed than Purple-rumped. Male has broad crimson breast-band and mantle. Female has crimson rump. Eclipse male has crimson back and purple rump. Calls include a flowerpecker-like *thlick-thlick*. Evergreen forest and plantations. GO: nr, KA: nr, KE: cr, MH: nr, TN: lcr

Purple Sunbird *Nectarinia asiatica* 10 cm
a MALE, **b** ECLIPSE MALE and **c** **d** FEMALE Male is metallic purple. Female has uniform yellowish underparts, with faint supercilium and darker mask; can have greyer upperparts and whiter underparts. Eclipse plumage male is similar to female but with dark stripe down centre of throat. Calls are buzzing *zit* and high-pitched, wheezy *swee*. Open forest and gardens. AN: cr, GO: nr, KA: cr, KE: cr, MH: cr, TN: cr

Loten's Sunbird *Nectarinia lotenia* 13 cm
a MALE, **b** FEMALE and **c** ECLIPSE MALE Sickle-shaped bill. Male has dusky-brown belly and vent. Female has dark olive-green upperparts; lacks supercilium and masked appearance of Purple. Call is a hard *chit chit*, lacking buzzing quality of Purple. Well-wooded country. AN: nr, GO: nr, KA: nr, KE: nr, MH: nr, TN: lcr

Crimson Sunbird *Aethopyga siparaja* 11 cm
a MALE and **b** FEMALE Male has crimson mantle, scarlet throat and breast, and grey belly. Female is rather plain, with uniform greyish underparts. Light forest, groves and gardens. AN: nr, GO: nr, KA: nr, KE: nr, MH: nr, TN: nr

Little Spiderhunter *Arachnothera longirostra* 16 cm
ADULT Very long downcurved bill, unstreaked upperparts, yellowish underparts. Wild banana plants in moist broadleaved forest. AN: nr, GO: nr, KA: nr, KE: nr, MH: nr, TN: nr

1 Forest Wagtail *Dendronanthus indicus* 18 cm
ADULT Broad yellowish-white wing-bars, double black breast-band, olive upperparts, white supercilium and whitish underparts. Paths and clearings in forest. AN: np, GO: nw, KA: nw, KE: nw, MH: nw, MV: v, TN: nw

2 White Wagtail *Motacilla alba* 19 cm
a MALE BREEDING and **b** 1ST-WINTER *M. a. personata*; **c** MALE *M. a. dukhunensis* Two races recorded in southern India, but others may occur. Black-and-white patterning to head (although never has head pattern of White-browed). First-winter birds have prominent black band across breast. Winters near water in open country. AN: cw, GO: nw, KA: cw, KE: nw, LS: v, MH: cw, TN: nw

3 White-browed Wagtail *Motacilla maderaspatensis* 21 cm
a ADULT and **b** JUVENILE Large black-and-white wagtail. Head black with white supercilium and black mantle. Juvenile has brownish-grey head, mantle and breast, with white supercilium. Banks of rivers, pools and lakes. AN: cr, GO: cr, KA: cr, KE: nr, MH: nr, TN: cr

4 Citrine Wagtail *Motacilla citreola* 19 cm
a MALE BREEDING, **b** ADULT FEMALE and **c** **d** 1ST-WINTER Broad white wing-bars in all plumages. Male breeding has yellow head and underparts, and grey mantle with black half-collar. Female breeding and adult non-breeding have broad yellow supercilium continuing around ear-coverts, grey upperparts and mainly yellow underparts. Juvenile lacks yellow, and has brownish upperparts, buffish supercilium (with dark upper edge) and ear-covert surround, and spotted black gorget. First-winter has grey upperparts; distinguished from Yellow by white surround to ear-coverts, dark border to supercilium, pale brown forehead, pale lores, all-dark bill, and white undertail-coverts; by early November, has yellowish supercilium, ear-covert surround and throat. Marshes and wet fields. AN: nw, GO: nw, KA: nw, KE: v, MH: cw, TN: nw

5 Yellow Wagtail *Motacilla flava* 18 cm
a MALE BREEDING, **b** ADULT FEMALE, **c** JUVENILE and **d** 1ST-WINTER *M. f. beema*; **e** MALE and **f** 1ST-WINTER *M. f. lutea*; **g** MALE *M. f. melanogrisea*; **h** MALE and **i** 1ST-WINTER *M. f. thunbergi* Four races have been recorded in the south. Male breeding has olive-green upperparts and yellow underparts, with considerable variation in coloration of head depending on race. Female extremely variable, but often has some features of breeding male. First-winter birds typically have brownish-olive upperparts, and whitish underparts with variable yellowish wash; in some races can closely resemble Citrine, but have narrower white supercilium that does not continue around ear-coverts. (*See also* Table 7 on p.233.) Damp grasslands and marshes. AN: nw, GO: nw, KA: cw, KE: cw, LS: np, MH: cw, MV: nwp, TN: lcw

6 Grey Wagtail *Motacilla cinerea* 19 cm

a MALE BREEDING, **b** ADULT FEMALE and **c** JUVENILE Longer-tailed than other wagtails. In all plumages, shows white supercilium, grey upperparts, and yellow vent and undertail-coverts. Male has black throat when breeding. Fast-flowing rocky streams in summer, slower streams in winter. AN: cw, GO: cw, KA: cw, KE: lcw, LS: v, MH: cw, MV: v, TN: lcw

Richard's Pipit *Anthus richardi* 17 cm
ADULT Large size with well-streaked upperparts and breast, pale lores, long and stout bill, and long hind-claw. When flushed, typically gains height with deep undulations (compared with Paddyfield). Loud *schreep* call. Moist grassland and cultivation. AN: nw, GO: nw, KA: nw, KE: nw, LS: v, MH: nw, TN: nw

Paddyfield Pipit *Anthus rufulus* 15 cm
ADULT Smaller than Richard's, with well-streaked breast; lores usually look pale. When flushed, has comparatively weak, rather fluttering flight. *Chip-chip-chip* call. Short grassland and cultivation. AN: cr, GO: cr, KA: lcr, KE: cr, LS: v, MH: cr, TN: cr

Tawny Pipit *Anthus campestris* 16 cm
a ADULT, **b** 1ST-WINTER and **c** JUVENILE Adult and first-winter have plain or faintly streaked upperparts and breast. Juvenile more heavily streaked. Useful features are dark lores, comparatively fine bill, rather horizontal stance, and wagtail-like behaviour. Stony semi-desert and fallow cultivation. Loud *tchilip* or *chep* call. AN: nw, GO: nw, KA: nw, MH: nw, TN: v

Blyth's Pipit *Anthus godlewskii* 16.5 cm
ADULT Smaller than Richard's, with shorter tail, and shorter and more pointed bill. Shape of centres to adult median coverts distinctive if seen well, but this feature is of no use in first-winter and juvenile plumage; these feathers have square-shaped, well-defined black centres with broad, pale tips (centres to median coverts are more triangular in shape, and more diffuse, in adult Richard's). Pale lores and well-streaked breast useful distinctions from Tawny. Call is a wheezy *spzeeu*. Grassland and cultivation. AN: nw, GO: nw, KA: nw, KE: nw, MH: nw, TN: nw

Long-billed Pipit *Anthus similis* 20 cm
a ADULT *A. s. similis*; **b** ADULT *A. s. travancoriensis* Considerably larger than Tawny, with very large bill and shorter-looking legs. Dark lores. Southernmost *travancoriensis* is more richly coloured and heavily streaked than *similis*. Call is a sparrow-like *chirp*. Breeds on rocky or scrubby slopes; winters in dry cultivation and scrub. KA: nr, KE: nr, MH: nr, TN: nr

Tree Pipit *Anthus trivialis* 15 cm
ADULT Buffish-brown to greyish ground colour to upperparts (lacking greenish-olive cast), and buffish fringes to greater coverts, tertials and secondaries. Call is a harsher *teez* than that of Olive-backed. Fallow cultivation and open country with scattered trees. AN: nw, GO: nw, KA: nw, LS: v, MH: nw, MV: v, TN: nw

Olive-backed Pipit *Anthus hodgsoni* 15 cm
ADULT *A. h. hodgsoni* Greenish-olive cast to upperparts, and greenish-olive fringes to greater coverts, tertials and secondaries. Typically, has more striking head pattern than Tree Pipit. Two races occur; *A. h. yunnanensis* is much less heavily streaked on upperparts than nominate race. Call is a *see*, less harsh than that of Tree. Open forest and shrubberies. AN: nw, GO: nw, KA: nw, KE: nw, MH: nw, TN: lcw

Red-throated Pipit *Anthus cervinus* 15 cm
a MALE BREEDING and **b** 1ST-YEAR Adult has reddish throat and upper breast, which tend to be paler on female and on autumn/winter birds. First-year has heavily streaked upperparts, pale 'braces', well-defined white wing-bars, strongly contrasting blackish centres and whitish fringes to tertials, pronounced dark malar patch, and boldly streaked breast and (especially) flanks. Call is a drawn-out *seeeeee*. Marshes, grassland and stubble. GO: nw, MV: nwp

Nilgiri Pipit *Anthus nilghiriensis* 17 cm
ADULT Large, heavily streaked pipit. Compared with Paddyfield, has shorter tail, more heavily streaked upperparts, and streaked upper belly and flanks, and lacks malar stripe and patch. Call is a weak *see-see*, quite unlike that of Paddyfield. Grassy slopes. KA: nr, KE: nr, TN: nr

House Sparrow *Passer domesticus* 15 cm

 MALE and  FEMALE Male has grey crown, black throat and upper breast, chestnut nape and brownish mantle. Female has buffish supercilium and unstreaked greyish-white underparts. Habitation, also nearby cultivation. AN: cr, GO: cr, KA: cr, KE: lcr, MH: cr, MV: ir, TN: cr

Eurasian Tree Sparrow *Passer montanus* 14 cm

ADULT Chestnut crown, and black spot on ear-coverts. Sexes similar. Habitation and nearby cultivation. AN: nr, KA: v

Chestnut-shouldered Petronia *Petronia xanthocollis* 13.5 cm

a MALE and b FEMALE Unstreaked brownish-grey head and upperparts, and prominent wing-bars. Male and some females have yellow on throat. Male has chestnut lesser coverts and white wing-bars; female has brown lesser coverts and buff wing-bars. Open dry forest and scrub. AN: nr, GO: nw, KA: nr, KE: nr, MH: cr, TN: nr

Black-breasted Weaver *Ploceus benghalensis* 14 cm

a b MALE BREEDING and c d NON-BREEDING Breeding male has yellow crown and black breast-band. In female and non-breeding plumages, breast-band can be broken by whitish fringes or restricted to small patches at sides, and may show indistinct, diffuse streaking on lower breast and flanks; head pattern as on female/non-breeding Streaked, except crown, nape and ear-coverts more uniform; rump also indistinctly streaked and, like nape, contrasts with heavily streaked mantle/back. Tall moist grassland and reedy marshes. AN: nr, KA: nr, MH: nr

Streaked Weaver *Ploceus manyar* 14 cm

a MALE BREEDING and b NON-BREEDING Breeding male has yellow crown, dark brown head-sides and throat, and heavily streaked breast and flanks. Other plumages typically show boldly streaked underparts; can be only lightly streaked on underparts, when it is best told from Baya by combination of yellow supercilium and neck-patch, heavily streaked crown, dark or heavily streaked ear-coverts, and pronounced dark malar and moustachial stripes. Reedbeds. AN: cr, GO: v, KA: nr, KE: nr, MH: v, TN: nr

Baya Weaver *Ploceus philippinus* 15 cm

a MALE BREEDING, b MALE NON-BREEDING and c FEMALE Breeding male has yellow crown, dark brown ear-coverts and throat, unstreaked yellow breast, and yellow on mantle and scapulars. Female/non-breeding birds usually have unstreaked buff to pale yellowish underparts; can show streaking as prominent as on some poorly marked Streaked, but generally has less distinct and buffish supercilium, lacks yellow neck-patch, and lacks pronounced dark moustachial and malar stripes. Head pattern of some (non-breeding males?) can, however, be rather similar to Streaked. Cultivation and grassland. AN: cr, GO: cr, KA: lcr, KE: nr, MH: cs, TN: cr

1 Red Avadavat *Amandava amandava* 10 cm
a MALE BREEDING, **b** FEMALE and **c** JUVENILE Breeding male is mainly red with white spotting. Non-breeding male and female have red bill, red rump and uppertail-coverts, and white tips to wing-coverts and tertials. Juvenile lacks red in plumage; has buff wing-bars, pink bill-base, and pink legs and feet. Tall wet grassland and reedbeds. AN: nr, KA: lcr, KE: nr, MH: nr, TN: lcr

2 Green Avadavat *Amandava formosa* 10 cm
a MALE and **b** FEMALE Breeding male is green and yellow, with red bill and barred flanks. Female is much duller, with weak flank barring. Grass and low bushes, also tall grassland. AN: nr, KA: nr?, KE: v, MH: nr

3 Indian Silverbill *Lonchura malabarica* 11–11.5 cm
a ADULT and **b** JUVENILE Adult has white rump and uppertail-coverts, black tail with elongated central feathers, and rufous-buff barring on flanks. Dry cultivation, grassland and thorn scrub. AN: cr, GO: nr?, KA: lcr, KE: nr, MH: cr, TN: cr

4 White-rumped Munia *Lonchura striata* 10–11 cm
ADULT Dark breast and white rump. Pale streaking on ear-coverts, rufous-brown to whitish fringes to brown breast, and dingy underparts with faint streaking. Open wooded areas and scrub. AN: nr, GO: nr, KA: lcr, KE: cr, MH: cr, TN: cr

5 Black-throated Munia *Lonchura kelaarti* 12 cm
ADULT Blackish face, throat and upper breast, and pinkish-cinnamon sides of neck and breast; underparts pinkish cinnamon. Juvenile lacks black on head and breast, and has uniform upperparts; underparts are warm buffish brown with diffuse buff streaking and mottling. Forest clearings, scrub and grassland. AN: nr, GO: v, KA: nr, KE: nr, MH: nr, TN: lcr

6 Scaly-breasted Munia *Lonchura punctulata* 10.5–12 cm
a ADULT and **b** JUVENILE Adult has chestnut throat and upper breast, and whitish underparts with dark scaling. Juvenile has brown upperparts and buffish underparts; bill black. Open forest, bushes and cultivation. AN: cr, GO: nr, KA: cr, KE: nr, MH: cr, TN: cr

7 Black-headed Munia *Lonchura malacca* 11.5 cm
a ADULT and **b** JUVENILE Black head, neck and upper breast, rufous-brown upperparts, white lower breast and flanks, and black belly centre and undertail-coverts. Juvenile has uniform brown upperparts and buff to whitish underparts; bill blue-grey. Cultivation and grassland. AN: nr, GO: np, KA: nr, KE: nr, MH: nr, TN: nr

Common Rosefinch *Carpodacus erythrinus* 14.5–15 cm
a MALE and **b** FEMALE *C. e. roseatus*; **c** MALE and **d** FEMALE *C. e. erythrinus* Compact, with short, stout bill. Male has red head, breast and rump. Female has streaked upperparts and underparts, and double wing-bar. The nominate Siberian race has less red in male, and female is less heavily streaked, compared with Himalayan *roseatus*. Winters in cultivation with bushes. AN: nw, GO: nw, KA: nw, KE: cw, MH: cw, TN: lcw

Crested Bunting *Melophus lathami* 17 cm
a MALE, **b** FEMALE and **c** 1ST-WINTER MALE Always has crest and chestnut on wing and tail; tail lacks white. Dry rocky and grassy hillsides, and terraced cultivation. MH: nr

Grey-necked Bunting *Emberiza buchanani* 15 cm
a MALE, **b** FEMALE and **c** 1ST-WINTER Pinkish-orange bill, plain head and whitish eye-ring. Adult has blue-grey head, buffish submoustachial stripe and throat, and rusty-pink underparts. First-winter and juvenile often have only slight greyish cast to head and buffish underparts; light streaking on breast. *See* Appendix for comparison with Ortolan Bunting. Dry rocky and bushy hills. AN: nw, GO: nw, KA: nw, MH: nw

House Bunting *Emberiza striolata* 13–14 cm
a MALE and **b** FEMALE Has black eye-stripe and moustachial stripe, and white supercilium and submoustachial stripe; throat and breast streaked, and underparts brownish buff with variable rufous tinge. Female duller than male, with less striking head pattern. Dry rocky hills; also sandy plains in winter. MH: nr

Black-headed Bunting *Emberiza melanocephala* 16–18 cm
a MALE BREEDING, **b** MALE NON-BREEDING, **c** WORN FEMALE and **d** IMMATURE Male has black on head and chestnut on mantle. Female when worn may show ghost pattern of male; fresh female almost identical to Red-headed, but indicative features include rufous fringes to mantle and/or back, slight contrast between throat and greyish ear-coverts, and more uniform yellowish underparts. Immature has buff underparts and yellow undertail-coverts. Cultivation, bushes at field edges. AN: v, GO: np, KA: np, MH: cw

Red-headed Bunting *Emberiza bruniceps* 16 cm
a MALE BREEDING, **b** MALE NON-BREEDING, **c** FRESH FEMALE and **d** IMMATURE Smaller than Black-headed, with shorter, more conical bill. Male is rufous on head with yellowish-green mantle. Female when worn may be rufous on head and breast, with yellowish cast to crown and mantle, and is distinguishable from female Black-headed. Fresh female has paler throat than breast, with suggestion of buffish breast-band; forehead and crown are often virtually unstreaked (indicative features separating it from Black-headed). Immature often not separable from Black-headed, but may exhibit some of the features mentioned above. Cultivation. AN: v, GO: np, KA: nw, MH: nw, TN: v

APPENDIX

Vagrants (very irregular visitors that have only been recorded once or on few occasions) are listed below.

Mute Swan *Cygnus olor* 125–155 cm
Adult is white and has orange bill with black base and knob. Juvenile is mottled sooty-brown, and has grey bill with black base. Large rivers and lakes. MH

Lesser White-fronted Goose *Anser erythropus* 53–66 cm
Adult has white band at front of head, black barring on belly, orange-pink bill and orange legs and feet. Smaller and more compact, with squarer head and stouter bill, compared with Greater White-fronted *A. albifrons* (not recorded in Southern India). White frontal band of adult extends onto forehead. Both adult and juvenile have yellow eye-ring, and darker head and neck than Greater White-fronted. Wet grassland and lakes. MH

Greylag Goose *Anser anser* 75–90 cm
Large grey goose with pink bill and legs. Lacks white frontal band of Greater and Lesser White-fronted. Shows pale grey forewing in flight. Crops, lakes and large rivers. AN, MH

Falcated Duck *Anas falcata* 48–54 cm
Male has bottle-green head with maned hind-neck, and elongated black-and-grey tertials; shows pale grey forewing in flight. Female has rather plain greyish head, a dark bill, dark spotting and scalloping on brown underparts, and greyish-white fringes to exposed tertials; shows greyish forewing and white greater-covert bar in flight, but does not show striking white belly (compare with female Eurasian Wigeon). Lakes and large rivers. MH

Baikal Teal *Anas formosa* 39–43 cm
Grey forewing and broad white trailing edge to wing in flight in both sexes (recalling Northern Pintail). Male has striking head pattern of black, yellow, bottle-green and white; also black-spotted pinkish breast, black undertail-coverts, and chestnut-edged scapulars. Female superficially resembles female Common Teal; has dark-bordered white loral spot and buff supercilium that is broken above eye by dark crown; some females have white half-crescent on cheeks. Lakes and large rivers. GO

Marbled Duck *Marmaronetta angustirostris* 39–42 cm
Pale sandy-brown-coloured duck. Has shaggy hood, dark mask and diffusely spotted body. Upperwing rather uniform and underwing very pale. Shallow freshwater lakes and ponds. MH

Baer's Pochard *Aythya baeri* 41–46 cm
Greenish cast to dark head and neck, which contrast with chestnut-brown breast. White patch on foreflanks visible above water. Female and immature male have duller head and breast than adult male. Female has dark iris and pale and diffuse chestnut-brown loral spot. Lakes and large rivers. Globally threatened. GO

Greater Scaup *Aythya marila* 40–51 cm
Larger and stockier than Tufted, and lacking any sign of crest. Male is superficially similar to Tufted but has grey upperparts contrasting with black rear end. Female is very similar in plumage to Tufted but has broad white face-patch, which is less extensive on juvenile/immature. Lakes and large rivers. MH

Common Merganser *Mergus merganser* 58–72 cm
Slim head, neck and body, with long slim bill and spiky crest. Male has dark green head and whitish breast and flanks (with variable pink wash). Female and immature male have chestnut head and greyish body. Lakes, rivers and streams. MH

Ruddy Kingfisher *Halcyon coromanda* 26 cm
Entirely rufous-orange with violet iridescence on upperparts, and striking coral-red bill. Flashes bluish-white rump in flight. Dense, broadleaved, evergreen forest. TN

Oriental Cuckoo *Cuculus saturatus* 30–32 cm
Broader dark barring on buffish-white underparts compared with Eurasian Cuckoo; upperparts are a shade darker; paler head. Hepatic female is slightly more heavily barred than Eurasian. Call a

resonant *ho...ho...ho...ho*, easily confused with the call of Common Hoopoe. Forest and well-wooded country. MH

Plaintive Cuckoo *Cacomantis merulinus* 23 cm

Similar in size, shape and general appearance to Grey-bellied Cuckoo, but adult has orange underparts. On hepatic female, compared with Grey-bellied, base colour of underparts is pale rufous (rather than white), and upperparts and tail are strongly barred. Juvenile has bold streaking on rufous-orange head and breast. Song is a mournful *tay...ta...tee*. Forest and wooded country. AN, KA

Asian Emerald Cuckoo *Chrysococcyx maculatus* 18 cm

Small cuckoo. Male is mainly emerald-green, with barred upperparts. Female has rufous-orange crown and nape, barred underparts, and unbarred bronze-green mantle and wings. Juvenile has unbarred rufous-orange crown and nape, rufous-orange barring on mantle and wing-coverts, and rufous-orange wash to barred throat and breast. Song is a loud, descending *kee-kee-kee-kee* and a sharp *chweek* uttered in flight. Broadleaved evergreen forest. TN

Violet Cuckoo *Chrysococcyx xanthorhynchus* 17 cm

Small cuckoo. Male is mainly purple, with barred underparts. Female has uniform bronze-brown upperparts, with only slight greenish tinge, and white underparts with brownish-green barring. Juvenile has extensive dark barring on crown and nape, and lacks rufous-orange wash to throat and breast compared with juvenile Asian Emerald. Call is a disyllabic and repeated *che-wick*, particularly in flight, and an accelerating trill. Secondary evergreen forest and orchards. TN

Himalayan Swiftlet *Collocalia brevirostris* 14 cm

Stocky brownish swiftlet with paler grey-brown underparts and diffuse greyish rump-band. Compared with Indian Swiftlet, is slightly larger, with more distinct indentation to tail, and more pronounced greyish rump-band (rump-band lacking, or indistinctly paler in Indian). Banking and gliding flight, interspersed with bat-like fluttering. Open areas near forest. MV

White-throated Needletail *Hirundapus caudacutus* 20 cm

Compared with Brown-backed Needletail, has striking white throat, more prominent pale 'saddle', and white patch on tertials. Ridges, cliffs, upland grassland and river valleys. MV

Pallid Swift *Apus pallidus* 17 cm

Very similar in appearance to Common Swift but with paler grey-brown upperparts and underparts, darker eye-patch, and more extensive pale throat. Shows slight contrast between dark outer primaries and inner wing-coverts and paler rest of wing, and has dark-saddled, pale-headed appearance (not apparent in Common). Underparts more distinctly scaled than in Common. Coastal areas. MV

Eurasian Scops Owl *Otus scops* 19 cm

Occurs as grey and brown morphs. Not safely distinguishable in the field from Oriental Scops, although has different call and longer primary projection (usually shows six or seven primaries extending beyond tertials when the wing is closed; four to five in Oriental). Browner or darker grey in coloration compared with Pallid Scops. Compared with that species has pronounced darkening around eyes, more prominent white spots on scapulars, pale horizontal bars across streaked underparts, and narrower and more numerous pale barring on tail (five to seven bars compared to two to four in Pallid). Scrub in dry rocky hills and valleys. MH

Long-eared Owl *Asio otus* 35–37 cm

Superficially resembles Short-eared Owl. Has heavily streaked underparts and long ear-tufts. Orange-brown facial discs and orange eyes. Forests and groves. TN

Eurasian Nightjar *Caprimulgus europaeus* 25 cm

Medium-sized, grey nightjar with regular, bold lanceolate streaking on crown, nape and scapulars (latter with buffish outer edges). Rocky slopes with scattered bushes. *See* Table 1 on p.230. MH, TN

Sykes's Nightjar *Caprimulgus mahrattensis* 23 cm

Small, grey nightjar. Has finely streaked crown, black 'inverted anchor-shaped' marks on scapulars, large white patches on sides of throat, and irregular buff spotting on nape forming indistinct collar. Wide variety of habitats in winter. *See* Table 1 on p.230. KA, MH

European Turtle Dove *Streptopelia turtur* 33 cm

Has white sides and tip to tail. Told from *meena* race of Oriental Turtle by smaller size and slimmer build; broader, paler rufous-buff fringes to scapulars and wing-coverts; more buffish- or brownish-grey rump and uppertail-coverts; and greyish-pink breast, becoming whitish on belly and undertail-coverts. Cultivation in drier mountains and valleys. MV

Macqueen's Bustard *Chlamydotis macqueenii* 55–65 cm

Medium-sized bustard (larger than Lesser Florican). Adult has slight crest (elongated white crown feathers tipped with black) and dark vertical stripe down neck. In flight, extensive white patch on outer primaries (contrasting with black primary coverts and inner primaries). Sexes similar, but female is smaller, has less pronounced crest and neck stripe. Male has whitish panel across greater coverts, lacking in female. Juvenile very similar to female, but lacks black-tipped crest, neck stripe is finer, and white on wing is washed with buff and less prominent. Semi-desert with scattered shrubs and sandy grassland. KE

Siberian Crane *Grus leucogeranus* 120–140 cm

Adult is white, with bare red face, pinkish-red legs and noticeably downcurved reddish bill. Immature has brownish bill and fully feathered head at first, and is strongly marked with cinnamon-brown on head, neck, mantle and wings, with some white body feathers by first winter; by third winter, red mask is apparent and body feathers are mainly white. In flight, both adult and immature show black primaries that contrast with rest of wing. Freshwater marshes. MH

Little Crake *Porzana parva* 20–23 cm

Very similar in size and appearance to Baillon's Crake. Longer wings than Baillon's (primaries extending noticeably beyond tertials at rest), with less extensive barring on flanks, and pronounced pale edges to scapulars and tertials (features for all plumages). Adult also with red at base of bill. Male has grey underparts. Female has buff underparts. Juvenile is similar to female but has more extensive barring on flanks (but less than on Baillon's). Marshes. GO, KA, MH

Black-bellied Sandgrouse *Pterocles orientalis* 33–35 cm

Both sexes have black belly. Stocky and shorter-tailed compared with Chestnut-bellied. Best distinguished from Chestnut-bellied by white underwing-coverts which contrast with black flight feathers. Male has black and chestnut throat and grey neck and breast. Female is very heavily marked, as is female Chestnut-bellied; belly of female Black-bellied is solid black (dark-barred in Chestnut bellied) and has narrow black throat collar. Semi-desert. KA, MH

Great Snipe *Gallinago media* 27–29 cm

Medium-sized, bulky snipe, with broader wings than Common and Pintail Snipes, and slower and more direct flight. Additional features include heavily barred underwing, narrow but distinct white wing-bars, and prominent white at sides of tail (latter two features less pronounced in juvenile). White wing-bars and white belly help to distinguish from Wood Snipe. Marshes. KA, TN

Buff-breasted Sandpiper *Tryngites subruficollis* 18–20 cm

Recalls a tiny Ruff, with shorter and straighter bill, large eyes and bright yellow legs. Upperwing lacks wing-bar, and shows no white on rump or tail. White underwing has dark crescent on primary coverts (underwing entirely white in Ruff). In all plumages, face and underparts are buff, and dark upperparts are neatly fringed with buff. Short grass, mud and seashore. GO

Grey-tailed Tattler *Heteroscelus brevipes* 24–27 cm

Uniform grey upperparts, including rump/tail and grey underwing. Stocky, with short yellow legs. Prominent supercilium, usually extending beyond eye; primaries extend to tail-tip. Adult breeding has barring on breast and flanks. Adult non-breeding uniform grey on upperparts and breast. Juvenile has indistinct white spotting on upperparts. Coastal wetlands. GO

Caspian Plover *Charadrius asiaticus* 18–20 cm

A medium-sized, long-legged and long-winged plover. In non-breeding plumage, best told from Greater Sand Plover by slimmer appearance, slimmer bill, narrower wing-bar, complete breast-band, and more pronounced supercilium with dark-capped appearance. Male in breeding plumage has chestnut breast-band with a black lower border; female in breeding plumages similar to adult non-breeding but with some chestnut on breast. White underwing-coverts and greenish or brownish legs are best distinctions from the similar Oriental Plover *C. veredus* (although this species has not been recorded from Southern India). Mudflats and coast. MH, MV, TN

Black-fronted Dotterel *Elseyornis melanops* 16–18 cm
Adult has red eye-ring; short, black-tipped red bill; black stripe through eye and white supercilium; black breast-band and purplish scapular patch. In flight, shows black wing-tips and greyish panel across wing-coverts on upperwing, and mainly white underwing-coverts contrasting with black flight feathers. Juvenile similar to adult, although duller, and breast-band is incomplete; lacks purplish scapular patch. Mainly stony beds of rivers and streams in Australian breeding areas. TN

Northern Lapwing *Vanellus vanellus* 28–31 cm
Black crest, white (or buff) and black face pattern, black breast-band and dark green upperparts. Shows all-dark upperwing, and whitish rump and blackish tail-band in flight. Has very broad, rounded wing-tips, with distinctive slow-flapping flight with rather erratic wing beats. Wet grassland, marshes, fallow fields and wetland edges. AN

Grey-headed Lapwing *Vanellus cinereus* 34–37 cm
Yellow bill with black tip, and yellow legs. Grey head, neck and breast, latter with diffuse black border, and black tail-band. In flight, secondaries are all-white. Call is a plaintive *chee-it, chee-it*. River banks, marshes and wet fields. AN, GO, KA

Collared Pratincole *Glareola pratincola* 16–19 cm
Distinguished from Oriental Pratincole in all plumages by white trailing edge to secondaries on both upperwing and underwing (although this can be difficult to see). Adult breeding has deeper fork to tail than Oriental (with elongated outer feathers reaching at least to end of closed primaries at rest), paler brown mantle and wing-coverts contrasting more with flight feathers, and more extensive red at base of bill (reaching to nostril of upper mandible). Adult non-breeding and juvenile are similar to those plumages of Oriental and best told by white trailing edge to wing. Dry bare ground around wetlands. MH, TN

Brown Skua *Catharacta antarctica* 63 cm
Larger and more powerful than South Polar Skua, with broader-based wings and larger bill. Usually darker, lacking contrast between pale head and underbody and darker upperbody; can be very similar to South Polar in general colour and appearance, but upperparts of adult are more heavily and irregularly splashed with pale markings. Juvenile warmer, more rufous-brown, in coloration, and upperparts more uniform (lacking pronounced pale splashes of adult). Coastal waters. KE, MH, MV, TN

South Polar Skua *Catharacta maccormicki* 53 cm
Marginally smaller and slighter than Brown Skua, with finer bill. Pale morph distinctive: pale sandy-brown head and underbody contrasting with dark brown mantle and upperwing- and underwing-coverts. Dark morph lacks heavy pale streaking/mottling of Brown, and usually has pale forehead, dark cap/head and paler hind-neck; uniform (unbarred) underwing-coverts, axillaries and uppertail- and undertail-coverts differentiate from dark juvenile Pomarine Jaeger. Intermediates also occur. Juvenile has pale to mid-grey head and underparts, and dark grey upperparts. Coastal waters. KA, LS, MV

White-eyed Gull *Larus leucophthalmus* 39 cm
Similar to Sooty Gull, with dark mantle and upperwing and blackish underwing. Best told from that species in all plumages by slimmer, all-dark bill, prominent crescents above and below eye, and is slightly smaller and slimmer. Adult has black hood, and grey mantle and upperwing; bill is reddish. First-year has grey-brown mantle and upperwing, and dark ear-coverts and nape. Fishing ports and harbours. MV

Mew Gull *Larus canus* 43 cm
Smaller and daintier than Caspian, with shorter and finer bill. Adult has darker grey mantle than Caspian, with more black on wing-tips; bill yellowish green, with dark subterminal band in non-breeding plumage, and dark iris. Head and hind-neck heavily marked in non-breeding (unlike adult non-breeding Caspian). First-winter/first-summer have uniform grey mantle. Distinctions from second-year Caspian (which also has grey mantle) include unbarred greyish greater coverts forming mid-wing panel, narrow black subterminal tail-band, and well-defined dark tip to greyish/pinkish bill. Lakes and large rivers. GO

Black Tern *Chlidonias niger*   22–24 cm
In breeding plumage, has black head and underbody, and uniform grey upperwing and underwing. Non-breeding and juvenile have dark patch on side of breast (lacking in Whiskered and White-winged terns); distinguished from juvenile White-winged by less contrast between mantle and upperwing-coverts and by grey rump and tail. Marshes, pools and lakes. AN, GO, TN

White-tailed Eagle *Haliaeetus albicilla*   70–90 cm
Huge, with broad parallel-edged wings, short wedge-shaped tail, and protruding head and neck. Soars and glides with wings level. Adult has large yellow bill, pale head and white tail. Juvenile is all dark with whitish centres to tail feathers, pale patch on axillaries, and variable pale band across underwing-coverts. Catches fish and waterfowl by flying low over the water surface. Large rivers and lakes. KA, KE

Lesser Fish Eagle *Ichthyophaga humilis*   64 cm
Adult differs from Grey-headed in smaller size, greyish tail, paler grey upperparts, white patch at base of outer primaries on underwing, and greyer underparts. Juvenile browner than adult, with paler underwing and paler base to tail; lacks prominent streaking of juvenile Grey-headed, and has clear-cut white belly and different tail pattern. As Grey-headed, usually seen perched above water, and rarely soars above the tree canopy. Forested streams and lakes. KA, MH

Himalayan Griffon *Gyps himalayensis*   115–125 cm
Larger than Eurasian Griffon, with broader body and slightly longer tail. Wing-coverts and body pale buffish white, contrasting strongly with dark flight feathers and tail; underparts lack pronounced streaking; legs and feet pinkish with dark claws, and has yellowish cere. Immature has brown feathered ruff, with bill and cere initially black (yellowish on adult), and has dark brown body and upperwing-coverts boldly and prominently streaked with buff (wing-coverts almost concolorous with flight feathers), and back and rump also dark brown; streaked upperparts and underparts and pronounced white banding across underwing-coverts are best distinctions from Cinereous Vulture. Very similar in plumage to juvenile White-rumped Vulture, but much larger and more heavily built, with broader wings and longer tail, underparts more heavily streaked, and streaking on mantle and scapulars. Open country in mountains. TN

Cinereous Vulture *Aegypius monachus*   100–110 cm
Very large vulture with broad, parallel-edged wings. Soars with wings flat. At a distance appears typically uniformly dark, except for pale areas on head and bill. Adult blackish brown with paler brown ruff; may show paler band across greater underwing-coverts, but underwing darker and more uniform than on *Gyps* species. Juvenile blacker and more uniform than adult. Open country. AN, KA, KE, MH, TN

Japanese Sparrowhawk *Accipiter gularis*   25–31.5 cm
Very small. Long primary projection. In all plumages, pale bars on tail generally broader than dark bars (reverse on Besra). Underpart patterning of adults rather different from Besra; juveniles more similar. Male has dark bluish-grey upperparts, pale rufous to pale grey underparts (some with fine grey barring) and dark crimson iris. Female has browner upperparts, whitish underparts with distinct barring, indistinct gular stripe, and yellow iris. Juvenile has brown to rufous streaking and barring on underparts. Probably forest. AN

Chinese Sparrowhawk *Accipiter soloensis*   25–30 cm
Narrow and pointed wings, with long primary projection at rest. Adult has blue-grey head and upperparts, indistinct grey gular stripe, and rufous-orange breast; distinctive underwing pattern, with unbarred remiges and coverts, blackish wing-tips and dark grey trailing edge. Sub-adults show some dark barring on underside of flight feathers. Juvenile has dark brown upperparts, pronounced dark gular stripe, and rufous-brown spotting and barring on underparts; compared with juvenile Japanese Sparrowhawk, crown is darker slate-grey than mantle, lacks distinct supercilium and has distinctive underwing pattern (dark grey wing-tips and trailing edge, largely unmarked greyish-brown to pale rufous coverts). Forest and wooded country. AN

Northern Goshawk *Accipiter gentilis*   50–61 cm
Very large, with heavy, deep-chested appearance. Wings comparatively long, with bulging secondaries. Male has grey upperparts (greyer than female Eurasian Sparrowhawk), white supercilium

and finely barred underparts. Female considerably larger, with browner upperparts. Juvenile has heavy streaking on buff-coloured underparts. Forest. GO, KA, KE, MH, TN

Imperial Eagle *Aquila heliaca* 72–83 cm

Large, stout-bodied eagle with long and broad wings, longish tail, and distinctly protruding head and neck. Wings flat when soaring and gliding. Adult has almost uniform upperwing, small white scapular patches, golden-buff crown and nape, and two-toned tail. Juvenile has pronounced curve to trailing edge of wing, pale wedge on inner primaries, streaked buffish body and wing-coverts, uniform pale rump and back (lacking distinct pale crescent shown by other species except Tawny), and white tips to median and greater upperwing-coverts. Large rivers and lakes, open country. Globally threatened. KE, MH, TN

Saker Falcon *Falco cherrug* 50–58 cm

Large falcon with long wings and long tail. Wing-beats slow in level flight, with lazier flight action than Peregrine. At rest, tail extends noticeably beyond closed wings (wings fall just short of tail-tip on Laggar and are equal to tail on Peregrine). Adult has paler crown, less clearly defined mous-tachial stripe and paler rufous-brown upperparts than Laggar; underparts generally not so heavily marked as on Laggar, with flanks and thighs usually clearly streaked and not appearing wholly brown (although some overlap exists); outer tail feathers more prominently barred. Juvenile has greyish cere and greyish legs and feet; otherwise similar to adult, but crown more heavily marked, moustachial stripe stronger, underparts more heavily streaked and upperparts darker brown. *F. c. milvipes* has broad orange-buff barring on upperparts and is rather different in plumage from Laggar. Semi-desert in hills and mountains, and open dry scrubby areas. MH

Great Crested Grebe *Podiceps cristatus* 46–51 cm

Large and slender-necked grebe. Has white cheeks and foreneck in non-breeding plumage. Rufous-orange ear-tufts, white cheeks and foreneck, and rufous flanks in breeding plumage. Lakes and large rivers. AN, MH

Black-necked Grebe *Podiceps nigricollis* 28–34 cm

Slightly larger than Little Grebe, with longer neck. Steep forehead, and bill appears upturned. Dusky ear-coverts contrast with white throat and sides of head in non-breeding plumage. Yellow ear-tufts, black neck and breast and rufous flanks in breeding plumage. Lakes and large rivers. MH

Goliath Heron *Ardea goliath* 135–150 cm

Superficially resembles Purple Heron. Huge size and large, dark bill. Black legs and feet. Rufous on head and neck. Adult has purplish-chestnut underparts and underwing-coverts; lacks black head stripes of Purple. Juvenile has black crown, indistinct stripes down foreneck, and rufous fringes to upperparts. Rivers. MH

Little Bittern *Ixobrychus minutus* 33–38 cm

Small size. Buffish wing-coverts contrast with dark flight feathers in all plumages. Male is best told from Yellow Bittern by black mantle/scapulars, and paler buffish face and hind-neck. Female is similar but with brown mantle/scapulars, and brownish-buff streaking on foreneck (mantle col-oration is best feature separating it from female Yellow). Juvenile has warm buff upperparts streaked with dark brown, and brown streaking on underparts; very similar to juvenile Yellow but streak-ing on foreneck and breast of Yellow is generally more rufous-orange. Reedbeds. KA, MH

Dalmatian Pelican *Pelecanus crispus* 160–180 cm

In all plumages, has greyish underside to secondaries and inner primaries (becoming darker on outer primaries) lacking strong contrast with pale underwing-coverts, and often with whiter cen-tral panel. Forehead feathering broader across upper mandible (orbital skin more restricted than on Great White). Legs and feet always dark grey (pinkish on Great White). Larger than Spot-billed Pelican, with cleaner and whiter appearance at all ages; lacks 'spotting' on upper mandible, and bill usually darker than pouch. Adult breeding has orange pouch and purple skin around eye, and curly or bushy crest. Adult non-breeding more dirty white; pouch and skin around eye paler. Immature dingier than adult non-breeding, with some pale grey-brown on upperwing-coverts and scapulars. Juvenile has pale grey-brown mottling on hind-neck and upperparts, including upper-wing-coverts; pouch greyish yellow. Large inland waters and coastal lagoons. AN

Bulwer's Petrel *Bulweria bulwerii* 26–27 cm
Small and all dark, with long tail. Smaller than Jouanin's, with finer bill, and more prominent pale band across greater coverts (although Jouanin's in worn plumage may show this). Has weaker flight, with rapid beats interspersed with twisting glides; becoming shallow arcs in strong wind. Pelagic. MV

Jouanin's Petrel *Bulweria fallax* 30–32 cm
All dark, with long, pointed tail. Larger and broader-winged than Bulwer's, with stouter bill. Flight more powerful, with 'shearing' or long glides interspersed with steady flapping. Smaller and with less languid flight than Wedge-tailed Shearwater. Pelagic. LS, MV

Barau's Petrel *Pterodroma baraui* 38 cm
Whitish forehead and dark grey cap, blackish M-mark across grey upperwing, dark rump and tail contrasting with grey lower mantle and back, and dark patches on sides of breast. Underparts otherwise largely white. Largely white underwing with black band on leading and trailing edges. Pelagic. LS

Streaked Shearwater *Calonectris leucomelas* 48 cm
Brown upperparts, white underparts and underwing-coverts, and large size. Variable whitish streaking on head, and pale bill with dark tip. Flight typically rather relaxed and gull-like with wings slightly angled at carpal joints. Pelagic, inshore waters. MV, TN

Persian Shearwater *Puffinus persicus* 30–33 cm
Slightly larger than Audubon's, with browner coloration to upperparts, longer bill, less extensive white on underwing, and brownish axillaries and flanks. There may also be differences in leg and bill colour. Offshore and pelagic waters. GO, KE, MH

White-faced Storm-petrel *Pelagodroma marina* 20 cm
White supercilium and dark mask, greyish-brown upperwing-coverts with paler grey greater-covert bar, white underparts, grey rump and peculiar bounding flight. Feet project noticeably beyond tail, and wings appear broad and oval-shaped. Pelagic. KA, KE, MV

White-bellied Storm-petrel *Fregetta grallaria* 20 cm
Black head, and white underbody and underwing-coverts. Only likely to be confused with Black-bellied Storm-petrel *F. tropica* (although this species has not been recorded); this species has a black line down the centre of belly and black undertail-coverts. Pelagic. MV

Leach's Storm-petrel *Oceanodroma leucorhoa* 20 cm
Similar in shape and appearance to Swinhoe's Storm-petrel, but has white band across rump. Pelagic. MV

Grey-backed Shrike *Lanius tephronotus* 25 cm
Compared with Long-tailed Shrike, adult has dark grey upperparts (no rufous on scapulars and upper back). Also usually lacks, or has only very indistinct, white patch at base of primaries, and lacks, or has very narrow, black forehead band. Juvenile has cold grey base colour to upperparts. Bushes in cultivation, scrub and secondary growth. MH

Common Raven *Corvus corax* 58–69 cm
Distinguished from Large-billed Crow, by larger size, long and angular wings, prominent throat hackles and pronounced wedge-shaped tail. Call is a loud, deep, resonant croaking *wock...wock*, different from other crows (Large-billed has a dry *kaaa-kaaa* call). Head and bill shape are also different from Large-billed (flatter crown and straighter ridge to culmen in Common Raven). Dry rocky areas. MH

Long-tailed Minivet *Pericrocotus ethologus* 20 cm
Male is glossy black above and red below. Similar to Scarlet Minivet, but is smaller and slimmer, with deeper red underparts and different wing pattern, and lacking red circular patch at tip of tertials and inner secondaries (has a red line that extends along edge of tertials from red wing-covert panel, which is the best feature to distinguish it from Short-billed Minivet *P. brevirostris* – although this species has not been recorded in Southern India). Female best told by combination of narrow, indistinct yellow wash on forehead and supercilium (extensive yellow forehead in female Scarlet and Short-billed), grey ear-coverts (wholly or partly yellow in Scarlet and Short-billed), and paler

yellow throat than breast. Distinctive *pi-ru* whistle. Lacks circular yellow patch on wings (as shown in female Scarlet). Forest; also well-wooded areas in winter. MH

Marshall's Iora *Aegithina nigrolutea* 14 cm
Extensive white on black tail is best feature separating it from Common Iora in all plumages. Breeding male has black crown and nape, yellow hind-collar (not usually shown by any race of Common) and blackish mantle with yellowish-green mottling. Apart from tail pattern, non-breeding male and female are similar to Common. Scrub and groves. MH

Siberian Thrush *Zoothera sibirica* 22 cm
Adult male slate-grey, with white supercilium (lacks wing bars and white belly of Pied Thrush). First-winter male is similar to adult male but with buff supercilium, throat and greater-covert bar. Female has buff supercilium and dark scaling on underparts; lacks buff tips to tertials of Pied, wing-bars are much less prominent or non-existent, while scaling on flanks is partly obscured by olive-brown (flanks whiter, and scaling more prominent, in female Pied). Forest. MH

Eyebrowed Thrush *Turdus obscurus* 23 cm
In all plumages has white supercilium and white crescent below eye, and peachy-orange flanks contrasting with white belly. Male has blue-grey head. Female and first-winter have browner crown and ear-coverts and dark malar stripe. Open forest. KA, MV, TN

Dark-throated Thrush *Turdus ruficollis* 25 cm
Uniform grey upperparts and wings, with pale supercilium either absent or very indistinct. *T. r. atrogularis* (the race recorded) has black throat and/or breast; first-winter has grey streaking on breast and flanks. Forest, forest edges, cultivation and pastures with scattered trees. AN, MH

Ferruginous Flycatcher *Muscicapa ferruginea* 13 cm
Similar in shape and appearance to Asian Brown Flycatcher, but with rufous-orange uppertail-coverts and tail, rufous-orange flanks and undertail-coverts, and grey cast to head. Moist forest. AN

Yellow-rumped Flycatcher *Ficedula zanthopygia* 13 cm
Yellow rump, and white on wing in all plumages. Male has white supercilium, black upperparts and yellow underparts. Female and first-winter have greyish-olive upperparts. Undergrowth along rivers and streams. GO, MH

Little Pied Flycatcher *Ficedula westermanni* 10 cm
Small, compact flycatcher. Male black above and white below, with broad white supercilium and white wing-bar. Female has grey-brown upperparts, brownish-grey wash to breast, and rufous cast to rump/uppertail-coverts. Broadleaved forest and open wooded country. AN, MH, TN

White-tailed Rubythroat *Luscinia pectoralis* 14 cm
Male similar to male Siberian Rubythroat with ruby-red throat; main differences are black breast-band, white on tail, and greyer upperparts. Female White-tailed has greyer upperparts than female Siberian Rubythroat, with a grey breast-band and white tip to tail. Legs are black (brown in Siberian). Scrub and tall grass in marshes. KA

Variable Wheatear *Oenanthe picata* 14.5 cm
Very variable, with three races occurring in the subcontinent. Males can be mainly black, have black head with white underparts, or white crown and white underparts. Females can be mainly sooty-brown or have greyish upperparts with variable greyish-white underparts. Both sexes show extensive white at sides of tail. Cultivation and rocky areas. MH, TN

Pied Wheatear *Oenanthe pleschanka* 14.5 cm
Different tail pattern than Variable; always shows black edge to outer feathers (lacking in Variable) and often has only a narrow and broken terminal black band (broad and even on Variable). Finer features of breeding male are that white of nape extends to mantle, black of throat does not extend to upper breast, and breast is washed with buff (but is otherwise very similar to *capistrata* race of Variable). Non-breeding and first-winter male and female have pale fringes to upperparts and wings (not apparent on fresh-plumaged Variable). Open stony ground. MV

Northern Wheatear *Oenanthe oenanthe* 15 cm
Breeding male has blue-grey upperparts, black mask and pale orange breast. Breeding female greyish to olive-brown above. Compared with Isabelline, adult winter and first-winter have blackish centres to wing-coverts and tertials, and show more white at sides of tail. Open stony ground and cultivation. MV

Rufous-tailed Wheatear *Oenanthe xanthoprymna* 14.5 cm
Similar in appearance to Isabelline Wheatear but with rufous-orange lower back and rump, and rufous tail sides. Male has black lores. Semi-desert. GO, MH

Asian Glossy Starling *Aplonis panayensis* 20 cm
Adult is entirely glossy greenish black, with bright red iris. Juvenile has blackish-brown upperparts with variable greenish gloss, and streaked underparts. Groves and forest edges. TN

Purple-backed Starling *Sturnus sturninus* 19 cm
Male has pale grey head and underparts, purplish-black hind-crown patch and mantle, and white tips to median coverts and rear scapulars. Female and juvenile duller; wing-bars and tips to scapulars less prominent in juvenile. Open wooded areas. TN

Fire-capped Tit *Cephalopyrus flammiceps* 10 cm
Flowerpecker-like, with greenish upperparts and yellowish to whitish underparts. Lacks crest. Breeding male has bright orange-scarlet forecrown. Deciduous forest and deciduous/coniferous forest. MH

Asian House Martin *Delichon dasypus* 12 cm
Very similar to Northern House Martin; has dusky-white underparts and rump, shallower tail-fork, dusky underwing and (not always) dusky centres to undertail-coverts. Grassy slopes with cliffs, and forest around mountain villages. TN

White-eared Bulbul *Pycnonotus leucotis* 20 cm
A white-cheeked bulbul with black crown and nape, and short or non-existent crest. Upperparts are brown, and underparts whitish with yellow vent. Has white tip to tail. Thorn scrub and dry, open cultivation. KA, MH

Grey Hypocolius *Hypocolius ampelinus* 25 cm
Bulbul-like in shape. Crested, with long tail and white on primaries. Male is mainly grey with black mask and tail-band. Female rather uniform sandy-brown. Thorn scrub and date-palm groves in semi-desert. MH

Rusty-rumped Warbler *Locustella certhiola* 13.5 cm
Streaked upperparts. Superficially similar to Grasshopper Warbler. By comparison with that species, has more distinct supercilium, greyish crown, rufous rump and uppertail-coverts, and rather dark tail with white tips. Juvenile has yellowish wash to underparts and light spotting on breast. Reedbeds. KE

Yellow-browed Warbler *Phylloscopus inornatus* 10–11 cm
Uncommon winter visitor and passage migrant; 915–2590 m. Very similar to Hume's Warbler. Has yellowish wing-bars and supercilium (although these become whiter in worn plumage). Bill has orange at base. Call is a piercing *cheweest*. Groves and open forest. *See* Table 4 on p.232. GO, KE, MH, TN

Blyth's Leaf Warbler *Phylloscopus reguloides* 11 cm
Very similar in appearance to Western Crowned Warbler, with prominent wing-bars and pale crown-stripe. Is slightly smaller in size, typically with head pattern more striking, yellower underparts and more prominent wing-bars. Winters in bushes and open forest. *See* Table 5 on p.232. TN

Whistler's Warbler *Seicercus whistleri* 10 cm
Very similar in plumage to Golden-spectacled; dark sides of crown are not as black and are diffuse on forehead, and yellow eye-ring is broader at rear. Generally, upperparts are duller greyish green, underparts are duller yellow, and wing-bar is usually more distinct. Shows more white in outertail feathers; in particular there is much white on basal half of outer web of outermost tail feathers (Golden-spectacled generally lacks white in this area). Forest understorey and secondary growth. AN

Bimaculated Lark *Melanocorypha bimaculata*   17 cm
A very large lark, with stout bill and short tail. Has prominent white supercilium, black patch on
side of breast, and white tip to tail. Semi-desert and fallow cultivation. MH

Sand Lark *Calandrella raytal*   12 cm
Distinguished from other *Calandrella* larks by smaller size and stockier appearance, shorter tail and
rounded wings, colder sandy-grey upperparts, whitish underparts with fine sparse streaking on breast
(lacking any patches on breast), and pale rump and uppertail-coverts. Sandy river banks. TN

Ortolan Bunting *Emberiza hortulana*   16 cm
Pinkish-orange bill, plain head and prominent eye-ring. Adult has olive-grey head and breast, and
yellow submoustachial stripe and throat. Female streaked on crown and breast. First-winter and
juvenile more heavily streaked on mantle, malar region and breast than Grey-necked; submoustachial stripe and throat are buffish, but often with touch of yellow which helps separate it from
Grey-necked. Orchards and open woodland. MH

White-capped Bunting *Emberiza stewarti*   15 cm
Male has grey head, black supercilium and throat, and chestnut breast-band; pattern obscured
in winter. Female has rather plain head with pale supercilium; crown and mantle uniformly and
diffusely streaked, and underparts finely streaked and washed with buff. Cultivation, grass and
scrub. MH

Chestnut-eared Bunting *Emberiza fucata*   16 cm
Adult has chestnut ear-coverts, black breast streaking, and chestnut on breast sides. Some nondescript;
plain head with warm brown ear-coverts and pale eye-ring distinctive. Dry rocky and bushy hills. MH

Yellow-breasted Bunting *Emberiza aureola*   15 cm
Male in breeding plumage has black face and chestnut breast-band, and white inner wing-coverts;
patterning is obscured by pale fringes in fresh, non-breeding plumage. Female has strikingly patterned
head and mantle, yellowish underparts and white median-covert bar. Juvenile is similar to female
but with streaking on underparts. Cultivation and grassland. GO

TABLES

Table 1. Nightjars
(+ = vagrant)

Species	Size/structure	General Coloration	Crown/nape	Scapulars/coverts	Primaries	Tail	White throat patch
Grey Nightjar +	Medium. Well-proportioned, longish wings and tail, and large head	Uniform cold grey to grey-brown heavily marked with black.	Variable. Heavily to very heavily marked with black drop-shaped streaks. Some with irregular patches of rufous on nape. Streaking less regular and more extensive than Large-tailed	Scapulars heavily but irregularly marked with black, usually lacking well-defined buff or white edges (although pronounced pale edges to these feathers may be prominent in some). Coverts with variable greyish-white to buffish spotting	Male has small white spots on three or four primaries. On female, spots either lacking or small and rufous	Male variable, usually with white at tips of all but central tail feathers, with diffuse greyish margin at end	Large, central white spot in male, or buff in female
Eurasian Nightjar +	Medium. Long wings and tail, and small head	Grey, neat lanceolate streaking	Regular, bold, black lanceolate streaking	Bold lanceolate streaking to scapulars, with buff outer edge. Well-defined, regular pale buff spots on coverts	Male has large white spots on three primaries and female has no spots	Outermost two tail feathers have broad white tips in male. No white tips in female	Indistinct, but generally complete, white throat-crescent
Sykes's Nightjar +	Small. Shortish wings and tail, and large head	Grey with buff mottling and restricted dark vermiculations	Variable, small dark arrowhead markings. Irregular buff spotting on nape gives suggestion of collar	Scapulars relatively unmarked, with a few black inverted 'anchor-shaped' marks. Coverts with irregular and small buff markings	Male has large white spots on three or four primaries. Female primary spots are buffish	In male, two outermost pairs have broad white tips. In female, tail is unmarked or has buffish tip to outertail	Broken, large white patches on sides. Some have complete crescent
Indian Nightjar	Small. Short wings and tail, and small head	Grey, with bold buff, black and some rufous markings. Resembles small version of Large-tailed	Bold, broad, black streaking to crown. Nape marked with rufous-buff forming distinct collar	Bold, triangular black centres and broad rufous-buff fringes to scapulars. Coverts with bold buff or buffish spotting	Both sexes have small white or buffish spots on four primaries	Both sexes have broad white tips to outer two tail feathers	Generally broken. Large white patches on sides. Lacking in some
Large-tailed Nightjar	Large. Long-winged and long, broad tail. Large head	Large head. More warmly coloured than Grey with buff-brown tones, heavily marked with black and buff	Brownish grey with bold black streaks down centre. Diffuse pale rufous-brown band across nape	Scapulars have well-defined buff edges with bold, wedge-shaped, black centres. Coverts boldly tipped buff	Male has white spots on four primaries; female lacks these or has smaller buff spots	Male has extensive white tips to two outermost feathers. Female has less extensive buff tips to outer two feathers	Large central white throat patch in both sexes
Jerdon's Nightjar	Medium. Relatively short-winged and short-tailed with large head	Warmly coloured as Large-tailed, though generally darker	As Large-tailed. More extensive rufous coloration to nape and upper mantle	Much as Large-tailed	As Large-tailed	As Large-tailed	As Large-tailed
Savanna Nightjar	Medium. Shortish wings and tail, and large head	Dark brownish grey, intricately patterned (without bold, dark streaking) but with variable rufous-buff markings	Variable. Some only finely vermiculated, others with black, 'arrowhead' markings and others with irregular-shaped, black markings	Scapulars variably marked but most show rufous-buff outer web. Coverts variably marked with rufous-buff, showing as distinct spotting in some	Male has large white spots on four primaries. Female's spots have buff to rufous-buff wash	Outer two tail feathers are mainly white in male, but not in female	Large white patches on sides

Table 2. Small to medium-sized Phylloscopus warblers, lacking wing-bars and crown-stripe

Species	Head pattern	Upperparts including wings	Underparts	Call	Additional features
Common Chiffchaff	Whitish or buffish supercilium, and prominent crescent below eye	Greyish to brownish with olive-green cast to rump and edges of remiges and rectrices	Whitish with variable buffish or greyish cast to breast-sides and flanks	Plaintive *peu*, more disyllabic *sie-u*	Blackish bill and legs (compare with Greenish and Dusky)
Dusky Warbler	Broad, buffish-white supercilium with strong dark eye-stripe	Dark brown to paler greyish brown; never shows any greenish in plumage	White with buff on sides of breast and flanks	Hard *chack chack*	Pale brown legs, and orangish base to lower mandible. Typically skulking
Tickell's Leaf Warbler	Prominent yellow supercilium concolorous with throat; well-defined eye-stripe	Dark greenish to greenish-brown upperparts, and with greenish edges to remiges	Bright lemon-yellow underparts, lacking strong buff tones	A *chit*, or *sit*; not as hard as that of Dusky	
Sulphur-bellied Warbler	Prominent, bright sulphur-yellow supercilium, distinctly brighter than throat	Cold brown to brownish grey, lacking greenish tones, and with greyish edges to remiges	Yellowish buff with strong buff tones to breast and flanks and sulphur-yellow belly	Soft *quip* or *dip*	Climbs about rocks, or nuthatch-like on tree trunks
Tytler's Leaf Warbler	Prominent, fine white to yellowish-white supercilium, with broad dark olive eye-stripe	Greenish, becoming greyer when worn	Whitish, with variable yellowish wash when fresh	A double *y-it*	Long, slender, mainly dark bill; shortish tail

Table 3. Medium-sized to large Phylloscopus warblers, with narrow wing-bars, and lacking crown-stripe

Note: Wing-bars may be missing when plumage is worn (when confusion is then possible with species in Table 2)

Species	Head pattern	Upperparts including wings	Underparts	Bill	Call	Other features
Greenish Warbler *T. t. viridanus*	Prominent yellowish-white supercilium usually extends to forehead; eye-stripe usually falls short of base of bill	Olive-green, becoming duller and greyer when worn; generally lacking darker crown. Single narrow but well-defined white wing-bar	Whitish with faint yellowish suffusion	Lower mandible orangish, usually lacking prominent dark tip	Loud, slurred *chit-wee*	
Greenish Warbler *T. t. nitidus*	Prominent yellowish supercilium, and yellow wash to cheeks	Upperparts brighter and purer green than *viridanus*, with one or two slightly broader and yellower wing-bars	Strongly suffused with yellow, which can still be apparent in worn plumage	As *viridanus*	More trisyllabic than that of *viridanus*, a *chis-ru-weet*	
Large-billed Leaf Warbler	Striking yellowish-white supercilium contrasting with broad, dark eye-stripe, with greyish mottling on ear-coverts	Dark oily-green with noticeably darker crown; one or two yellowish-white wing-bars	Dirty, often with diffuse streaking on breast and flanks and oily-yellow wash on breast and belly; however, can appear whitish	Large and mainly dark, with orange at base of lower mandible; often with pronounced hooked tip	Loud, clear, upward-inflected *der-tee*	Large size

Table 4. Small Phylloscopus *warblers with broad, generally double, wing-bars, most having pale crown-stripe* (+ = vagrant)

Species	Head pattern	Wing-bars	Underparts	Call	Other features
Yellow-browed Warbler +	Lacks well-defined crown-stripe, although can show diffuse paler line; broad yellowish-white supercilium and cheeks	Broad, yellowish or whitish wing-bars; median-covert wing-bar is prominent	White with variable amounts of yellow	A loud *cheeweest*, with distinct rising inflection	Brighter greenish-olive upperparts (in fresh plumage) compared with Hume's. Bill has extensive pale (usually orangish) base to lower mandible, and legs are paler (compared with Hume's)
Hume's Warbler	Lacks well-defined crown-stripe, although can show diffuse paler line; broad, buffish-white supercilium and cheeks	Broad, buffish or whitish median- and greater-covert wing-bar; median-covert wing-bar tends to be poorly defined, but can be prominent	White, often sullied with grey	A rolling, disyllabic *whit-hoo* or *visu-visu*, and a flat *chwee*	Greyish-olive upperparts, with variable yellowish-green suffusion, and browner crown. Bill appears all dark and legs are normally blackish brown

Table 5. Large Phylloscopus *warblers with crown-stripe, prominent wing-bars, and large bill with orange lower mandible*
(+ = vagrant)

Species	Head pattern	Upperparts including wings	Underparts	Call	Additional features
Western Crowned Warbler	Greyish-white to pale yellow crown-stripe, contrasting with dusky olive sides of crown, which may be darker towards nape; prominent dull yellow supercilium	Generally duller greyish green compared with Blyth's, with stronger grey cast to nape; wing-bars narrower and less prominent than Blyth's, because bases not so dark	Whitish, strongly suffused with grey, especially on throat and breast; can show traces of yellow on breast and belly	A repeated *chit-weei*	Larger and more elongated than Blyth's, with larger and longer bill
Blyth's Leaf Warbler +	Tends to be more striking than Western Crowned, with yellow supercilium and crown-stripe contrasting with darker sides of crown	Usually darker and purer green than Western Crowned, although may be similar. Wing-bars are more prominent than Western Crowned, being broader and often divided by dark panel across greater coverts	Generally has distinct yellowish wash, especially on cheeks and breast	*Kee-kew-i* repeated constantly	

Table 6. Unstreaked Acrocephalus warblers and Booted Warbler

Species	Bill/feet	Head pattern	Upperparts	Underparts	Additional features
Paddyfield Warbler	Shorter bill than Blyth's Reed, usually with well-defined dark tip to pale lower mandible. Yellowish-brown to pinkish-brown legs and feet	Prominent white supercilium, often broadening behind eye, becoming almost square-ended, with dark eye-stripe; supercilium can appear to be bordered above by diffuse dark line (supercilium less distinct on some)	More rufescent than Blyth's Reed. Typically shows dark centres and pale fringes to tertials. Greyer or sandier when worn but usually retains rufous cast to rump	Warm buff flanks; underparts whiter when worn. Often shows whitish sides to neck	Typically looks longer-tailed than Blyth's Reed, with tail often held cocked
Blyth's Reed Warbler	Bill longer than Paddyfield. Lower mandible entirely pale or has diffuse dark tip	Comparatively indistinct supercilium; often does not extend beyond eye, or barely does so, and never reaches rear of ear-coverts. Lacks dark upper border to supercilium and dark eye-stripe	Tertials rather uniform. Generally colder olive-grey to olive-brown than Paddyfield. Noticeable warm olive cast to upperparts when fresh (more rufescent in first-winter)	Can have light buffish wash on flanks when fresh; otherwise cold whitish	Shorter-looking, more-rounded tail than Booted, and longer upper- and undertail-coverts; more skulking and lethargic than that species
Booted Warbler *H. c. rama*	Longer-billed than *caligata*. Legs and feet paler and browner than Blyth's Reed	Supercilium more distinct than Blyth's Reed and lores can appear pale	Paler and greyer than *caligata* and all *Acrocephalus* (although can be rather similar to Blyth's Reed)	Off-white	More arboreal than *caligata*; behaviour often *Phylloscopus*-like compared to *Acrocephalus*. Longer-looking square-ended tail than *Acrocephalus* with shorter undertail-coverts
Booted Warbler *H. c. caligata*	Comparatively short and fine bill	Supercilium more prominent than *rama*; can appear to have dark border	Warmer brown than *rama*. Fine whitish fringes to remiges and edges of outertail feathers often apparent (also shown by *rama*)	Off-white	Rather *Phylloscopus*-like in appearance, often feeding on ground. Squarer tail and short undertail-coverts compared with *Acrocephalus*

Table 7. Yellow Wagtails (breeding males only)

Subspecies	Head pattern
M. f. beema	Pale bluish-grey head, complete and distinct white supercilium, white chin, and usually a white submoustachial stripe contrasting with yellow throat; ear-coverts are grey or brown, usually with some white feathers
M. f. melanogrisea	Black head, lacking any supercilium, and white chin and poorly defined submoustachial stripe contrasting with yellow throat
M. f. thunbergi	Dark slate-grey crown with darker ear-coverts, lacking supercilium (although may show faint trace behind eye)
M. f. lutea	Mainly yellow head, with variable amounts of yellowish green on crown, nape and ear-coverts (concolorous with mantle)

INDEX

* = vagrant to southern India.

English Names

Adjutant Greater 158
Lesser 158
Avadavat Green 216
Red 216
Avocet Pied 106
Babbler Abbott's 202 *(Heard only)*
Common 204
Dark-fronted 202
Indian Scimitar 202
Jungle 204
Large Grey 204
Puff-throated 202
Rufous 204
Rufous-fronted 202
Striped Tit 204
Tawny-bellied 202
Yellow-billed 204
Yellow-eyed 204
Barbet Brown-headed 62
Coppersmith 62
Crimson-fronted 62
White-cheeked 62
Baza Black 122
Jerdon's 122
Bee-eater Blue-bearded 70
Blue-cheeked 70
Blue-tailed 70
Chestnut-headed 70
European 70
Green 70
Besra 132
Bittern Black 152
Cinnamon 152
Great 152
Little* 225
Yellow 152
Blackbird Eurasian 176
Bluebird Asian Fairy 164
Bluethroat 182
Booby Brown 146
Masked 146
Red-footed 146
Bulbul Black 192
Black-crested 192
Grey-headed 192
Red-vented 192
Red-whiskered 192
White-browed 192
White-eared* 228
Yellow-browed 192
Yellow-throated 192
Bunting Black-headed 218
Chestnut-eared* 229
Crested 218
Grey-necked 218
House 218
Ortolan* 229
Red-headed 218
White-capped* 229
Yellow-breasted* 229
Bushchat Pied 184
Bushlark Indian 206
Jerdon's 206

Singing 206
Bustard Indian 90
Macqueen's* 222
Buttonquail Barred 48
Small 48
Yellow-legged 48
Buzzard Common 134 *(honey)*
Long-legged 134
White-eyed 134
Chiffchaff Common 198
Cisticola Bright-headed 194
Zitting 194
Coot Common 94
Cormorant Great 144
Indian 144
Little 144
Coucal Greater 76
Lesser 76
Courser Indian 110
Jerdon's 110
Crab-plover 106
Crake Baillon's 92
Brown 92
Little* 225
Ruddy-breasted 92
Slaty-legged 92
Spotted 92
Crane Common 90
Demoiselle 90
Sarus 90
Siberian* 222
Creeper Spotted 188
Crow House 166
Large-billed 166
Cuckoo Asian Emerald* 221
Banded Bay 72
Chestnut-winged 72
Common Hawk 72
Drongo 74
Eurasian 72
Grey-bellied 74
Indian 72
Large Hawk 72
Lesser 72
Oriental* 220
Pied 72
Plaintive* 221
Violet* 221
Cuckooshrike Black-headed 168
Black-winged 168
Large 168
Curlew Eurasian 98

Darter 144
Dollarbird 66
Dotterel Black-fronted* 223
Dove Emerald 88
Eurasian Collared 86
European Turtle* 222
Laughing 86
Oriental Turtle 86
Red Collared 86

Spotted 86
Dowitcher Asian 100
Drongo Ashy 170
Black 170
Bronzed 170
Greater Racket-tailed 170
Spangled 170
White-bellied 170
Duck Comb 52
Falcated* 220
Marbled* 220
Pink-headed 56
Spot-billed 54
Tufted 58
Dunlin 104
Eagle Black 128
Bonelli's 138
Booted 138
Changeable Hawk 138
Crested Serpent 128
Greater Spotted 136
Grey-headed Fish 124
Imperial* 225
Indian Spotted 136
Lesser Fish* 224
Mountain Hawk 138
Pallas's Fish 124
Rufous-bellied 138
Short-toed Snake 128
Steppe 136
Tawny 136
White-bellied Sea 124
White-tailed* 224
Egret Cattle 148
Great 148
Intermediate 148
Little 148
Western Reef 148
Falcon Amur 140
Laggar 142
Peregrine 142
Red-necked 140
Saker* 225
Fantail White-browed 172
White-throated 172
Flameback Black-rumped 62
Common 62
Greater 62
Himalayan 62
Flamingo Greater 154
Lesser 154
Florican Lesser 90
Flowerpecker Pale-billed 208
Plain 208
Thick-billed 208
Flycatcher Asian Brown 178
Black-and-orange 178
Blue-throated 180
Brown-breasted 178
Ferruginous* 227
Grey-headed Canary 180

Kashmir 178
Little Pied* 227
Nilgiri 180
Pale-chinned 180
Red-throated 178
Rusty-tailed 178
Tickell's Blue 180
Ultramarine 178
Verditer 180
White-bellied Blue 180
Yellow-rumped* 227
Flycatcher-shrike Bar-
winged 168
Francolin Grey 46
Painted 46
Frigatebird Great 160
Lesser 160
Frogmouth Sri Lanka 84
Fulvetta Brown-cheeked 204

Gadwall 54
Garganey 56
Godwit Bar-tailed 98
Black-tailed 98
Goose Bar-headed 52
Greylag* 220
Lesser White-fronted* 220
Goshawk Crested 132
Northern* 224
Grassbird Bristled 200
Broad-tailed 200
Striated 200
Grebe Black-necked* 225
Great Crested* 225
Little 144
Greenshank Common 98
Griffon Eurasian 126
Himalayan* 224
Gull Black-headed 114
Brown-headed 114
Caspian 112
Heuglin's 112
Mew* 223
Pallas's 112
Slender-billed 114
Sooty 112
White-eyed* 223

Harrier Eurasian Marsh 128
Hen 130
Montagu's 130
Pallid 130
Pied 130
Heron Black-crowned Night
150
Goliath* 225
Grey 150
Indian Pond 150
Little 150
Malayan Night 152
Purple 150
Hobby Eurasian 142
Oriental 142
Honey-buzzard Oriental 134
Hoopoe Common 66
Hornbill Great 64
Indian Grey 64
Malabar Grey 64
Malabar Pied 64
Oriental Pied 64

Hypocolius Grey* 228

Ibis Black 154
Black-headed 154
Glossy 154
Iora Common 172
Marshall's* 227

Jacana Bronze-winged 106
Pheasant-tailed 106
Jaeger Parasitic 112
Pomarine 112
Junglefowl Grey 50
Red 50

Kestrel Common 140
Lesser 140
Kingfisher Black-capped 68
Blue-eared 68
Collared 68
Common 68
Oriental Dwarf 68
Pied 68
Ruddy* 220
Stork-billed 68
White-throated 68
Kite Black 122
Black-shouldered 122
Brahminy 122
Knot Great 100
Red 100
Koel Asian 74

Lapwing Grey-headed* 223
Northern* 223
Red-wattled 110
River 110
Sociable 110
White-tailed 110
Yellow-wattled 110
Lark Ashy-crowned Sparrow
206
Bimaculated* 229
Crested 206
Greater Short-toed 206
Malabar 206
Rufous-tailed 206
Sand* 229
Sykes's 206
Laughingthrush Grey-
breasted 202
Nilgiri 202
Wynaad 202
Leafbird Blue-winged 164
Golden-fronted 164

Malkoha Blue-faced 74
Green-billed 74
Sirkeer 74
Mallard 54
Martin Asian House* 228
Dusky Crag 190
Eurasian Crag 190
Northern House 190
Pale 188
Plain 188
Sand 188
Merganser Common* 220
Minivet Ashy 168
Long-tailed* 226

Rosy 168
Scarlet 168
Small 168
White-bellied 168
Monarch Black-naped 172
Moorhen Common 94
Munia Black-headed 216
Black-throated 216
Scaly-breasted 216
White-rumped 216
Myna Bank 186
Common 186
Hill 186
Jungle 186

Needletail Brown-backed 78
White-rumped 78
White-throated* 221
Nightjar Eurasian* 221
Great Eared 84
Grey 84
Indian 84
Jerdon's 84
Large-tailed 84
Savanna 84
Sykes's* 221
Noddy Brown 120
Lesser 120
Nuthatch Chestnut-bellied
188
Velvet-fronted 188

Openbill Asian 156
Oriole Black-hooded 166
Black-naped 166
Eurasian Golden 166
Osprey 122
Owl Barn 80
Brown Fish 82
Brown Hawk 82
Brown Wood 82
Collared Scops 80
Dusky Eagle 82
Eurasian Eagle 82
Eurasian Scops* 221
Grass 80
Long-eared* 221
Mottled Wood 82
Oriental Bay 80
Oriental Scops 80
Pallid Scops 80
Short-eared 82
Spot-bellied Eagle 82
Owlet Forest 80
Jungle 80
Spotted 80
Oystercatcher Eurasian 106

Painted-snipe Greater 96
Paradise-flycatcher Asian
172
Parakeet Alexandrine 76
Malabar 76
Plum-headed 76
Rose-ringed 76
Parrot Vernal Hanging 76
Peafowl Indian 50
Pelican Dalmatian* 225
Great White 160
Spot-billed 160

Petrel Barau's* 226
  Bulwer's* 226
  Jouanin's* 226
Petronia Chestnut-shouldered 214
Phalarope Red-necked 104
Piculet Speckled 60
Pigeon Green Imperial 88
  Mountain Imperial 88
  Nilgiri Wood 86
  Orange-breasted Green 88
  Pale-capped 86
  🖝 Pompadour Green 88
  Rock 86
  Yellow-footed Green 88
Pintail Northern 56
Pipit Blyth's 212
  Long-billed 212
  Nilgiri 212
  Olive-backed 212
  Paddyfield 212
  Red-throated 212
  Richard's 212
  Tawny 212
  Tree 212
Pitta Indian 164
Plover Caspian* 222
  Common Ringed 108
  Greater Sand 108
  Grey 108
  Kentish 108
  Lesser Sand 108
  Little Ringed 108
  Pacific Golden 108
Pochard Baer's* 220
  Common 58
  Ferruginous 58
  Red-crested 58
Pratincole Collared* 223
  Oriental 110
  Small 110
Prinia Ashy 194
  Grey-breasted 194
  Jungle 194
  Plain 194
  Rufescent 194
  Rufous-fronted 194
Pygmy-goose Cotton 56

Quail Blue-breasted 48
  Common 46
  Jungle Bush 48
  Painted Bush 48
  Rain 46
  Rock Bush 48

Rail Slaty-breasted 92
  Water 92
Raven Common* 226
Redshank Common 98
  Spotted 98
Redstart Black 184
Robin Indian 184
  Indian Blue 182
  Oriental Magpie 182
Rock-chat Brown 182
Roller European 66
  Indian 66
Rosefinch Common 218
Rubythroat Siberian 182

White-tailed* 227
Ruff 104

Sanderling 102
Sandgrouse Black-bellied* 222
  Chestnut-bellied 94
  Painted 94
Sandpiper Broad-billed 104
  Buff-breasted* 222
  Common 100
  Curlew 104
  Green 100
  Marsh 98
  Spoon-billed 104
  Terek 100
  Wood 100
Scaup Greater* 220
Shama White-rumped 182
Shearwater Audubon's 162
  Flesh-footed 162
  Persian* 226
  Streaked* 226
  Wedge-tailed 162
Shelduck Common 52
  Ruddy 52
Shikra 132
Shortwing White-bellied 182
Shoveler Northern 54
Shrike Bay-backed 164
  Brown 164
  Grey-backed* 226
  Long-tailed 164
  Rufous-tailed 164
  Southern Grey 164
Silverbill Indian 216
Skimmer Indian 114
Skua Brown* 223
  South Polar* 223
Skylark Oriental 206
Snipe Common 96
  Great* 222
  Jack 96
  Pintail 96
  Swinhoe's 96
  Wood 96
Sparrow Eurasian Tree 214
  House 214
Sparrowhawk Chinese* 224
  Eurasian 132
  Japanese* 224
Spiderhunter Little 208
Spoonbill Eurasian 154
Spurfowl Painted 46
  Red 46
Starling Asian Glossy* 228
  Asian Pied 186
  Brahminy 186
  🖉 Chestnut-tailed 186
  Common 186
  Purple-backed* 228
  Rosy 186
Stilt Black-winged 106
Stint Little 102
  Long-toed 102
  Red-necked 102
  Temminck's 102
Stonechat Common 184
Stork Black 158
  Black-necked 158

Painted 156
White 156
Woolly-necked 156
Storm-petrel Leach's* 226
  Swinhoe's 162
  White-bellied* 226
  White-faced* 226
  Wilson's 162
Sunbird Crimson 208
  Crimson-backed 208
  Loten's 208
  Purple 208
  Purple-rumped 208
  Ruby-cheeked 208
Swallow Barn 190
  Pacific 190
  Red-rumped 190
  Streak-throated 190
  Wire-tailed 190
Swamphen Purple 94
Swan Mute* 220
Swift Alpine 78
  Asian Palm 78
  Common 78
  Fork-tailed 78
  House 78
  Pallid* 221
Swiftlet Himalayan* 221
  Indian 78

Tailorbird Common 196
Tattler Grey-tailed* 222
Teal Baikal* 220
  Common 56
Tern Black* 224
  Black-bellied 118
  Black-naped 118
  Bridled 120
  Caspian 116
  Common 118
  Great Crested 116
  Gull-billed 116
  Lesser Crested 116
  Little 118
  River 116
  Roseate 118
  Sandwich 116
  Saunders's 118
  Sooty 120
  Whiskered 120
  White 120
  White-cheeked 118
  White-winged 120
Thick-knee Eurasian 106
  Great 106
Thrush Blue Rock 174
  Blue-capped Rock 174
  Dark-throated* 227
  Eyebrowed* 227
  Malabar Whistling 174
  Orange-headed 174
  Pied 174
  Scaly 174
  Siberian* 227
  Tickell's 176
Tit Black-lored 188
  Fire-capped* 228
  Great 188
  White-naped 188
Treepie Grey 166

Rufous 166
White-bellied 166
Treeswift Crested 78
Trogon Malabar 66
Tropicbird Red-billed 146
White-tailed 146
Turnstone Ruddy 100

Vulture Cinereous* 224
Egyptian 124
Indian 126
Red-headed 126
White-rumped 126

Wagtail Citrine 210
Forest 210
Grey 210
White 210
White-browed 210
Yellow 210
Warbler Blyth's Leaf* 228
Blyth's Reed 196
Booted 196
Clamorous Reed 196
Dusky 198

Golden-spectacled 200
Grasshopper 196
Greenish 198
Hume's 198
Large-billed Leaf 198
Orphean 200
Paddyfield 196
Pale-footed Bush 196
Rusty-rumped* 228
Sulphur-bellied 198
Thick-billed 196
Tickell's Leaf 198
Tytler's Leaf 198
Western Crowned 200
Whistler's* 228
Yellow-browed* 228
Watercock 94
Waterhen White-breasted 92
Weaver Baya 214
Black-breasted 214
Streaked 214
Wheatear Desert 184
Isabelline 184
Northern* 228
Pied* 227

Rufous-tailed* 228
Variable* 227
Whimbrel 98
Whistling-duck Fulvous 52
Lesser 52
White-eye Oriental 194
Whitethroat Lesser 200
Wigeon Eurasian 54
Woodcock Eurasian 96
Woodpecker Brown-capped Pygmy 60
Fulvous-breasted 60
Heart-spotted 60
Rufous 60
Streak-throated 62
White-bellied 60
White-naped 62
Yellow-crowned 60
Woodshrike Common 172
Large 172
Woodswallow Ashy 168
Wryneck Eurasian 60

Yellownape Greater 60
Lesser 60

Scientific Names

Accipiter badius 132
badius badius 132
badius dussumier 132
*gentilis** 224
*gularis** 224
nisus 132
*soloensis** 224
trivirgatus 132
virgatus 132
Acridotheres fuscus 186
ginginianus 186
tristis 186
Acrocephalus aedon 196
agricola 196
dumetorum 196
stentoreus 196
Actitis hypoleucos 100
*Aegithina nigrolutea** 227
tiphia 172
tiphia humei 172
tiphia multicolor 172
*Aegypius monachus** 224
Aethopyga siparaja 208
Alauda gulgula 206
gulgula australis 206
gulgula gulgula 206
Alcedo atthis 68
meninting 68
Alcippe poioicephala 204
Amandava amandava 216
formosa 216
Amaurornis akool 92
phoenicurus 92
Ammomanes phoenicurus 206
Anas acuta 56
Anas clypeata 54
crecca 56
*falcata** 220
*formosa** 220
penelope 54
platyrhynchos 54

poecilorhyncha 54
querquedula 56
strepera 54
Anastomus oscitans 156
Anhinga melanogaster 144
Anous stolidus 120
tenuirostris 120
*Anser anser** 220
*erythropus** 220
indicus 52
Anthracoceros albirostris 64
coronatus 64
Anthreptes singalensis 208
Anthus campestris 212
cervinus 212
godlewskii 212
hodgsoni 212
hodgsoni hodgsoni 212
hodgsoni yunnanensis 212
nilghiriensis 212
richardi 212
rufulus 212
similis 212
similis similis 212
similis travancoriensis 212
trivialis 212
*Aplonis panayensis** 228
Apus affinis 78
apus 78
pacificus 78
*pallidus** 221
Aquila clanga 136
clanga 'fulvescens' 136
hastata 136
*heliaca** 225
nipalensis 136
rapax 136
Arachnothera longirostra 208
Ardea cinerea 150
*goliath** 225
purpurea 150

Ardeola grayii 150
Ardeotis nigriceps 90
Arenaria interpres 100
Artamus fuscus 168
Asio flammeus 82
*otus** 221
Athene blewitti 80
brama 80
Aviceda jerdoni 122
leuphotes 122
*Aythya baeri** 220
ferina 58
fuligula 58
*marila** 220
nyroca 58

Batrachostomus moniliger 84
Botaurus stellaris 152
Brachypteryx major 182
major albiventris 182
major major 182
Bubo bubo 82
coromandus 82
nipalensis 82
Bubulcus ibis 148
Buceros bicornis 64
*Bulweria bulwerii** 226
*fallax** 226
Burhinus oedicnemus 106
Butastur teesa 134
Buteo buteo 134
buteo japonicus 134
buteo refectus 134
rufinus 134
Butorides striatus 150

*Cacomantis merulinus** 221
passerinus 74
sonneratii 72
Calandrella brachydactyla
dukhunensis 206

brachydactyla longipennis 206
raytal* 229
Calidris alba 102
  alpina 104
  canutus 100
  ferruginea 104
  minuta 102
  pygmea 104
  ruficollis 102
  subminuta 102
  temminckii 102
  tenuirostris 100
Calonectris leucomelas* 226
Caprimulgus affinis 84
  asiaticus 84
  atripennis 84
  europaeus* 221
  indicus 84
  macrurus 84
  mahrattensis* 221
Carpodacus erythrinus 218
  erythrinus erythrinus 218
  erythrinus roseatus 218
Casmerodius albus 148
Catharacta antarctica* 223
  maccormicki* 223
Celeus brachyurus 60
Centropus bengalensis 76
  sinensis 76
Cephalopyrus flammiceps* 228
Cercomela fusca 182
Ceryle rudis 68
  rudis leucomelanura 68
  rudis travancoreensis 68
  rudis travancoreensis   68
Cettia pallidipes 196
Ceyx erithacus 68
Chaetornis striatus 200
Chalcophaps indica 88
Charadrius alexandrinus 108
  alexandrinus alexandrinus 108
  alexandrinus seebohmi 108
  asiaticus* 222
  dubius 108
  hiaticula 108
  leschenaultii 108
  mongolus 108
Chlamydotis macqueenii* 222
Chlidonias hybridus 120
  leucopterus 120
  niger* 224
Chloropsis aurifrons 164
  cochinchinensis 164
Chrysococcyx maculatus* 221
  xanthorhynchus* 221
Chrysocolaptes festivus 62
  lucidus 62
Chrysomma sinense 204
Ciconia ciconia 156
  episcopus 156
  nigra 158
Circaetus gallicus 128
Circus aeruginosus 128
  cyaneus 130
  macrourus 130
  melanoleucos 130
  pygargus 130
Cisticola exilis 194
  juncidis 194
Clamator coromandus 72

jacobinus 72
Collocalia brevirostris* 221
  unicolor 78
Columba elphinstonii 86
  livia 86
  punicea 86
Copsychus malabaricus 182
  saularis 182
Coracias benghalensis 66
  garrulus 66
Coracina macei 168
  melanoptera 168
  melaschistos 168
Corvus corax* 226
  macrorhynchos 166
  splendens 166
Coturnix chinensis 48
  coromandelica 46
  coturnix 46
Cuculus canorus 72
  micropterus 72
  poliocephalus 72
  saturatus* 220
Culicicapa ceylonensis 180
Cursorius coromandelicus 110
Cygnus olor* 220
Cyornis pallipes 180
  poliogenys 180
  rubeculoides 180
  tickelliae 180
Cypsiurus balasiensis 78

Delichon dasypus* 228
  urbica 190
Dendrocitta formosae 166
  leucogastra 166
  vagabunda 166
Dendrocopos macei 60
  mahrattensis 60
  nanus 60
Dendrocygna bicolor 52
  javanica 52
Dendronanthus indicus 210
Dicaeum agile 208
  concolor 208
  erythrorynchos 208
Dicrurus aeneus 170
  caerulescens 170
  hottentottus 170
  leucophaeus 170
  macrocercus 170
  paradiseus 170
Dinopium benghalense 62
  javanense 62
  shorii 62
Dromas ardeola 106
Dryocopus javensis 60
Ducula aenea 88
  badia 88
Dumetia hyperythra 202
  hyperythra albogularis 202
  hyperythra hyperythra 202
Dupetor flavicollis 152

Egretta garzetta 148
  gularis 148
Elanus caeruleus 122
Elseyornis melanops* 223
Emberiza aureola* 229
  bruniceps 218

buchanani 218
  fucata* 229
  hortulana* 229
  melanocephala 218
  stewarti* 229
  striolata 218
Ephippiorhynchus asiaticus 158
Eremopterix grisea 206
Esacus recurvirostris 106
Eudynamys scolopacea 74
Eumyias albicaudata 180
  thalassina 180
Eurostopodus macrotis 84
Eurystomus orientalis 66

Falco amurensis 140
  cherrug* 225
  chicquera 140
  jugger 142
  naumanni 140
  peregrinus 142
  peregrinus babylonicus 142
  peregrinus calidus 142
  peregrinus peregrinator 142
  severus 142
  subbuteo 142
  tinnunculus 140
Ficedula nigrorufa 178
  parva 178
  parva albicilla 178
  parva parva 178
  subrubra 178
  superciliaris 178
  westermanni* 227
  zanthopygia* 227
Francolinus pictus 46
  pondicerianus 46
Fregata ariel 160
  minor 160
Fregetta grallaria* 226
Fulica atra 94

Galerida cristata 206
  deva 206
  malabarica 206
Gallicrex cinerea 94
Gallinago gallinago 96
  media* 222
  megala 96
  nemoricola 96
  stenura 96
Gallinula chloropus 94
Gallirallus striatus 92
Galloperdix lunulata 46
  spadicea 46
  spadicea spadicea 46
  spadicea stewarti 46
Gallus gallus 50
  sonneratii 50
Garrulax cachinnans 202
  delesserti 202
  jerdoni 202
  jerdoni fairbanki 202
  jerdoni jerdoni 202
  jerdoni meridionale 202
Gelochelidon nilotica 116
Glareola lactea 110
  maldivarum 110
  pratincola* 223
Glaucidium radiatum 80

radiatum malabaricum 80
radiatum radiatum 80
Gorsachius melanolophus 152
Gracula religiosa 186
Grus antigone 90
grus 90
leucogeranus* 222
virgo 90
Gygis alba 120
Gyps bengalensis 126
fulvus 126
himalayensis* 224
indicus 126

Haematopus ostralegus 106
Halcyon capensis 68
coromanda* 220
pileata 68
smyrnensis 68
Haliaeetus albicilla* 224
leucogaster 124
leucoryphus 124
Haliastur indus 122
Harpactes fasciatus 66
Hemicircus canente 60
Hemiprocne coronata 78
Hemipus picatus 168
Heteroscelus brevipes* 222
Hieraaetus fasciatus 138
kienerii 138
pennatus 138
Hierococcyx sparverioides 72
varius 72
Himantopus himantopus 106
Hippolais caligata 196
caligata caligata 196
caligata rama 196
Hirundapus caudacutus* 221
giganteus 78
Hirundo concolor 190
daurica 190
fluvicola 190
rupestris 190
rustica 190
smithii 190
tahitica 190
Hydrophasianus chirurgus 106
Hypocolius ampelinus* 228
Hypothymis azurea 172
Hypsipetes leucocephalus 192

Ichthyophaga humilis* 224
ichthyaetus 124
Ictinaetus malayensis 128
Iole indica 192
Irena puella 164
Ixobrychus cinnamomeus 152
minutus* 225
sinensis 152

Jynx torquilla 60

Ketupa zeylonensis 82

Lanius cristatus 164
isabellinus 164
schach 164
schach caniceps 164
schach erythronotus 164
schach tricolor 164

tephronotus* 226
vittatus 164
Larus brunnicephalus 114
cachinnans 112
canus* 223
genei 114
hemprichii 112
heuglini 112
ichthyaetus 112
leucophthalmus* 223
ridibundus 114
Leptoptilos dubius 158
javanicus 158
Limicola falcinellus 104
Limnodromus semipalmatus 100
Limosa lapponica 98
limosa 98
Locustella certhiola* 228
naevia 196
Lonchura kelaarti 216
malabarica 216
malacca 216
punctulata 216
striata 216
Loriculus vernalis 76
Luscinia brunnea 182
calliope 182
pectoralis* 227
svecica 182
Lymnocryptes minimus 96

Macronous gularis 204
Malacocincla abbotti 202
Marmaronetta angustirostris*
220
Megalaima haemacephala 62
rubricapilla 62
viridis 62
zeylanica 62
Megalurus palustris 200
Melanocorypha bimaculata* 229
Melophus lathami 218
Mergus merganser* 220
Merops apiaster 70
leschenaulti 70
orientalis 70
persicus 70
philippinus 70
Mesophoyx intermedia 148
Metopidius indicus 106
Milvus migrans 122
Mirafra affinis 206
cantillans 206
erythroptera 206
Monticola cinclorhynchus 174
solitarius 174
Motacilla alba 210
alba dukhunensis 210
alba personata 210
cinerea 210
citreola 210
flava 210
flava beema 210
flava lutea 210
flava melanogrisea 210
flava thunbergi 210
maderaspatensis 210
Muscicapa dauurica 178
ferruginea* 227
muttui 178

ruficauda 178
Mycteria leucocephala 156
Myophonus horsfieldii 174

Nectarinia asiatica 208
lotenia 208
minima 208
zeylonica 208
Neophron percnopterus 124
Nettapus coromandelianus 56
Ninox scutulata 82
Numenius arquata 98
phaeopus 98
Nycticorax nycticorax 150
Nyctyornis athertoni 70

Oceanites oceanicus 162
Oceanodroma leucorhoa* 226
monorhis 162
Ocyceros birostris 64
griseus 64
Oenanthe deserti 184
isabellina 184
oenanthe* 228
picata* 227
pleschanka* 227
xanthoprymna* 228
Oriolus chinensis 166
oriolus 166
xanthornus 166
Orthotomus sutorius 196
Otus bakkamoena 80
brucei 80
scops* 221
sunia 80

Pandion haliaetus 122
Parus major 188
nuchalis 188
xanthogenys 188
xanthogenys aplonotus 188
xanthogenys travancoreensis
188
Passer domesticus 214
montanus 214
Pavo cristatus 50
Pelagodroma marina* 226
Pelecanus crispus* 225
onocrotalus 160
philippensis 160
Pellorneum ruficeps 202
Perdicula argoondah 48
asiatica 48
erythrorhyncha 48
Pericrocotus cinnamomeus 168
cinnamomeus cinnamomeus
168
cinnamomeus malabaricus 168
divaricatus 168
erythropygius 168
ethologus* 226
flammeus 168
roseus 168
Pernis ptilorhyncus 134
Petronia xanthocollis 214
Phaenicophaeus leschenaultii 74
tristis 74
viridirostris 74
Phaethon aethereus 146
lepturus 146

Phalacrocorax carbo 144
  fuscicollis 144
  niger 144
Phalaropus lobatus 104
Philomachus pugnax 104
Phodilus badius 80
Phoenicopterus minor 154
  ruber 154
Phoenicurus ochruros 184
Phylloscopus affinis 198
  collybita 198
  fuscatus 198
  griseolus 198
  humei 198
  inornatus* 228
  magnirostris 198
  occipitalis 200
  reguloides* 228
  trochiloides 198
  trochiloides nitidus 198
  trochiloides viridanus 198
  tytleri 198
Picumnus innominatus 60
Picus chlorolophus 60
  flavinucha 60
  xanthopygaeus 62
Pitta brachyura 164
Platalea leucorodia 154
Plegadis falcinellus 154
Ploceus benghalensis 214
  manyar 214
  philippinus 214
Pluvialis fulva 108
  squatarola 108
Podiceps cristatus* 225
  nigricollis* 225
Pomatorhinus horsfieldii 202
Porphyrio porphyrio 94
Porzana fusca 92
  parva* 222
  porzana 92
  pusilla 92
Prinia buchanani 194
  hodgsonii 194
  inornata 194
  inornata franklinii 194
  inornata inornata 194
  rufescens 194
  socialis 194
  sylvatica 194
Pseudibis papillosa 154
Psittacula columboides 76
  cyanocephala 76
  eupatria 76
  krameri 76
Pterocles exustus 94
  indicus 94
  orientalis* 222
Pterodroma baraui* 226
Puffinus carneipes 162
  lherminieri 162
  pacificus 162
  persicus* 226
Pycnonotus cafer 192
  jocosus 192
  leucotis* 228
  luteolus 192
  melanicterus 192
  melanicterus flaviventris 192
  melanicterus gularis 192

priocephalus 192
xantholaemus 192

Rallina eurizonoides 92
Rallus aquaticus 92
Recurvirostra avosetta 106
Rhinoptilus bitorquatus 110
Rhipidura albicollis 172
  aureola 172
Rhodonessa caryophyllacea 56
  rufina 58
Rhopocichla atriceps 202
Riparia diluta 188
  paludicola 188
  riparia 188
Rostratula benghalensis 96
Rynchops albicollis 114

Salpornis spilonotus 188
Sarcogyps calvus 126
Sarkidiornis melanotos 52
Saxicola caprata 184
  torquata 184
Saxicoloides fulicata 184
Schoenicola platyura 200
Scolopax rusticola 96
Seicercus burkii 200
  whistleri* 228
Sitta castanea 188
  frontalis 188
Spilornis cheela 128
Spizaetus cirrhatus 138
  nipalensis 138
Stachyris rufifrons 202
Stercorarius parasiticus 112
  pomarinus 112
Sterna acuticauda 118
  albifrons 118
  albifrons sinensis 118
  anaethetus 120
  aurantia 116
  bengalensis 116
  bergii 116
  caspia 116
  dougallii 118
  fuscata 120
  hirundo 118
  repressa 118
  sandvicensis 116
  saundersi 118
  sumatrana 118
Streptopelia chinensis 86
  decaocto 86
  orientalis 86
  orientalis erythrocephala 86
  orientalis meena 86
  senegalensis 86
  tranquebarica 86
  turtur* 222
Strix leptogrammica 82
  ocellata 82
Sturnus contra 186
  malabaricus 186
  malabaricus blythii 186
  malabaricus malabaricus 186
  pagodarum 186
  roseus 186
  sturninus* 228
  vulgaris 186
Sula dactylatra 146

leucogaster 146
  sula 146
Surniculus lugubris 74
Sylvia curruca 200
  curruca althaea 200
  curruca blythi 200
  hortensis 200
Sypheotides indica 90

Tachybaptus ruficollis 144
Tachymarptis melba 78
Tadorna ferruginea 52
  tadorna 52
Tephrodornis gularis 172
  pondicerianus 172
Terpsiphone paradisi 172
Threskiornis melanocephalus 154
Todiramphus chloris 68
Treron bicincta 88
  phoenicoptera 88
  pompadora 88
Tringa erythropus 98
  glareola 100
  nebularia 98
  ochropus 100
  stagnatilis 98
  totanus 98
Tryngites subruficollis* 222
Turdoides affinis 204
  caudatus 204
  malcolmi 204
  striatus 204
  striatus orientalis 204
  striatus somervillei 204
  subrufus 204
Turdus merula 176
  merula bourdilloni 176
  merula nigropileus 176
  merula simillimus 176
  obscurus* 227
  ruficollis* 227
  unicolor 176
Turnix suscitator 48
  sylvatica 48
  tanki 48
Tyto alba 80
  capensis 80

Upupa epops 66

Vanellus cinereus* 223
  duvaucelii 110
  gregarius 110
  indicus 110
  leucurus 110
  malabaricus 110
  vanellus* 223

Xenus cinereus 100

Zoonavena sylvatica 78
Zoothera citrina 174
  citrina citrina 174
  citrina cyanotus 174
  dauma 174
  dauma dauma 174
  dauma neilgherriensis 174
  sibirica* 227
  wardii 174
Zosterops palpebrosus 194